WOR
**A
Vocabulary
Power Workbook**

WORDS!

A Vocabulary Power Workbook

Michael J. Sheehan
City Colleges of Chicago

HARCOURT BRACE COLLEGE PUBLISHERS

Fort Worth   Philadelphia   San Diego   New York   Orlando   Austin   San Antonio
Toronto   Montreal   London   Sydney   Tokyo

Publisher	Ted Buchholz
Editor in Chief	Christopher P. Klein
Senior Acquisitions Editor	Carol Wada
Senior Developmental Editor	Meera Dash
Project Editor	John Haakenson
Production Manager	Cynthia Young
Senior Art Director	Don Fujimoto

Cover design and illustrations by Terry Rasberry

ISBN: 0-15-5025708
Library of Congress Catalog Card Number: 95-079771

Copyright © 1996 by Harcourt Brace & Company

All rights reserved. No part of this publication may be reproduced or transmitted in any form or by any means, electronic or mechanical, including photocopying, recording or any information storage and retrieval system, without permission in writing from the publisher, except that, until further notice, the contents or parts whereof may be reproduced for instructional purposes by users of *WORDS! A Vocabulary Power Workbook* by Michael J. Sheehan, provided each copy contains a proper copyright notice as follows: 1996 by Harcourt Brace & Company.

Requests for permission to make copies of any part of the work should be mailed to: Permissions Department, Harcourt Brace & Company, 6277 Sea Harbor Drive, Orlando, Florida 32887-6777.

Address for Editorial Correspondence:
Harcourt Brace College Publishers
301 Commerce Street, Suite 3700
Fort Worth, Texas 76102

Address for Orders:
Harcourt Brace & Company
6277 Sea Harbor Drive
Orlando, FL 32887-6777
1-800-782-4479, or 1-800-433-0001 (in Florida)

(Copyright Acknowledgments begin on page 401, which constitutes a continuation of this copyright page.)

Printed in the United States of America

5 6 7 8 9 0 1 2 3 4   016   10 9 8 7 6 5 4 3 2 1

To Michael J. Sheehan, Jr.:

Hic est filius meus dilectus, in quo mihi bene complacui.

CONTENTS

Chapter 1 INTRODUCTION *1*

Chapter 2 NUMBERS *19*

Chapter 3 DIRECTION *51*

Chapter 4 RELATIONSHIP *83*

Chapter 5 DIMENSION *117*

Chapter 6 SHAPE *149*

Chapter 7 TIME *181*

Chapter 8 THE SENSES *215*

Chapter 9 ACTION *247*

Chapter 10 QUALITIES *279*

Chapter 11 BODY PARTS *313*

Chapter 12 NATURE *345*

Appendix A HOW TO MEMORIZE *377*

Appendix B NEGATIVE WORD PARTS *387*

Appendix C SUFFIXES *393*

Index to Word Parts *397*

PREFACE

Words! A Vocabulary Power Workbook is designed to help students increase their reading vocabulary—the words that are essential when reading textbooks or magazines, for instance. It is a *recognition* vocabulary. While recognition vocabulary is the first step to a more active and self-initiated formal vocabulary, it comes into play primarily when we decode thoughts presented by others.

GENERAL METHOD

Instead of presenting static, limited word lists to be memorized, this book takes a more flexible, long-range, and in-depth approach by presenting word *parts* to be memorized—letter combinations which show up in dozens of words, always with the same basic meaning. Word parts are important precisely because they are recycled constantly, especially in technical or professional terms. Memorizing them pays off in an almost geometric way. For example, once we know that the word part *eury-* means wide, then jawbreakers such as *eurybathic* and *euryphagous* hold only half the mystery and frustration. If we read these words in a sentence, their context—that is, the way that they are used—may unlock the other half. In addition, if we have also learned that the word part *-bathic* means depth and that *-phagous* means eating, it won't take us long to realize that someone is writing about sea creatures which can tolerate a wide variety of depths and eat a wide variety of foods.

Mindful of the theory of expectations, this book approaches vocabulary-building students in a positive, optimistic way. It forces them to reach, but it does so in measured, sequential doses which allow success, since building self-esteem must be a major component of the agenda for struggling students. Mindful of the theory of immersion, instead of repeating a mere handful of words per chapter as if students could handle no more, the exercises expose them to almost two hundred new words in context per chapter. This faster pace provides a larger spectrum of word parts in sentences as they are actually found in college textbooks and professional readings, saturates students in the assigned word parts with less chance of boredom, and gives them practice in handling new and unexpectedly difficult words in real-life settings. Finally, mindful of the theory of association as a memory technique, the chapters present word parts in meaningful categories. This thematic grouping makes it far easier to memorize word parts than if they were presented in less effective ways, such as mere front cover to back cover alphabetical listing without thematic grouping, or constant mechanical division into prefixes, roots, and suffixes.

GENERAL ORGANIZATION

As a glance at the Table of Contents will show, each working chapter is devoted to a specific theme or category of word parts that students will encounter in textbooks and courses in many different fields. Chapter 1 equips students with essential tools for learning vocabulary by reviewing context, dictionary use, and word parts as building blocks. Each subsequent chapter has three sections. Twice per chapter, a new list of word parts is presented. The student then tackles a varied array of exercises focusing on the word parts and meanings in those lists. A third section provides a review and exercises to end each chapter. These field-tested exercises can be used for at-large classroom discussions, for small peer group exercises, or for traditional individual desk work or homework. Some of the exercises depend only on word parts, some require the use of a dictionary, but most of them demand attention to context. In all cases, the point is not to learn a handful of sample words which probably will not be remembered out of context anyway, but to commit the word parts to memory for immediate and long-term academic and professional use. The book ends with three appendices: one on memory techniques, one on negative word parts, and one on suffixes.

THE EXERCISES

Parallel exercises are featured in each section within a chapter. Every chapter from 2 to 12 follows a uniform sequence to enhance student comfort and build confidence.

- Each list is accompanied by a unique pre-exercise. This listmaking activity forces students to pay close attention to the original list, invites them to participate in an analytical process, and gives them a second version of each list based on a complementary principle to aid memorization and to use with subsequent exercises.
- A warm-up exercise designed to establish trust in the usefulness of the list begins each exercise sequence.
- The two following exercises (one with visual cues and one without) require students to provide meanings for word parts used in context. They are followed by a matching column exercise which can serve as an interim quiz.
- The quiz is followed by two more exercises (again, one with visual cues and one without) which require students to reverse the earlier process by now completing words used in context with word parts which bear a designated meaning.
- The last exercise for each list gives five actual excerpts in paragraph form, mainly from textbooks, and asks students to use context principles in conjunction with word part recognition and dictionary use to uncover meaning.
- A review list, a combined form of the two earlier lists, begins the last section of each chapter. This review section features listmaking, matching columns which join word parts with their meanings, a dictionary-based crossout

exercise which serves to warn against word part look-alikes, an open-ended definition exercise, an exercise featuring synonyms and antonyms, and a final set of 10 excerpted paragraphs which stress the necessity of context, dictionary use, and word part recognition working in concert.

In summary, each working chapter has 23 separate exercises which require an average of 375 answers per chapter—a total of 4,134 participatory items for Chapters 2–12. Additional exercise items appear in the introductory chapter and in the appendices. In the course of doing these exercises and memorizing the word part lists upon which they are based, students will learn 329 separate word parts in Chapters 2–12 and 104 more new word parts in the appendices, a grand total of 433 dynamic, seminal word parts.

Although the direct focus of this text is word parts as building blocks, Chapters 2–12 each present students with 170 words in context, a total of 1,870 words or word variations. The appendices add 336 more words for a total of 2,206 words based on thematic word part lists, all of them either defined or used in context.

Visual imagery aids the learning of vocabulary. To that end, the chapters contain mnemonic illustrations which enhance the exercises and act as models of particular memory techniques (Appendix A explains these techniques).

SUPPLEMENTARY MATERIAL

A fully integrated package enhances the use of *WORDS! A Vocabulary Power Workbook*.

- The text itself provides a workbook format to help students learn and use the word parts.
- A substantial instructor's manual contains the following elements:
  √ Discussions of working assumptions and principles behind the text, detailed explanations of exercise organization, and hints for classroom use of the text
  √ An exhaustive and convenient answer key
  √ A test bank consisting of two 30-item tests for every working chapter
  √ A puzzle bank consisting of two puzzles for every chapter—one a word search puzzle, the other a simplified crossword puzzle

ACKNOWLEDGMENTS

The marvelous team at Harcourt Brace made this endeavor easier than it would otherwise have been. Thanks go to Jill Yuen, who got me off the dime and in front of my computer; to Carol Wada, Senior Acquisitions Editor, who helped me see the light at the end of the tunnel; to Meera Dash, Senior Developmental Editor, who always had a cogent suggestion and an encouraging word; to John Haakenson, Project Editor; to Cindy Young, Production Manager; and to Don Fujimoto, Art Director.

Thanks also to the reviewers: Gail Benchener, DeAnza College; Judith Cohen, University of Illinois at Chicago; Sue Hackett, Rio Hondo College; Dennis Keen, Spokane Community College; William Loflin, Catonsville College; Belinda Smith, Wake Technical Community College.

Comments about the text will be appreciated. They may be e-mailed to me at this Internet address: ak797@leo.nmc.edu

CHAPTER 1 INTRODUCTION

When you come upon a word that you do not know, there are three ways to find out what it means. You can look it up in a dictionary, you can figure out its meaning on your own by studying its surroundings (context), or you can use any recognizable letter sequence (word part) that you may find inside the unknown word.

These three methods can work for you in various situations. Sometimes the dictionary alone will see you through; it's all that you need. On the other hand, sometimes you can't use the dictionary—during a test, for instance—so you have to turn to the context of the word to unlock its meaning. And sometimes simply examining the word all by itself, ignoring for a moment the rest of the sentence or paragraph in which it is found, will make previously memorized word parts leap out at you.

Often, these methods must be combined. For instance, if the word that you are looking up in the dictionary has more than one meaning, you will find it absolutely necessary to use context. In addition, the dictionary often highlights word parts and uses them to help define a term. Such information is found regularly inside brackets in dictionary entries. And for those times when a dictionary is unavailable, even when you are examining an unknown word for its telltale parts, you cannot help but take into account the words that come before it and behind it and the relationships of meaning that are involved.

All in all, it's best to think of these three methods as partners rather than as competitors. It really doesn't matter which one way or which combination of ways leads you to the meaning of an unknown word. What counts is that you ultimately know what the word means.

To make sure that you are familiar with all three methods, let's review them at this point. Then, in the exercises that appear in the remaining chapters in this book, you will have a chance to practice them.

SECTION 1: USING THE DICTIONARY

If you look up a word in the dictionary and find that it has more than one meaning, don't just grab the first meaning that you see. Instead, search through the choices until you find the meaning that fits best in the sentence which sent you to the dictionary in the first place.

Consider a simple word such as **drive**. It doesn't always mean the same thing. For instance, you can drive a car, drive a golf ball, drive a nail in a wall, or drive a friend crazy. They are all very different in meaning, but the spelling stays the same each time: d-r-i-v-e.

Let's say that you've come across a sentence with yet another use of the word **drive**: *The Allied drive into Germany during World War II led to victory in Europe.* You might turn to a dictionary for help. The following dictionary entry shows what you would find. As you read it, notice that the definitions are grouped into three sections, one called *v.—tr.* (transitive verb, one that has an object), another called *v.—intr.* (intransitive verb, one that has no object), and a third called *—n.* (noun). Notice also that each section has its own separate sequence of numbers.

drive (drīv) *v.* **drove** (drōv) or *archaic* **drave** (drāv), **driven** (drĭvən), **driv·ing**, **drives**. —*tr.* **1.** To push, propel, or press onward forcibly; urge forward: *drove the horses into the corral.* **2.** To repulse forcefully; put to flight: *drove the attackers away; drove out any thought of failure.* **3.** To guide, control, or direct (a vehicle). **4.a.** To convey or transport in a vehicle: *drove the children to school.* **b.** To traverse in a vehicle: *drive the freeways to work.* **5.** To supply the motive force or power to and cause to function: *Steam drives the engine.* **6.** To compel or force to work, often excessively: *"Every serious dancer is driven by notions of perfection—perfect expressiveness, perfect technique"* (Susan Sontag). **7.** To force into or from a particular act or state: *Indecision drives me crazy.* **8.** To force to go through or penetrate: *drove the stake into the ground.* **9.** To create or produce by penetrating forcibly: *The nail drove a hole in the tire.* **10.** To carry through vigorously to a conclusion: *drove home his point.* **11.a.** *Sports.* To throw, strike, or cast (a ball, for example) hard or rapidly. **b.** *Basketball.* To move with the ball directly through: *drove the lane and scored.* **c.** *Baseball.* To cause (a run) to be scored. **12.a.** To chase (game) into the open or into traps or nets. **b.** To search (an area) for game in such a manner. —*intr.* **1.** To move along or advance quickly as if pushed by an impelling force. **2.** To rush, dash, or advance violently against an obstruction: *The wind drove into my face.* **3.** To operate a vehicle, such as a car. **4.** To go or be transported in a vehicle: *drove to the supermarket.* **5.a.** *Sports.* To hit, throw, or impel a ball or other missile forcibly. **b.** *Basketball.* To move directly to the basket with the ball. **6.** To make an effort to reach or achieve an objective; aim. —**drive** *n.* **1.** The act of driving. **2.** A trip or journey in a vehicle.

Copyright © 1996 Harcourt Brace & Company. All rights reserved.

3. *Abbr.* **Dr.** A road for automobiles and other vehicles. **4.a.** The means or apparatus for transmitting motion or power to a machine or from one machine part to another. **b.** The means by which automotive power is applied to a roadway: *four-wheel drive.* **c.** The means or apparatus for controlling and directing an automobile: *right-hand drive.* **5.** *Computer Science.* A device that reads data from and writes data onto a storage medium, such as a floppy disk. **6.** A strong organized effort to accomplish a purpose. See Synonyms at **campaign**. **7.** Energy, push, or aggressiveness. **8.** *Psychology.* A strong motivating tendency or instinct, especially of sexual or aggressive origin, that prompts activity toward a particular end. **9.** A massive, sustained military offensive. **10.a.** *Sports.* The act of hitting, knocking, or thrusting a ball very swiftly. **b.** *Sports.* The stroke or thrust by which a ball is driven. **c.** *Basketball.* The act of moving with the ball directly to the basket. **11.a.** A rounding up and driving of cattle to new pastures or to market. **b.** A gathering and driving of logs down a river. **c.** The cattle or logs thus driven.

[*Reproduced by permission from* THE AMERICAN HERITAGE DICTIONARY OF THE ENGLISH LANGUAGE. *Copyright 1992 by Houghton Mifflin Company.*]

Those are a lot of meanings for one little word, but it's not unusual for a word to have multiple meanings. Now, if you make the same mistake that many people do, you will be tempted to grab the very first definition and consider your work finished. You'll shut the dictionary with the idea that drive means "to push, propel, or press onward forcibly." But try substituting that idea in the original sentence above: Did the Allies *push* something? Did they *propel* something? Did they *press* something? No, what they did was to take part in something called a drive. In this case, you need to define what something was called, not what someone did. In other words, you need a noun meaning, not a verb meaning.

You'll have to keep searching until you find a definition that makes sense when substituted in the original sentence. When you finally get down to the third set of definitions—specifically, number 9—you'll find what you need. **Drive** in this sense is a term for a military operation. The context of the original sentence (its mention of Allies and World War II) will help you know when you have found a good fit.

There is a shortcut that you can use. Instead of reading through 40 separate definitions before coming across the one you needed, you could have skipped all the verb definitions and started reading only the noun definitions. This is because the word **drive** was used as a noun in that sentence about World War II, and if a word is used as a noun, only a noun meaning from the dictionary will fit.

You won't be able to find an accurate meaning of a noun in the verb section, the adjective section, or any other section.

So finding the meaning of a word in a dictionary is a sorting process, a selection process. You can't grab just any definition, and you can't lose sight of the original sentence that sent you to the dictionary in the first place.

STEP-BY-STEP PROCEDURE:

1. Before you even touch the dictionary, figure out the part of speech for the word as it is used in its sentence.
   — A noun tells what something is *called*. It may have markers such as *a*, *an*, or *the*. It may have adjectives (describing words) attached to it. Abbreviation: *n*.
     - My xxxxx once lived in xxxxx, where he owned an xxxxx.
     - We fixed the broken xxxxx as quickly as we could.
     - A small red xxxxx appeared on its xxxxx overnight.
   — A verb tells what someone or something *does* or has *done to* it. A verb's spelling may show time, and it may have a helping verb attached to it. Sometimes the dictionary will subdivide a verb into *v.t.* (transitive verb—one that takes an object) or *v.i.* (intransitive verb—one that doesn't take an object). Abbreviation: *v*.
     - He xxxxxs his hair whenever he xxxxxes a mirror.
     - I will not xxxxx the dog unless you xxxxx it first.
     - Your uncle should have been xxxxxed before he was xxxxxed.
   — An adjective is a describing word. It tells *what kind, how many,* or *which one*. Abbreviation: *adj*.
     - The xxxxx camper would not fit into the xxxxx garage.
     - We saw xxxxx people in xxxxx costumes doing a xxxxx dance.
     - xxxxx book has a xxxxx cover.
   — Other parts of speech (which you normally won't have to look up) include pronouns (*pron.*), adverbs (*adv.*), prepositions (*prep.*), conjunctions (*conj.*), and interjections (*interj.*).
2. After you have figured out the part of speech, *then* open your dictionary and find the word.
3. Now that you are looking at the proper entry, find the part of speech section that you need (*n.* or *v.* or whatever) and read only those definitions.

4. Keep comparing the definitions with the context of the original sentence until you find a match. If two different definitions sound so close that both of them seem to fit, at least you're in the right ballpark.

EXERCISE:

Using the dictionary entry for **drive** on pages 2–3, find the meaning that best fits each of the following sentences. Give the part of speech (*n.* or *v.*) in the first column and the definition number in the second column.

N/V   #

1. The **drive** to Milwaukee takes an hour and a half.
2. Marge can **drive** the nail through the pine board without splitting the wood.
3. Many old clocks used a worm gear **drive** to make the hands rotate.
4. Did you see him **drive** the bulldozer into the drainage ditch and tip over?
5. She has more **drive** and energy than any other student in her class.
6. Rodriguez can **drive** the ball straight down the fairway almost every time.
7. The disk **drive** suddenly crashed, losing all of the data that it contained.
8. This year's Red Cross **drive** hopes to raise millions of dollars in contributions.
9. In the movie *City Slickers*, three old friends go to a western dude ranch to participate in a **drive,** even though they don't know one end of a cow from another.
10. The constant noise and the lung-searing pollution are **driving** me crazy.
11. Front wheel **drive** seems to have an advantage in snowy road conditions.
12. The heavy wind **drove** the leaves across the yard and out of sight.

Copyright © 1996 Harcourt Brace & Company. All rights reserved.

_____ _____ 13. Professor Van Helsing **drove** the vampire back by holding up a crucifix.

_____ _____ 14. Freud taught us that the sex **drive** is one of our most powerful instincts.

_____ _____ 15. Will you **drive** me to the doctor this afternoon for my appointment?

Answers: (1) n. 2   (4) v. tr. 3   (7) n. 5   (10) v. tr. 7   (13) v. tr. 2
          (2) v. tr. 8   (5) n. 7   (8) n. 6   (11) n. 4.b.   (14) n. 8
          (3) n. 4.a.   (6) v. tr. 11.a. (9) n. 11.a.   (12) v. tr. 1   (15) v. tr. 4.a.

SECTION 2: USING CONTEXT

Sometimes, you won't be able to use a dictionary. When that happens, you will need to know about using context to find the meaning of a word.

Context means the total surroundings of a word—the ideas that lead up to a word and the ideas that follow a word. If you pay attention to these surrounding ideas, you can often figure out what a word means without going near a dictionary.

To use context well, you have to pay very close attention to context clues. Context clues are the signals that will lead you to the meaning of a word. These clues are placed there by the writer to help you figure out the word's meaning. Here are some of the more common context clues.

(A) WORD CLUES

In this situation, the writer actually includes a definition near a new or difficult word. Usually, the unknown word will come first, then certain word clues, then the definition. In other cases, the definition will come first, the word clues will follow, and the unknown word will show up last.

In either case, this is the basic formula: *word = definition*. The = sign gets translated into any of the following words or words like them:

is/are	*is/was termed*	*is/was called*	*refers to*
was/were	*may be defined as*	*is/was known as*	*is/was designated as*
means	*is/was defined as*	*is/was referred to as*	*that is*

EXAMPLES:

- **Serfdom** was the medieval system that bound peasants to their master's land and transferred them along with the land when it went to a new owner. [signal: *was*]
- Skill in using one's hands or body is called **dexterity**. [signal: *is called*]
- The practice of foretelling the future by consulting animal intestines was known as **haruspication**. [signal: *was known as*]
- **Tenacity** is defined as the ability to hold firm to one's beliefs under pressure. [signal: *is defined as*]
- A generalized feeling of ill-being with symptoms such as an abnormal feeling of anxiety, general discontent, or vague physical discomfort is termed **dysphoria**. [signal: *is termed*]
- The metal tip at the end of a shoelace is known as an **aglet**. [signal: *is known as*]
- A **hierarchy** may be defined as a body of persons, such as clergy, organized or classified according to rank or authority. [signal: *may be defined as*]
- **Stenoky** means the ability of an organism to live only under a very narrow range of environmental conditions. [signal: *means*]
- **Transmigration** refers to the belief that the human soul passes into another body after death and is reborn. [signal: *refers*]
- Some people are **contumelious**. That is, they are rude in a contemptuous way, often delighting in insulting and humiliating their victims. [signal: *that is*]

(B) PUNCTUATION CLUES

Sometimes the writer will include a definition near a new or difficult word and use punctuation marks as a signal instead of special words. The unknown word usually comes first, and the definition follows inside certain punctuation marks. These include commas, dashes, and parentheses. Occasionally, the order is reversed. In that case, the definition will come first, and then the unknown word will follow inside those punctuation marks.

EXAMPLES:

- **Duplicity**, deliberate deceptiveness in action or speech, is one of the surest ways to destroy a friendship.

- **Carcinoma**, or cancer, may occur in any part of the digestive tract. Surgery, radiation, or chemotherapy may be prescribed to treat it.
- Substances through which electrons will not flow well, **insulators**, include glass, hard rubber, porcelain, and plastic.
- **Appositives**—words, phrases, or clauses placed next to a noun—often contain definitions.
- A common characteristic of Christianity, Judaism, and Islamism is **monotheism**—the belief in one god.
- Certain energy waves of short wavelength and high frequency—**gamma waves**—are shorter than X-ray wavelengths.
- Many neurologists agree that **prosopagnosia**—difficulty in recognizing familiar faces—is associated primarily with damage to the right hemisphere of the brain.
- In the process of **mitosis** (cell reproduction), each cell replaces its chromosomes, along with some cytoplasm, and then divides into two new cells.
- Since a water molecule has a positive end and a negative end, it is called a **dipole** (two poles).
- **Lipomas** (fatty tumors) are usually benign and thus not a cause for alarm.
- Small molecules may be combined in complex ways to form larger molecules (**macromolecules**).

Note: Remember that commas, dashes, and parentheses can be used for purposes that have nothing to do with definition. But the fact that they are often used to signal a definition is what always warrants a closer look.

(C) SYNONYMS

A synonym is a word with a meaning very similar to the meaning of another word. It is able to replace the other word. When the synonym is simpler than the unknown word, it can be just as useful as a long definition.

Sometimes the synonym shows up in a cluster or group of words. Sometimes the synonym simply substitutes for the more difficult word in a later sentence. You must watch for equivalent terms.

EXAMPLES:

- She is one of the most perceptive, understanding, and **perspicacious** persons I have ever met. [*perspicacious* = perceptive and understanding]
- Beware of politicians who make **nebulous** and vague promises. [*nebulous* = vague]
- His reputation as a stubborn, **refractory**, and bullheaded individual made it difficult for him when he decided to run for public office. [*refractory* = stubborn and bullheaded]
- **Phobias** may be found in all age groups. These abnormal fears make life difficult for those who suffer from them. [*phobias* = abnormal fears]
- Ostriches are probably the most familiar of the **ratites**. Such flightless birds have a long history, dating back 135 million years to a huge, flightless bird called *Aepyornis*. [*ratites* = flightless birds]
- In regard to religion, Socrates seems to have spoken generally of gods in the plural and to have meant thereby the traditional Greek **deities**. [*deities* = gods]
- Physical **proximity** is important in determining friendship. Living near someone or working near someone is likely to produce interaction. [*proximity* = nearness]
- Scare tactics often work on children. Parents can **intimidate** youngsters into staying away from electrical outlets or can make them afraid of strangers. [*intimidate* = scare]
- Most of the people who die from falls are over 65. Middle-aged people and infants die most often in fires. Teenagers **succumb** primarily to poison and drugs. [*succumb* = die, surrender their lives]
- In the Middle East, **falciform** swords were standard during medieval times. The sickle-shaped blade was designed to behead enemies with a single blow. [*falciform* = sickle-shaped]

(D) EXAMPLES or DESCRIPTION

Quite often, the writer does not include an actual definition with a difficult word. However, if he or she has used examples or has described something closely connected with that word, this approach may be almost as good as an actual definition.

When it comes to examples, watch for word signals such as *for example, for instance, such as,* and *like*. On the other hand, some examples do not begin with any signal words at all.

Descriptions do not usually use signal words. Instead, you must look for words that have to do with seeing, touching, hearing, tasting, and smelling.

EXAMPLES:

- **Misdemeanors**, for example, include drunkenness, disorderly conduct, small or petty thefts, trespassing on private property, and loitering in a public place. [*misdemeanors* = minor crimes]
- Certain **impediments** may make a marriage invalid. For instance, being younger than the minimum age set by law or already being legally married to someone else are impediments to marriage. [*impediments* = obstacles, blocks]
- Delbert was **emaciated**. His clothes hung loosely from his frame. His arms and legs could have been used as toothpicks. His face looked like the mask of a Halloween skeleton. [*emaciated* = extremely thin]
- When the waiter said hello, Bonnie snapped at him for being too friendly. When she discovered that the menu did not list lobster, she let everyone around her know in a loud voice. When she paid her bill, she grew sarcastic because the cashier was too slow for her liking. Bonnie is a **querulous** person. [*querulous* = unpleasantly complaining]
- An **exoskeleton** feels hard to the touch, cannot easily be squashed by applied pressure, and offers a sort of armor by which a lobster, crab, or other creature can avoid the teeth, claws, or tentacles of an enemy. [*exoskeleton* = outer shell or hard covering]
- Pain is a warning that should be listened to, but most people rush to quiet it by taking aspirins, barbiturates, codeines, tranquilizers, sleeping pills, and other **analgesics**. [*analgesics* = painkillers]
- It didn't take us long to figure out that he was a **tyro** at golf. He didn't know where to tee off, he tried to use his putter as a driver, and he couldn't figure out how to start the golf cart. [*tyro* = beginner]
- Since the head-end of an embryo differentiates first and grows more rapidly in the womb than the foot-end, a newborn child has a relatively large head attached to a medium-sized body with **diminutive** legs and feet. This is later reversed through growth as legs and feet overtake the front end. [*diminutive* = small]
- He exhibited **misogynistic** tendencies, such as constantly belittling women, denying their intelligence, and claiming that the only

thing they were good for was having babies. [*mysogynistic* = woman-hating]
- If I had walked up to him and flipped back his parka, I know what I would have found. A shaggy thatch of bristly hair would have sprung into view. Then I would have seen his furtive face with its pointed ears, beady little red-rimmed eyes, long snout, prominent cheekbones, and sharp, razorlike teeth. Benny appears **racine**, you see. His head is constantly twisting in nervous little jerks, and he seems to be sniffing the air. You expect him to scurry back into a hole at any second, which is what he practically does if he spots a narc in the area. [*racine* = ratlike]

(E) CONTRAST or OPPOSITES

Sometimes the writer will contrast a word by using other words that mean the opposite. In those situations, you must reverse the meaning of the word that you already know to find the meaning of the word that you don't know.

Watch for contrast signal words such as these: *but, yet, however, nevertheless, in spite of, other,* and *on the other hand.*

Also watch for negative signal words such as these: *no, not, never,* and *nor.*

EXAMPLES:

- Some apartments are small and cramped and are no bargain. On the other hand, some are **commodious**. [*commodious* = spacious, the opposite of *small* and *cramped*]
- We might have given a favorable response if he had been polite and mannerly, but the fact that he was so **uncouth** made us turn down his request. [*uncouth* = impolite and unmannerly, the opposite of *polite* and *mannerly*]
- Some jobs are perfectly stable. They offer a secure and certain livelihood. Other jobs are **precarious**. They disappear in hard economic times. [*precarious* = unreliable, the opposite of *stable, secure,* and *certain*]
- Some events or experiences do not happen only once. They **recur**. [*recur* = happen again, the opposite of *happen only once*]
- People in authority should be very careful not to hire **mendacious** aides. Assistants who are not truthful and honest will pull a leader down. [*mendacious* = lying, the opposite of *truthful* and *honest*]

Copyright © 1996 Harcourt Brace & Company. All rights reserved.

- In mammals, the eyes are never set at the back of the head. They are always on the **anterior** side. [*anterior* = front, the opposite of *back*]
- Lee lived in a **static** society that could endure almost anything but change. Grant, on the other hand, fought because everything he lived by was tied to growth, expansion, and a constantly widening horizon. [*static* = unchanging or stable, the opposite of *change, growth, expansion*]
- Digestion can take place either outside or inside the cell itself. Digestion that takes place outside the cells is known as extracellular digestion. The other type of digestion is known as **intracellular** digestion. [*intracellular* = inside the cell, the opposite of *extracellular*]
- In a moment the ship changed from something **quiescent** into something fierce and desperate. [*quiescent* = peaceful or calm, the opposite of *fierce* and *desperate*]
- Instead of being organized and in good shape, his political campaign was now in a **shambles**. [*shambles* = disorder or mess, the opposite of *organized* and *in good shape*]

(F) PRIOR KNOWLEDGE, PAST EXPERIENCE, OR COMMON SENSE

Sometimes the clue that will lead you to the meaning of an unknown word lies within yourself, not on the page in front of you. Things that you have done or learned in the past survive in your memory and help you make useful applications. This is part of the reason why extensive experience, constant reading, and a broad base of knowledge are considered so valuable by teachers and employers alike.

EXAMPLES:

- If exposure to violence had the power to **immunize** our actions, Pasteur-like, we would not have to worry about the younger generation.
    [Louis Pasteur was the nineteenth-century French chemist who discovered that exposing patients to controlled doses of a virus could prevent catching a full-blown version of a disease. Thus, *immunize* in this context means to control or to protect from unhealthy effects, especially the effects of violence.]

- It doesn't take a lot of **perspicacity** to realize that not shutting a refrigerator door will lead to wasted electricity and spoiled food.

  [Having heard so many critical statements beginning with the words *It doesn't take a lot of brains to . . .*, it is not hard to make the connection between perspicacity and intelligence. This is particularly true in dealing with a refrigerator, a simple and obvious situation that we learned about as children.]

- There is nothing as frustrating as trying to change a flat tire and discovering that the lug nuts are **inextricable** when you attempt to use the jack handle supplied by the car manufacturer.

  [Those who have changed tires know that lug nuts are those thick nuts used to attach the wheel to the axle. Furthermore, these people have probably experienced the frustration of not being able to budge the lug nuts because of accumulated road dirt or rust. All this experience leads to the recognition that *inextricable* in this case must mean immovable or incapable of being turned.]

- If I should be so **fortuitous** as to win the lottery, I will quit my job, buy an expensive sailboat, and travel around the globe.

  [As we all know, winning a lottery is not a matter of skill or talent. It is a case of pure, raw luck. Therefore, it is easy to see that *fortuitous* can be replaced by the word *lucky* or *fortunate*.]

- The doctor warned her that if she did not cut back on her excessive consumption of alcohol, a **hepatectomy** might soon be necessary.

  [The first thing that catches my eye is the *-ectomy* ending. It immediately reminds me of similar words: *appendectomy, hysterectomy, tonsillectomy*. I know that they are all medical terms referring to operations, so I reason that a hepatectomy is a surgical operation. The mention of a doctor makes that all the more likely. Next, I become aware that the opening letters (*hepat-*) also remind me of something. I think of hepatitis. I know that it is a disease of the liver because an uncle of mine had it. Finally, drawing on the memory of a health class that I once took, I recall that one of the consequences of alcoholism is liver damage. Putting everything together, I conclude that *hepatectomy* means the surgical removal of the liver.]

14 CHAPTER 1 INTRODUCTION

EXERCISE:

Do not use a dictionary for this exercise. In the first blank, indicate what kind of context clue is available to help you. Sometimes there will be more than one clue, but just name the one that helped you most.
  Use this letter code for convenience:
  A. *word signals*   D. *examples or description*
  B. *punctuation signals*   E. *contrast or opposites*
  C. *synonyms (substitution)*   F. *prior knowledge; common sense*
In the second blank, write the meaning of the boldfaced word.

1. A good **mentor**, a wise and friendly advisor who is concerned about our future, is a real treasure in a business situation.
   Context Clue _____   Meaning _____

2. A **paradox** is a true statement that seems contradictory.
   Context Clue _____   Meaning _____

3. The governor was criticized for showing favoritism to her relatives by hiring them for highly paid jobs and for engaging in other types of **nepotism**.
   Context Clue _____   Meaning _____

4. The defendant retained his **sang-froid** during the trial, but when the jury declared him guilty, he screamed and cried and had to be carried away by the bailiffs.
   Context Clue _____   Meaning _____

5. She took the stopper out of the **flacon** and dabbed some of the expensive perfume behind each ear.
   Context Clue _____   Meaning _____

6. The billing error was **inadvertent**. We didn't mean to overcharge you.
   Context Clue _____   Meaning _____

7. Alcoholic, homeless, and practically starving, he found himself at the **nadir** of his life.
   Context Clue _____   Meaning _____

8. It would displease me greatly if you were to **divulge** the secrets that I shared with you. I wouldn't ever be able to trust you again.
   Context Clue _____   Meaning _____

Copyright © 1996 Harcourt Brace & Company. All rights reserved.

9. She tried to make her smile look real and heartfelt, but it still looked **factitious** to me.

   Context Clue _____ *Meaning* _____

10. Our thoughts are **covert**. They are hidden until we choose to reveal them.

    Context Clue _____ *Meaning* _____

Answers:
- (1) B   wise and friendly advisor
- (2) A   true statement that seems contradictory
- (3) C or D   favoritism to relatives
- (4) D or E   calmness; quiet behavior
- (5) D or F   bottle; container
- (6) C or E   not intentional; accidental
- (7) D   low point
- (8) D or F   reveal; tell
- (9) E   phony; not genuine
- (10) C   hidden; secret; private

*Note: In other classes and reading situations, you will not be asked to give the context clue that led you to the meaning of a word, but if you don't make it a habit to analyze the clue **first**, you will merely be guessing.*

SECTION 3: USING WORD PARTS

Word parts are letter combinations that show up frequently in words and mean the same basic thing each time. Learning word parts is one of the most efficient ways to increase your reading vocabulary. Word parts are multipliers. When you learn a single word part, you automatically memorize that portion of every word that uses it, which frequently turns out to be a dozen or more words. This process is much faster and easier than memorizing each of those words one at a time. Knowing word parts when you see them also means that your ability to use context will be that much keener. Context involves the ability to figure out the meaning of a word by its setting, its surroundings. If you already know a portion of a word, you can spend more time and energy decoding the context clues that may be present.

The following chapters will present lists of word parts organized by categories. As a preview, let's look at just a few examples of word parts in action.

EXAMPLES:

- As word parts, VID and VIS mean *sight*. Whenever you see these letter combinations as parts of actual words, you should immediately suspect that a portion of the meaning has to do with the act

of seeing. If you have any doubts, also use the context. Consider these words: *evident* (easily seen), *videotape* (magnetic tape used to record images), *vision* (the faculty of sight), *invisible* (unable to be seen), *envision* (to picture in the mind).
- As a word part, TRI means *three.* Consider these words: *tricycle* (vehicle with three wheels), *triennial* (occurring every third year), *triangle* (three-sided polygon), *triarchy* (government by three persons).
- As a word part, PHYLL means *leaf.* Consider these words: *chlorophyll* (green pigment found in leaves), *phylloid* (leaflike), *diphyllous* (having two leaves), *phyllotaxy* (the arrangement of leaves on a stem).
- As a word part, POST means *later* or *after.* Consider these words: *postmortem* (examination of a body after death), *posterior* (located behind or to the rear), *postpone* (to put off until later), *postgraduate* (further study after the bachelor's degree).
- As a word part, DERM means *skin.* Consider these words: *hypodermic* (introduced under the skin), *dermatologist* (a doctor who treats skin diseases), *endoderm* (innermost skin lining), *scleroderma* (disease in which the skin hardens).

Word parts can give you some problems if you treat them carelessly. First of all, letter combinations sometimes come together only accidentally. On first reading, they may seem to be word parts that you know, but further examination (through context or by using a dictionary) shows that they are not. Take the word part PORT, which normally means to *carry.* The word "s*port*ing" (athletic) has those four letters in the right order, but that is merely an accident. The same is true of the word "*port*rait" (formal painting or photo).

Second, word parts sometimes have more than one meaning. The word part PORT, for instance, can also mean *door,* as in *portal* or *porter.* The word *porter,* you will notice, can thus have two totally different meanings: a porter is someone hired to carry baggage, but a porter is also the title of a doorkeeper. To make things even worse, the word part PORT can also mean *part,* as in *portion,* and has several other meanings as well.

So what can you do? Never take anything for granted. Always study the context of a word. For instance, if a sentence reads "The porter wheeled my bags to the ticket counter," you can tell that this use of PORT means to *carry.* If another sentence reads "The porter refused to let them enter the lobby until they identified themselves as police officers," you can tell that this use of PORT is related to *door*.

The final and most secure judge, if you are in a situation where you can use it, is a dictionary. A dictionary will tell you if you are looking at a word part and what that word part means. It will do this in the numbered definitions by using the meaning of the word part to define the word. It may also give you, in square brackets, a quick historical background that will include any word parts and their meanings. For instance, here is a dictionary entry for *deport*. Both definition 2 and the information in brackets tell you that the PORT used in this word means to *carry*.

> **deport** (di pôrt′), *v.t.* **1.** to expel (an alien) from a country; banish. **2.** to send or carry off; transport, esp. forcibly. **3.** to bear, conduct, or behave oneself in a particular manner. [<MF *deporter* <L *deportare* to carry away, banish oneself]

You will find exercises in each chapter of this book (in the P sections) to help you understand how the dictionary can serve you in situations where you need to determine whether an accidental letter combination or multiple meanings are at work.

EXERCISE:

*Show how the meaning **carry** is involved in the following words, all of which have the letter combination PORT. You should use your dictionary.*

WORD	MEANING
portal vein:	a vein that **carries** blood from the digestive organs, spleen, pancreas, and gall bladder to the liver.

1. deportment: _____
2. export: _____
3. import: _____
4. portable: _____
5. portage: _____
6. porter: _____
7. portfolio: _____

Copyright © 1996 Harcourt Brace & Company. All rights reserved.

8. portmanteau: _____
9. report: _____
10. support: _____

Answers:
1. the way that you carry yourself in society; your conduct
2. to send or carry a commodity to other countries
3. to bring or carry in a commodity from another country
4. easily carried or moved
5. the carrying of boats and supplies overland between two waterways
6. a person employed to carry travelers' luggage
7. an easily carried case that holds documents, maps, etc.
8. a large leather suitcase that opens into two compartments and is carried by its handles
9. to carry an account or announcement to someone
10. to carry or bear the weight of something

SUMMARY

The point of this introductory chapter has been that three interdependent skills—word parts, context, and dictionary use—will help you as you attempt to cope with higher level vocabulary, especially in textbooks, source books, and professional journals.

In the following chapters, you will quickly discover that memory is a most important factor for success in vocabulary, especially where word parts are concerned. To help you review some principles and practical hints about memorizing, turn now to the mini-lesson in Appendix A.

CHAPTER 2 NUMBERS

SECTION 1

List 1
Here are some word parts that are used to signify numbers.

WORD PART	MEANING
BI	two
CENT	one hundred
DEC	ten
DU	two
MILLI	one thousand
MULTI	many; several
NONA	nine
NOV	nine
OCTO	eight
QUADR	four
QUART	four
QUINT	five
SEMI	half; partly
SEPT	seven
SEX	six
TER	three; threefold
UNI	one

PRE-EXERCISE ACTIVITY 1
- **List Making**
- **Skill: word parts**

*In the blanks that follow, rewrite List 1. This time, however, reverse the order by writing the **meanings** in the first column. Then gather all the word parts in the list which have that meaning and write them on one line in the second column. This will let you make necessary connections and help you in the process of long-term memorization. The first one has already been done to show you how.*

	MEANING	WORD PARTS	
1.	half, partly	semi	*Note:* This list will be more useful if you write it in numerical order.
2.	_____	_____	
3.	_____	_____	
4.	_____	_____	
5.	_____	_____	
6.	_____	_____	
7.	_____	_____	
8.	_____	_____	
9.	_____	_____	
10.	_____	_____	
11.	_____	_____	
12.	_____	_____	
13.	_____	_____	
14.	_____	_____	

EXERCISE 2-A
- **Multiple Choice**
- **Skill: word parts**

A meaning is in boldface for each of the following phrases. From the four choices given, pick the one answer which contains a word part with that meaning. Use both versions of List 1 to help you. **Do not use a dictionary**. *Do not focus on the size or difficulty of the words. Look only for the simple word part; it will lead you to the correct answer.*

Example: √A period of **ten** years
    (A) century   (C) millennium
    (B) generation   (D) decade

    Answer: (D) The reason for this answer is that the DEC part of *decade* means "ten."

1. A **seven**-sided figure
   (A) quintilateral   (C) bilateral
   (B) quadrilateral   (D) septilateral

2. **Five** children born at the same birth
   (A) triplets   (C) quadruplets
   (B) quintuplets   (D) sextuplets

3. Having **many** meanings or values
   (A) prevalent   (C) multivalent
   (B) bivalent   (D) univalent

4. A period of **one hundred** years
   (A) century   (C) decade
   (B) millennium   (D) generation

5. Multiplied by **eight**
   (A) decuple   (C) octuple
   (B) sextuple   (D) septuple

6. Having a **single** leaf
   (A) unifoliate   (C) septifoliate
   (B) multifoliate   (D) quinquefoliate

7. A unit of length equal to one-**thousandth** of a meter
   - (A) centimeter
   - (B) millimeter
   - (C) decimeter
   - (D) gravimeter

8. Having **four** sides
   - (A) quintilateral
   - (B) bilateral
   - (C) quadrilateral
   - (D) unilateral

9. People in their **nine**ties
   - (A) centenarians
   - (B) vegetarians
   - (C) sexagenarians
   - (D) nonagenarians

10. Celebrating **half** a century
    - (A) bicentennial
    - (B) sesquicentennial
    - (C) semicentennial
    - (D) quadricentennial

EXERCISE 2-B
- Fill in the Blank (one cue)
- Skill: word parts

*Use a **meaning** from List 1 to fill in the blank in each statement. The word part whose meaning you are defining will be found inside the boldfaced word. **Do not use a dictionary.** Do not focus on the size or difficulty of the words. Look only for the simple word part; it will lead you to the correct answer.*

Example: √A **semicircle** is _____ a circle.

   Answer: *half* [> SEMI]

1. A **unidirectional** microphone operates more effectively in _____ direction.
2. Something that is **multicellular** has _____ cells.
3. A **bilinear** equation has _____ variables.
4. A grouping of _____ items together is called a **septenary** grouping.
5. A **quintan** fever recurs every _____ days.
6. An **octosyllable** is a line of verse containing _____ syllables.

7. **Centesimal** means divided into _____ parts.
8. Something that is **sexennial** lasts for _____ years.
9. To multiply a number by _____ is to **decuple** it.
10. A **semiparasitic** insect can live _____ on live hosts and _____ on dead or decaying animal matter.
11. **Septentrion** refers to the northern regions of the earth and gets its name from a constellation known as the _____ plow oxen.
12. **Quadrivial** means having _____ ways or roads meeting in a point.
13. A **semipermeable** membrane _____ allows the passage of fluids through it.
14. A monastic prayer said at the _____ *th* hour of each day is named **sext**.
15. Motion that occurs in _____ plane surface is referred to as **uniplanar**.

EXERCISE 2-C
- Fill in the Blank (no cue)
- Skills: word parts, context

*Once again, use a **meaning** from List 1 to fill in the blank in each line. This time, however, you will have to find the word part yourself in the difficult or technical word. **Do not use a dictionary**. Do not focus on the size or difficulty of the words. Look only for the simple word part; it will lead you to the correct answer.*

Example: √A univalve is a mollusk with _____ shell.

    Answer: *one* [> UNI]

1. A centigrade thermometer is divided into _____ degrees.
2. A novennial observation recurs every _____ years.
3. A millimicron is a unit of length for measuring light waves; it is equal to one-_____ *th* of a micron.

4. Anything with _____ parts or divisions is called decamerous.
5. Multifarious activities involve _____ actions.
6. To quintuple something is to multiply it by _____ .
7. A bimetallic chain is made of _____ different metals.
8. A quadrant is one-_____th of the circumference of a circle.
9. Dualism is the belief that humans have _____ natures.
10. A sextan fever recurs every _____ days.
11. A nonagon is a polygon having _____ angles and _____ sides.
12. In music, ternary form is a musical form in _____ sections, with the last usually an exact repetition of the first.
13. A septuagenarian is _____ty years old.
14. In the religious stories of many ancient cultures, some creatures were described as semidivine, meaning that they were _____ divine.
15. A quarterly magazine appears _____ times a year.

Quint Eastwood wides again

EXERCISE 2-D
- **Matching Columns**
- **Skill: word parts**

Memory check. Do not look back at List 1 or use a dictionary.

1. _____ BI   (a) one hundred
2. _____ MULTI   (b) one thousand

3. ____ OCTO   (c) two
4. ____ QUART   (d) three
5. ____ SEMI   (e) many
6. ____ TER   (f) nine
7. ____ CENT   (g) eight
8. ____ MILLI   (h) half
9. ____ QUINT   (i) four
10. ____ NONA   (j) five

EXERCISE 2-E
- **Fill in (two cues)**
- **Skills: word parts, dictionary, context**

*To finish each word, fill in the blank with one of the **word parts** from your version of List 1. **You must use a college-level dictionary** to make sure that what you write really is a word and that it fits in the sentence. The boldfaced word will give you the meaning of the word part that you must write.*

Example: √An ____pus is a sea mollusk with **eight** sucker-bearing arms.

       Answer: *OCTO* [> eight]

1. In the Roman calendar, ____ember was the **seventh** month.
2. In the Roman calendar, ____ember was the **tenth** month.
3. In the Roman calendar, the **eighth** month was called ____ber.
4. In the Roman calendar, ____ember was the **ninth** month.
5. Social ____formity means that the members of a group act or appear as **one**.
6. A ____er is one-**fourth** of a dollar.
7. An event that happens every **two** weeks is called ____weekly.
8. A ____tet is a musical group with **six** members.
9. A **double** or an identical copy is called a ____plicate.
10. A ____imeter is **one hundredth** of a meter or .3937 inch.
11. A ____meter is **one thousandth** of a meter or .0397 inch.

12. A **four**-footed animal is a ___ruped.
13. Something ____farious is made up of **many** parts or kinds.
14. When a class reunion is held every **ten** years, it is called a ___ennial celebration.
15. In poetry, a ___cet consists of **three** lines that rhyme together.

EXERCISE 2-F
- Fill in (one cue)
- Skills: word parts, dictionary, context

*Continue filling in **word parts** from your version of List 1 as you have been doing, **using a college-level dictionary** to check accuracy. Now, however, there will be no word in boldface. You will have to search the sentence for a clue.*

Example: √A ___dome is half a dome.

   Answer: *SEMI* [> half]

1. Decisions made by one person without consulting others are ___lateral.
2. A ____volume encyclopedia consists of several volumes.
3. The metric unit of ten liters is called a ___iliter.
4. In statistics, one-fifth of the total sample is called a ____ile.
5. Many medicines use the ____gram as a measure, which is one thousandth of a gram.
6. Any animal with two feet is known as a __ped.
7. Any group, series, or set of seven identical copies is said to be in ____uplicate.
8. ___nary means third in order or rank.
9. A ____ennial is an anniversary of one hundred years.
10. An ____pus has eight tentacles—elongated parts that act like arms.
11. In music, any group of five singers or players is known as a _____et.
12. Something __que is the only one of its kind.

13. When a circle is divided into four parts, each part is called a ___rant.
14. A period of one thousand years is a ___ennium.
15. A worker who is ___skilled is partly trained, but not a specialist or expert.

EXERCISE 2-G
- **Paragraph Examples**
- **Skills: word parts, dictionary, context**

Answer these four questions after each paragraph:

(a) *What word part inside the boldfaced word helps you to understand that word? What does that word part mean?*

(b) *Using only the context of the word and the word part that it contains, what do you think the boldfaced word means? (See Chapter 1, Section 2.)*

(c) *Choose one context clue that helped you. (See Chapter 1, Section 2.)*

    1. *word signals*   4. *examples or description*
    2. *punctuation signals*   5. *contrast or opposites*
    3. *synonyms (substitution)* 6. *prior knowledge; common sense*
       If 6, explain: _____

(d) *How does the dictionary define the boldfaced word as it is used in the paragraph?*

---

1. If we were to go to Africa, where the bones of the petite mother of us all, Lucy, lie, just where she fell **millennia** ago, and look out across the valley, we would recognize in the distance the same mountains she knew. Indeed, they may well have been the last thing Lucy saw before she died. Many features of her physical world have changed: The constellations have shifted position a little, the landscape and weather have changed some, but

the outlines of that mountain still look much the same as when she stood there. She would have seen them as we do.

[Diane Ackerman, *A Natural History of the Senses*, xvi]

(a) _____
(b) _____
(c) _____
(d) _____

2. Community psychologists tend to focus on preventing rather than treating problems. Primary prevention aims to deter problems before they start, and community psychologists consult with community leaders, agencies and institutions, and lawmakers to try to change stressful conditions that contribute to abnormal behavior. Secondary prevention aims to catch psychological problems in their formative stages, as through school counseling. **Tertiary** prevention deals with psychological problems that have ripened.

[Spencer A. Rathus, *Psychology*, 5th Ed., 743]

(a) _____
(b) _____
(c) _____
(d) _____

3. With Germany gone and with Wellington advancing across the Pyrenees from Spain, Napoleon fought a last brilliant campaign to the north and east of Paris in the spring of 1814. He himself now suffered from a variety of ailments, his troops were green and badly outnumbered, and his subjects despairing from never-ending war. But he proved as dangerous as ever on the battlefield. The coalition nevertheless held. Viscount Castlereagh, the British Foreign Secretary, welded together the unlikely allies—Britain, Austria, Russia, Prussia—with the Treaty of Chaumont (March 1814). That **Quadruple** Alliance pledged to fight to restore the balance of power and confine France to its traditional boundaries, and to remain united for twenty years after war's end.

[Chodorow et al., *The Mainstream of Civilization*, 6th Ed., 607]

(a) _____
(b) _____
(c) _____
(d) _____

4. When an organization chooses a multidomestic strategy, it means that competition in each country is handled independently of industry competition in other countries. Thus, the **multinational** corporation is present in many countries, but it encourages marketing, advertising, and product design to be modified and adapted to the specific needs of each country. Many companies reject the idea of a single global market. They have found that the French do not drink orange juice for breakfast, that laundry detergent is used to wash dishes in parts of Mexico, and that people in the Middle East prefer toothpaste that tastes spicy.
   [Richard L. Daft, *Management,* 2nd Ed., 616]

   (a) _____
   (b) _____
   (c) _____
   (d) _____

5. Western forms of government, such as that of the United States, of course, are state governments, and their organization and workings are undoubtedly familiar to almost everyone. An example of a state not so familiar is afforded by the Swazi of Swaziland, a Bantu-speaking people who live in southeast Africa. The Swazi authority system is characterized by a highly developed **dual** monarchy, a hereditary aristocracy, and elaborate rituals of kinship, as well as by statewide age sets. The king and his mother are the central figures of all national activity, linking all the people of the Swazi state; they preside over higher courts, summon national gatherings, control age classes, allocate land, disburse national wealth, take precedence in ritual, and help organize important social events.
   [William A. Haviland, *Cultural Anthropology,* 7th Ed., 320–21]

   (a) _____
   (b) _____
   (c) _____
   (d) _____

SECTION 2

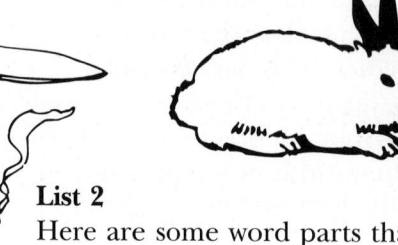

List 2
Here are some word parts that are used to signify numbers.

WORD PART	MEANING
AMBI	both; two
AMPHI	both; two
DEKA	ten
DI	two
HECTO	one hundred
HEMI	half; partly
HEPTA	seven
HEX	six
KILO	one thousand
MONO	one
OCTA	eight
PENTA	five
POLY	many; several
TETRA	four
TRI	three

PRE-EXERCISE ACTIVITY 2
- **List Making**
- **Skill: word parts**

*In the blanks that follow, rewrite List 2. This time, however, reverse the order by writing the **meanings** in the first column. Then gather all the word parts in the list which have that meaning and write them on one line in the second column. This will let you make necessary connections and help you in the process of long-term memorization. The first one has already been done to show you how.*

	MEANING	WORD PARTS	
1.	half, partly	hemi	*Note:* This list will be more useful if you write it in numerical order.
2.			
3.			
4.			
5.			
6.			
7.			
8.			
9.			
10.			
11.			
12.			
13.			
14.			

EXERCISE 2-H
- **Multiple Choice**
- **Skill: word parts**

A meaning is in boldface for each of the following phrases. From the four choices given, pick the one answer which contains a word part with that meaning. Use both versions of List 2 to help you. **Do not use a dictionary.** *Do not focus on the size or difficulty of the words. Look only for the simple word part; it will lead you to the correct answer.*

Example: √A polygon with **five** angles and five sides
    (A) dekagon   (C) pentagon
    (B) hexagon   (D) octagon

Answer: (C) The reason for this answer is that the PENTA part of *pentagon* means "five."

1. Poetry with **three** beats or stress points per line
    (A) monometer   (C) pentameter
    (B) trimeter   (D) octameter

2. A polygon with **six** angles and **six** sides
    (A) pentagon   (C) heptagon
    (B) hexagon   (D) enneagon

3. Certain animals, such as beach fleas, that have feet on **both** sides instead of underneath
    (A) tripods   (C) amphipods
    (B) monopods   (D) hexapods

4. Metric unit of mass equal to **one hundred** grams
    (A) hectogram   (C) decagram
    (B) kilogram   (D) polygram

5. In biology, having **eight** similar parts
    (A) tetramerous   (C) pentamerous
    (B) octamerous   (D) heptamerous

6. Polyhedron with **four** faces
    (A) enneahedron   (C) tetrahedron
    (B) decahedron   (D) heptahedron

7. Producing **one**-color light of a single wavelength
   - (A) polychromatic
   - (B) monochromatic
   - (C) semichromatic
   - (D) trichromatic

8. Paralysis of **half** the body
   - (A) hemiplegia
   - (B) diplegia
   - (C) quadriplegia
   - (D) triplegia

9. Unit of measurement worth **one-thousand** cycles
   - (A) kilocycle
   - (B) nanocycle
   - (C) ambicycle
   - (D) hectocycle

10. Having **many** colors
    - (A) semichromatic
    - (B) monochromatic
    - (C) polychromatic
    - (D) trichromatic

EXERCISE 2-I
- Fill in the Blank (one cue)
- Skill: word parts

*Use a **meaning** from List 2 to fill in the blank in each statement. The word part whose meaning you are defining will be found inside the boldfaced word. **Do not use a dictionary**. Do not focus on the size or difficulty of the words. Look only for the simple word part; it will lead you to the correct answer.*

Example: √**Polytheism** is the belief in _____ gods.

　　　　　Answer: *several* or *many* [> POLY]

1. **Monoculture** refers to the practice of growing _____ farm product.
2. A **hemihydrate** is a hydrate containing _____ a molecule of water to every one of the compound forming the hydrate.
3. A **hexarchy** is a political federation composed of _____ allied governments.
4. A **kilowatt** is a unit of electrical power equivalent to _____ watts.

5. An object or creature that is **trichroic** has _____ colors.
6. A **hexapod** is an invertebrate, _____-footed animal.
7. A **hectogram** is equal to _____ grams.
8. A **dekameter** equals _____ meters.
9. A **dipetalous** plant has _____ petals.
10. A _____-pointed star is called a **pentacle**.
11. Historically, a **heptarchy** referred to a group of _____ allied kingdoms.
12. The _____-handled jar with a narrow neck used by the ancient Greeks and Romans to carry wine or oil is called an **amphora**.
13. A statement with _____ meanings is called **polysemy**.
14. Anything that is **hemitrope** is _____ inverted; that is, it is _____ turned round.
15. Certain insects are **tetrapterous**. They have _____ wings.

EXERCISE 2-J
- Fill in the Blank (no cue)
- Skills: word parts, context

*Once again, use a **meaning** from List 2. This time, however, you will have to find the word part yourself in the difficult or technical word.* **Do not use a dictionary.** *Do not focus on the size or difficulty of the words. Look only for the simple word part; it will lead you to the correct answer.*

Example: √Tetrachloride contains _____ atoms of chlorine to one atom of the other element.

Answer: *four* [> TETRA]

1. An octachord is a musical instrument with _____ strings.
2. A _____-stringed musical instrument used to determine musical intervals is known as a monochord.

3. A pentangular figure has _____ angles.
4. A hex nut has _____ sides.
5. A lens with _____ different focal lengths is called a trifocal.
6. An ambiguous statement has _____ meanings.
7. A kiloton is an explosive force equal to _____ tons of dynamite.
8. Monomania is an exaggerated interest in _____ subject.
9. A pentatonic musical scale has only _____ tones.
10. A hemicycle is another name for a _____ circle.
11. A hectogram is a metric unit of mass equal to _____ grams.
12. In chemical analysis, a substance that is amphichroic can give off _____ colors.
13. Polyphagia refers to the ability of some animals to live on _____ kinds of food.
14. An altarpiece or panel with _____ folds or leaves is called a polyptych.
15. Flowers on a stalk arranged in _____ vertical rows are called tetrastichous.

EXERCISE 2-K
- Matching Columns
- Skill: word parts

Memory check. Do not look back at List 2 or use a dictionary.

1. ____	AMPHI	(a)	seven
2. ____	HECTO	(b)	three
3. ____	PENTA	(c)	many
4. ____	HEMI	(d)	six
5. ____	TETRA	(e)	both
6. ____	MONO	(f)	half
7. ____	POLY	(g)	one

DEC the halls . . .

Copyright © 1996 Harcourt Brace & Company. All rights reserved.

36 CHAPTER 2 NUMBERS

8. ____ TRI (h) one hundred
9. ____ HEX (i) four
10. ____ HEPTA (j) five

EXERCISE 2-L
- Fill in (two cues)
- Skills: word parts, dictionary, context

To finish each word, fill in the blank with one of the **word parts** *from your version of List 2.* **You must use a college-level dictionary** *to make sure that what you write really is a word and that it fits in the sentence. The boldfaced word will give you the meaning of the word part that you must write.*

Example: √_____pods are creatures that have feet on **both** sides.

Answer: *AMPHI* [> both]

1. _____gamy means marriage to **many** partners at the same time.
2. The northern _____sphere is the upper **half** of the earth as divided by the equator.
3. A star-shaped figure that has **five** sides is called a _____gram.
4. A starlike figure that has **six** sides is known as a ____agram.
5. A ____logue is a long speech by **one** person.
6. A __alogue is a conversation between **two** people.
7. A __pod is a **three**-legged support, as for a camera.
8. ____nesia consists of **several** island groups in the Pacific lying east of Micronesia.
9. People who have conflicting feelings at the same time, such as **both** love and hate, are experiencing ____valence.
10. Electric bills are measured in ____watts, which equal **one thousand** watts.
11. ____chloride is a chemical compound containing **four** chlorine atoms per molecule.
12. An ___gonal shape has **eight** sides and angles.
13. A ___plane is an aircraft with **one** pair of wings.

Copyright © 1996 Harcourt Brace & Company. All rights reserved.

14. The liquid measure equal to **one hundred** liters is called a _ _ _ _ _liter.
15. Someone who is _ _ _ _glot is able to speak or write **several** languages.

EXERCISE 2-M
- Fill in (one cue)
- Skills: word parts, dictionary, context

*Continue filling in **word parts** from your version of List 2 as you have been doing, **using a college-level dictionary** to check accuracy. Now, however, there will be no word in boldface. You will have to search the sentence for a clue.*

Example: √_ _ _ _dystrophy is underdevelopment of half the body.

        Answer: *HEMI* [> half]

1. Poetry that has four beats per line is written in _ _ _ _ _ meter.
2. Any situation that forces a person to choose between two equally balanced alternatives is a _ _lemma.
3. _ _ _ _theism is the belief that there is only one God.
4. A _ _ _ _hlon is an athletic contest comprising five different track and field events.
5. At different stages in its life, an _ _ _ _ bian is able to live both in water and on land.
6. _ _ _apod is the name given to an insect with six feet.
7. A _ _oxide is an oxide containing two atoms of oxygen in the molecule.
8. The unit of mass and weight equal to one thousand grams is a _ _ _ _gram.
9. A solid contained by four plane faces is given the name _ _ _ _ _hedron.
10. In ancient Rome, a government of three persons jointly holding the same authority was called a _ _ _umvirate.

11. _____gamy is the practice of having many spouses at the same time.
12. An _____hedron is a solid figure with eight plane surfaces.
13. The unit of length equal to one hundred meters is called the _____meter.
14. The _____teuch consists of the first seven books of the Old Testament.
15. Half of a line of poetry, especially as divided by a pause, is called a _____stich.

EXERCISE 2-N
- **Paragraph Examples**
- **Skills: word parts, dictionary, context**

Answer these four questions after each paragraph:

(a) *What word part inside the boldfaced word helps you to understand that word? What does that word part mean?*

(b) *Using only the context of the word and the word part that it contains, what do you think the boldfaced word means? (See Chapter 1, Section 2.)*

(c) *Choose one context clue that helped you. (See Chapter 1, Section 2.)*
   1. *word signals*
   2. *punctuation signals*
   3. *synonyms (substitution)*
   4. *examples or description*
   5. *contrast or opposites*
   6. *prior knowledge; common sense*
      If 6, explain: _____

(d) *How does the dictionary define the boldfaced word as it is used in the paragraph?*

1. George Simmel (1950) was the first sociologist to emphasize the importance of the size of a group on the interaction process. He suggested that small groups have distinctive qualities and patterns

of interaction that disappear when the group grows larger. For example, dyads resist change in their group size: on the one hand, the loss of one member destroys the group leaving the other member alone; but on the other hand a **triad**, or the addition of a third member, creates uncertainty because it introduces the possibility of two-against-one alliances.

    [Henry L. Tischler, *Introduction to Sociology,* 4th Ed., 109]

(a) _____
(b) _____
(c) _____
(d) _____

2. Where some form of conjugal or extended family is the norm, family exogamy requires that either the husband or wife, if not both, must move to a new household upon marriage. There are five common patterns of residence that a newly married couple may adopt. As among the Maya, a woman may go to live with her husband in the household in which he grew up; this is known as patrilocal residence. As among the Hopi, the man may leave the family in which he grew up to go live with his wife in her parents' household; this is called matrilocal residence. As in the case of extended families on the coast of Maine, a married couple may have the option of choosing whether to live matrilocally or patrilocally, an arrangement that is labelled **ambilocal** residence. As in most of modern North America, a married couple may form a household in an independent location, an arrangement referred to as neolocal residence. . . .

    [William A. Haviland, *Cultural Anthropology,* 7th Ed., 249]

(a) _____
(b) _____
(c) _____
(d) _____

3. There's been this received wisdom that because insects aren't durably calcified like mollusks or the bones of vertebrates, there wouldn't be much of a fossil record. In fact, the literature from old German, Russian and Chinese sources was rich enough to gather information about 1,263 extinct and extant insect families. Only about 825 families of four-legged animals (vertebrate **tetrapods**) have been documented as fossils.

    [John Rennie, "Insects Are Forever," *Scientific American,* November 1993, 18]

40 CHAPTER 2 NUMBERS

(a) _____
(b) _____
(c) _____
(d) _____

4. A number of patients suffering from severe cases of epilepsy have undergone split-brain operations, in which the corpus callosum is severed. The purpose of the operation is to try to confine epilepsy to one **hemisphere** of the cerebral cortex, rather than allow one hemisphere to agitate the other by transmitting a "violent storm of neural impulses" (Carlson 1988). These operations do seem to help epilepsy patients. People who have undergone them can be thought of as winding up with two brains, yet under most circumstances their behavior remains perfectly normal. However, some of the effects of two hemispheres that have stopped talking to one another can be rather intriguing.
[Spencer A. Rathus, *Psychology,* 4th Ed., 68]

(a) _____
(b) _____
(c) _____
(d) _____

SEMI
HEMI
POLY
MULTI

SEMI, HEMI—half or part;
POLY, MULTI—off the chart

5. The Irish potato famine was a major disaster caused by a fungal disease, late blight of potatoes. The potato, native to South America, was brought to Europe in the sixteenth century. Potatoes require little labor and produce high yields of one of the most nutritious crops. By the nineteenth century, they were almost the only crop grown in Ireland. However, **monocultures** (plantings of only one crop) are especially susceptible to the rapid spread of disease. In 1845 and 1846, late blight destroyed virtually the whole Irish potato crop, leading to a devastating famine. From 1845 to 1851, a million people died in Ireland and a million and a half emigrated, mainly to the United States and Canada.
[Arms et al., *A Journey into Life,* 3rd Ed., 399]

(a) _____
(b) _____
(c) _____
(d) _____

Copyright © 1996 Harcourt Brace & Company. All rights reserved.

SECTION 3: CHAPTER REVIEW (LISTS 1 AND 2 COMBINED)

Word Parts Covered in This Chapter:

WORD PART	MEANING	COMMON EXAMPLE	TEXTBOOK EXAMPLE
AMBI	both	*ambidextrous*	*ambiversion*
AMPHI	both	*amphibian*	*amphicoelous*
BI	two	*bicycle*	*bilineate*
CENT	one hundred	*century*	*centimeter*
DEC	ten	*December*	*decennary*
DEKA	ten	*dekameter*	*dekaliter*
DI	two	*dioxide*	*digraph*
DU	two	*duet*	*dualistic*
HECTO	one hundred	*hectometer*	*hectoliter*
HEMI	half; partly	*hemisphere*	*hemitrope*
HEPTA	seven	*heptagon*	*heptarchy*
HEX	six	*hexagon*	*hexameter*
KILO	one thousand	*kilogram*	*kilocalorie*
MILLI	one thousand	*millimeter*	*millimicron*
MONO	one	*monorail*	*mononeural*
MULTI	many; several	*multiply*	*multivalent*
NONA	nine	*nonagon*	*nonagenarian*
NOV	nine	*November*	*novennial*
OCT	eight	*October*	*octahedral*
PENTA	five	*pentagon*	*pentamerous*
POLY	many; several	*polygraph*	*polyandry*
QUAD	four	*quadrangle*	*quadruped*
QUART	four	*quarter*	*quartile*
QUINT	five	*quintet*	*quintile*
SEMI	half; partly	*semiconscious*	*semipalmate*
SEPT	seven	*September*	*septenary*
SEX	six	*sextet*	*sexagenarian*
TER	three; threefold	*ternary*	*tercet*
TETRA	four	*tetralogy*	*tetrachloride*
TRI	three	*tricycle*	*trinomial*
UNI	one	*uniform*	*unigravida*

Copyright © 1996 Harcourt Brace & Company. All rights reserved.

PRE-EXERCISE ACTIVITY 3
- **List Making**
- **Skill: word parts**

*In the blanks that follow, rewrite the combined word parts list. This time, however, reverse the order by writing the **meanings** in the first column. Then gather all the word parts in the list which have that meaning and write them on one line in the second column. This will let you make necessary connections and help you in the process of long-term memorization. The first one has already been done to show you how. (Note: You do not need to rewrite the examples.)*

	MEANING	WORD PARTS	
1.	half, partly	hemi, semi	*Note:* This list will be more useful if you write it in numerical order.
2.	_____	_____	
3.	_____	_____	
4.	_____	_____	
5.	_____	_____	
6.	_____	_____	
7.	_____	_____	
8.	_____	_____	
9.	_____	_____	
10.	_____	_____	
11.	_____	_____	
12.	_____	_____	
13.	_____	_____	
14.	_____	_____	
15.	_____	_____	

EXERCISE 2-O
- **Matching Columns**
- **Skill: word parts**

Memory check. Do not look back at the combined list or use a dictionary.

1. ____ DEKA	(a) six
2. ____ POLY	(b) one
3. ____ QUINT	(c) three
4. ____ UNI	(d) many
5. ____ KILO	(e) eight
6. ____ SEPT	(f) four
7. ____ TER	(g) seven
8. ____ OCTA	(h) ten
9. ____ HEX	(i) one thousand
10. ____ QUAD	(j) five

EXERCISE 2-P
- **Cross Out**
- **Skills: dictionary, word parts, context**

One word in each set does not contain the word part and meaning that is given, even though it has a set of similar letters. **Use a college-level dictionary** *to find the one that does* **not** *fit.*

Example:

	WORD PART	MEANING	CROSS OUT THE ONE WORD THAT DOES NOT FIT
	√BI	two	binary, bilious, binomial

Answer: The dictionary shows that *binary* and *binomial* have the word *two* in their definitions. *Bilious* does not; cross it out.

WORD PART	MEANING	CROSS OUT THE ONE WORD THAT DOES NOT FIT
1. DEC	ten	decade, decent, decathlon
2. CENT	one hundred	centralize, century, centesimal

Copyright © 1996 Harcourt Brace & Company. All rights reserved.

3. POLY   many   polytechnic, polymer, polyp
4. SEX   six   sextuplet, sexism, sextet
5. TRI   three   trilogy, tributary, triptych
6. SEMI   partly   seminal, semiskilled, semiprivate
7. DU   two   dualism, duplex, ducal
8. SEPT   seven   septic, September, septilateral
9. UNI   one   unilateral, uninhibited, univalent
10. NONA   nine   nonagon, nonagenarian, nonage

EXERCISE 2-Q
- **Extended Answer**
- **Skills: word parts, dictionary, context**

Answer the following questions by using a college-level dictionary.

Example: √How is the meaning *four* involved in the word **tetrapod**?

    Answer: Tetrapod means having four feet, legs, or leglike appendages.

1. How is the meaning *many* involved in the word **polyhedron**?

2. How is the meaning *seven* involved in the word **septuple**?

3. How is the meaning *two* involved in the word **digraph**?

4. How is the meaning *four* involved in the word **quadraphonic**?

5. How is the meaning *nine* involved in the word **nonagon**?

6. How is the meaning *partly* involved in the word **hemihedral**?

7. How is the meaning *three* involved in the word **ternary**?

8. How is the meaning *one thousand* involved in the term **kilowatt-hour?**

9. How is the meaning *five* involved in the word **pentadactyl?**

10. How is the meaning *both* involved in the word **ambidextrous?**

EXERCISE 2-R
- Fill in the Blank
- Skill: word parts

Memory check. Do not look back at the combined list or use a dictionary.

1. Name two word parts that mean *seven*: _____ and _____.
2. Name two word parts that mean *two*: _____ and _____.
3. Name two word parts that mean *100*: _____ and _____.
4. Name two word parts that mean *one*: _____ and _____.
5. Name two word parts that mean *five*: _____ and _____.
6. Name two word parts that mean *1,000*: _____ and _____.
7. Name two word parts that mean *nine*: _____ and _____.
8. Name two word parts that mean *many*: _____ and _____.
9. Name two word parts that mean *four*: _____ and _____.
10. Name two word parts that mean *half*: _____ and _____.

46 CHAPTER 2 NUMBERS

EXERCISE 2-S
- **Paragraph Examples**
- **Skills: word parts, dictionary, context**

Answer these four questions after each paragraph:

(a) *What word part inside the boldfaced word helps you to understand that word? What does that word part mean?*

(b) *Using only the context of the word and the word part that it contains, what do you think the boldfaced word means? (See Chapter 1, Section 2.)*

(c) *Choose one context clue that helped you. (See Chapter 1, Section 2.)*
   1. *word signals*
   2. *punctuation signals*
   3. *synonyms (substitution)*
   4. *examples or description*
   5. *contrast or opposites*
   6. *prior knowledge; common sense*
      If 6, explain: _____

(d) *How does the dictionary define the boldfaced word as it is used in the paragraph?*

1. Seahorses provide the only known example of **monogamy** in fishes living in sea grasses or mangroves. As far as we know, our pairs never divorce. Nor do they cheat. This is exceptional: new genetic research techniques are revealing that animals we thought of as firmly paired, including many birds, are often not sexually faithful after all. We can be sure of seahorse fidelity because a female's body visibly deflates when she transfers eggs, while the male's pouch inflates; these changes always occur simultaneously. In very few, if any, animals do both sexes make it so obvious they have mated.
   [Amanda Vincent, "The Improbable Seahorse," *National Geographic*, October 1994, 135]

   (a) _____
   (b) _____
   (c) _____
   (d) _____

2. You learn **ambidexterity**. Skills with your natural dominant side will always be somewhat better than with the non-dominant side,

but we've all seen athletes, such as switch-hitters in baseball, who make using both hands look easy. Translated, that means they've been persistent in practice. Ambidexterity is a good idea, not just for baseball hitters, but for any athletic endeavor you can think of. Those who work with weights in muscle development should be careful not to exercise one arm or leg with greater intensity than they do the other. For golfers, **ambidexterity** can help prevent back pain. A golfer who does warm-up swings with his or her nondominant arm will provide some balanced strength for the back muscles on that side.

[Dr. Donohue, *Traverse City Record-Eagle*, 12 Nov. 1994, 3B]

(a) _____
(b) _____
(c) _____
(d) _____

3. In 1971, astronomers recognized a class of bizarre, x-ray-emitting stars, known as x-ray binaries. Theorists have deduced that these objects consist of a normal star orbiting a collapsed stellar corpse, usually a neutron star. The study of x-ray binaries provides a glimpse into the life cycle of some of the most exotic and dynamic stellar systems in the sky. In these stellar **duos,** one or both members spends some time feeding off its partner. That transfer of material stunningly alters both stars' development.

[Edward P. J. van den Hueval and Jan van Paradijs, "X-Ray Binaries," *Scientific American*, November 1993, 64]

(a) _____
(b) _____
(c) _____
(d) _____

4. Genes are the basic building blocks of heredity. They are the biochemical materials that regulate the development of traits. Some traits, such as blood type, are transmitted by a single pair of genes—one of which is derived from each parent. Other traits, referred to as **polygenic**, are determined by complex combinations of genes.

[Spencer A. Rathus, *Psychology*, 4th Ed., 78]

(a) _____
(b) _____
(c) _____
(d) _____

5. If you can discriminate the colors of the visible spectrum, you have normal color vision and are labeled a **trichromat**. This means that you are sensitive to red-green, blue-yellow, and light-dark. People who are totally color-blind are called monochromats and are sensitive to light-dark only. Total color blindness is quite rare. The fully color-blind see the world as trichromats would on a black-and-white television set or in a black-and-white movie. Partial color blindness is more common than total color blindness. Partial color blindness is a sex-linked trait that strikes mostly males. The partially color-blind are called dichromats. Dichromats can discriminate only two colors—red and green, or blue and yellow—and the colors that are derived from mixing these colors.

[Spencer A. Rathus, *Psychology,* 4th Ed., 108]

(a) _____
(b) _____
(c) _____
(d) _____

6. In addition to his monohybrid crosses, Gregor Mendel performed **dihybrid** crosses. These involved plants with two different pairs of contrasting alleles. In one experiment, Mendel crossed plants homozygous for seeds that were both smooth and yellow with plants homozygous for wrinkled, green seeds. All the F_1 offspring were smooth and yellow, showing that smooth was dominant to wrinkled and yellow was dominant to green.

[Karen Arms, et al. *A Journey into Life,* 3rd Ed., 234]

(a) _____
(b) _____
(c) _____
(d) _____

7. Talismans were wonder-working objects—like relics, rosaries, images of the saints—and mainly concerned with healing. At the time of the Crusades, the most famous of talismans was the philosopher's stone. Anyone who possessed this touchstone would be able to perform many wonders, such as changing base metals into gold. Other talismanic symbols were the Egyptian ankh, a T-shaped cross with a looped top that promoted wisdom and well-being; the five-pointed star of the pentagram; and the **hexagram**. This six-pointed star was also known as Solomon's seal, and it was used as an amulet against fever.

[Mary Agnes O'Donnell, *Seething Cauldrons,* 73]

(a) _____
(b) _____
(c) _____
(d) _____

8, 9, 10. On the basis of structural differences, neurons can be classified into three major groups. **Multipolar** neurons have many processes arising from their cell bodies. Only one process of each neuron is an axon; the rest are dendrites. Most neurons whose cell bodies lie within the brain or spinal cord are of this type. The cell body of a **bipolar** neuron has only two processes, one arising from either end. Although these processes have similar structural characteristics, one serves as an axon and the other as a dendrite. Such neurons are found within specialized parts of the eyes, nose, and ears. Each **unipolar** neuron has a single process extending from its cell body. Unipolar neurons occur in specialized masses of nerve tissue called ganglia, which are located outside the brain and spinal cord.
   [John W. Hole, Jr., *Human Anatomy and Physiology*, 337–38]

(a) _____
(b) _____
(c) _____
(d) _____

(a) _____
(b) _____
(c) _____
(d) _____

(a) _____
(b) _____
(c) _____
(d) _____

CHAPTER 3 DIRECTION

SECTION 1

List 1
Here are some word parts that are used to signify direction.

WORD PART	MEANING
AB	away from
ANA	up(ward); going back
CATA	(going) down
DE	away from; down
E	out of; away from
EC	out of; away from
EF	out of; away from
EM	into
EN	into
EX	out of; away from
PER	through
RE	going back; again
SE	away from
-WARD	in the direction of; toward

51

PRE-EXERCISE ACTIVITY 1
- **List Making**
- **Skill: word parts**

*In the blanks that follow, rewrite List 1. This time, however, reverse the order by writing the **meanings** in the first column. Then gather all the word parts in the list which have that meaning and write them on one line in the second column. This will let you make necessary connections and help you in the process of long-term memorization. The first one has already been done to show you how.*

MEANING	WORD PARTS
1. again	re
2. _____	_____
3. _____	_____
4. _____	_____
5. _____	_____
6. _____	_____
7. _____	_____
8. _____	_____
9. _____	_____
10. _____	_____

Note: This list will be more useful if you write it in alphabetical order.

EXERCISE 3-A
- **Multiple Choice**
- **Skill: word parts**

A meaning is in boldface for each of the following phrases. From the four choices given, pick the one answer which contains a word part with that meaning. Use both versions of List 1 to help you. **Do not use a dictionary**. *Do not focus on the size or difficulty of the words. Look only for the simple word part; it will lead you to the correct answer.*

Example: √A taking **back** or cancellation
    (A) invocation   (C) revocation
    (B) provocation   (D) avocation

Answer: (C) The reason for this answer is that the RE part of *revocation* means "back."

1. Spread **through** every part
   - (A) invasive
   - (B) pervasive
   - (C) evasive
   - (D) derisive

2. To pour **out of**
   - (A) effuse
   - (B) refuse
   - (C) confuse
   - (D) infuse

3. To move **away from** the specific, practical, or applied
   - (A) protract
   - (B) contract
   - (C) abstract
   - (D) retract

4. Pertaining to wind currents that go **up**
   - (A) retrobatic
   - (B) acrobatic
   - (C) anabatic
   - (D) catabatic

5. To send goods **out of** a country
   - (A) import
   - (B) report
   - (C) comport
   - (D) export

6. To shut oneself **away from** others
   - (A) include
   - (B) conclude
   - (C) seclude
   - (D) preclude

7. Bringing **back** news of an event
   - (A) supporting
   - (B) reporting
   - (C) deporting
   - (D) purporting

8. Putting something **in** position
   - (A) displacing
   - (B) preplacing
   - (C) replacing
   - (D) emplacing

9. Fish migrating **down**-river to breed
   - (A) catadromous
   - (B) anadromous
   - (C) hippodromous
   - (D) syndromous

10. To keep someone **away from** a desired activity
    (A) maintain
    (B) pertain
    (C) detain
    (D) sustain

EXERCISE 3-B
- Fill in the Blank (one cue)
- Skill: word parts

*Use a **meaning** from List 1 to fill in the blank in each statement. The word part whose meaning you are defining will be found inside the boldfaced word. **Do not use a dictionary**. Do not focus on the size or difficulty of the words. Look only for the simple word part; it will lead you to the correct answer.*

Example: √A **recapitulation** involves _____ over material in a summarizing way.

   Answer: *going back* [> RE]

1. **Abrasion** is a wearing or rubbing _____ .
2. **Windward** means moving _____ from which the wind blows.
3. To **percolate** is to pass liquid, such as coffee, gradually _____ a filter system.
4. **Sedition** is an illegally organized movement _____ the government in power.
5. **Resilience** is the ability to get _____ into shape.
6. To **extricate** someone is to get him or her _____ difficulty.
7. A **depilatory** is a substance which takes _____ hair.
8. To **exculpate** is to take blame _____ a situation.
9. **Ablactation** means weaning an infant _____ mother's milk.
10. Something **anabiotic** is capable of bringing _____ animation or energy.
11. To **ensconce** is to settle _____ a secure place.

12. The geological term **cataclinal** means coming _____ in the same direction as the incline of the strata.
13. A **sequestrum** is a piece of dead tissue, especially bone, that has moved _____ the surrounding healthy tissue.
14. When a disease **recrudesces**, it breaks out _____ .
15. An **anadromous** fish goes _____ river to spawn.

EXERCISE 3-C
- **Fill in the Blank (no cue)**
- **Skills: word parts, context**

*Once again, use a **meaning** from List 1 to fill in the blank in each statement. This time, however, you will have to find the word part yourself in the difficult or technical word. **Do not use a dictionary**. Do not focus on the size or difficulty of the words. Look only for the simple word part; it will lead you to the correct answer.*

Example:　√A perspicuous idea is clear and easy to see _____ .

　　　　Answer: *through* [> PER]

1. An eccentric person has moved _____ the mainstream of social practice.
2. Segregation is the attempt to keep a group _____ the general body of society.
3. Denudation of the landscape takes place when the forces of erosion remove soil _____ the underlying rock.
4. Perennials are plants that last _____ three or more seasons.
5. Entanglements involve the victim _____ difficulties and complications.
6. An exclusionist wants to keep certain people _____ their rights and privileges.
7. A rezoning hearing involves _____ over old zoning laws to update them.

Copyright © 1996 Harcourt Brace & Company. All rights reserved.

8. Severance pay is given to those who are going _____ their job.
9. A sailboat moving leeward is moving _____ toward which the wind blows.
10. To resorb means to swallow or suck in _____ .
11. An anaglyph is an ornament carved with features that thrust _____ and are thus slightly three-dimensional.
12. Cataclastic refers to the break _____ of rock because of extreme pressure.
13. The abductor is a muscle that draws a body part _____ the body axis.
14. The breaking _____ in the body of complex chemical compounds into simpler ones is called catabolism.
15. Anagoge is a scriptural interpretation meant to lead the reader _____ to hidden spiritual meanings.

EXERCISE 3-D
- **Matching Columns**
- **Skill: word parts**

Memory check. Do not look at the list. Special note: This time, some answers are used more than once.

1. _____ RE   (a) down
2. _____ -WARD   (b) away from
3. _____ SE   (c) again
4. _____ ANA   (d) into
5. _____ AB   (e) in the direction of
6. _____ PER   (f) upward
7. _____ EM   (g) through
8. _____ EX
9. _____ CATA
10. _____ EN

AB, DE, EC and EF, EX, SE
Say it's time to get away.

EXERCISE 3-E
- Fill in (two cues)
- Skills: word parts, dictionary, context

*To finish each word, fill in the blank with one of the **word parts** from your version of List 1. **You must use a college-level dictionary** to make sure that what you write really is a word and that it fits in the sentence. The boldfaced word will give you the meaning of the word part that you must write.*

Example: √"West_ _ _ _ ho the wagons!" was the cry of many pioneers as they headed **in the direction of** the western United States in the nineteenth century.

Answer: -WARD [> in the direction of]

1. An _ _cerpt is a passage taken **out of** a longer book, speech, etc.
2. To _ _andon something is to go **away from** it.
3. The doctors tried to _ _vive the child, to bring him to consciousness **again**.
4. The bulletproof vest _ _flected the bullet, directing it **away from** the police officer's body.
5. The judge _ _questered the jury, ordering its members **away from** all outside contact.
6. The king _ _dicated his throne and walked **away from** his ruling position.
7. A _ _motion moves you **down** in the corporate power structure.
8. She _ _haled forcefully, pushing the air **out of** her lungs.
9. He _ _flected on his childhood, living the memories once **again**.
10. _ _cadence is a move **away from** quality.
11. Wind_ _ _ _ describes the location of a sailboat moving **in the direction** from which the wind blows.
12. To _ _fetter is to bind **in** chains.
13. One meaning of the word _ _ _ _ract is a great **down**pour of water.
14. The keen ability to see **through** or understand something is known as _ _ _spicacity.
15. _ _ _leptic treatment brings a patient's strength **back up** after a disease.

EXERCISE 3-F
- **Fill in (one cue)**
- **Skills: word parts, dictionary, context**

*Continue filling in **word parts** from your version of List 1 as you have been doing, **using a college-level dictionary** to check accuracy. Now, however, there will be no word in boldface. You will have to search the sentence for a clue.*

Example: √_ _lation means taking away unhealthy growths from the body by surgery.

   Answer: *AB* [> away from]

1. Prisoners of war who are allowed to go back to their homeland again are said to be _ _patriated.
2. When a volcano _rupts, lava and other materials come out of it.
3. When a liquid such as water passes through a porous substance, it is said to _ _ _colate.
4. Going back to an earlier, inferior, or less complex condition is called _ _gression.
5. Taking away the respect or care due to a sacred object is _ _secration.
6. Soldiers are discharged from the armed forces at a _ _paration center.
7. An _ _plosion is a more or less violent energy release outward.
8. _ _bedded memories are firmly fixed in the brain.
9. Giving something back again to its rightful owner is known as _ _stitution.
10. An _ _voy is sent into a foreign country on a special diplomatic mission.
11. An _ _ _chronism places something back in a time where it does not belong.
12. The foul-smelling vapors or fumes that come out of decaying matter are called _ _fluvia.
13. _ _hydrogenation is the chemical process of taking hydrogen away from a substance.

14. The natural stripping away of an outer layer of skin, as in snakes, is called ___dysis.
15. Humans fall into the group of primates called ____rrhine because their close-set nostrils are directed downward.

EXERCISE 3-G
- **Paragraph Examples**
- **Skills: word parts, dictionary, context**

Answer these four questions after each paragraph:

(a) *What word part inside the boldfaced word helps you to understand that word? What does that word part mean?*

_____

(b) *Using only the context of the word and the word part that it contains, what do you think the boldfaced word means? (See Chapter 1, Section 2.)*

_____

(c) *Choose one context clue that helped you. (See Chapter 1, Section 2.)*

   1. *word signals*   4. *examples or description*
   2. *punctuation signals*   5. *contrast or opposites*
   3. *synonyms (substitution)*   6. *prior knowledge; common sense*
       If 6, explain: _____

(d) *How does the dictionary define the boldfaced word as it is used in the paragraph?*

_____

1. Regardless of its source, most water we now drink has been used many times before. Mississippi River water, for instance, gets spewed out upstream as Natchez, Mississippi **effluent**, only to be pumped in downstream as Baton Rouge, Louisiana's drinking water. Other communities repeat the process, right on down to the Gulf of Mexico. Colorado River water that Southern Californians drink is a blend that includes waste water from 187 municipalities.
     [David Clarke, "Let Them Drink Waste Water," *Garbage*, Summer 1994, 10]

(a) _____
(b) _____
(c) _____
(d) _____

2. Centralization and decentralization pertain to the hierarchical level at which decisions are made. Centralization means that decision authority is located near the top of the organization. With decentralization, decision authority is pushed downward to lower organization levels. Organizations may have to experiment to find the correct hierarchical level at which to make decisions. In the United States and Canada, the trend over the last 30 years has been toward greater decentralization of organizations. **Decentralization** is believed to make greater use of human resources, unburden top managers, ensure that decisions are made close to the action by well-informed people, and permit more rapid response to external changes.

[Richard L. Daft, *Management,* 2nd Ed., 252]

(a) _____
(b) _____
(c) _____
(d) _____

3. In fifteenth century Europe, progressive landlords tried to introduce capitalism into agriculture by producing only the most profitable crops and animal products. Particularly in England—where wool production was well established—many landlords fenced in, or enclosed, open fields that had formerly been reserved for the use of villagers, and some of them even enclosed cultivated land to accommodate huge flocks of sheep. At the beginning of the sixteenth century, Thomas More, chancellor of England, complained that the **enclosure** movement was ruining the small farmers and was creating a class of "sturdy beggars" or "vagabonds" who posed a problem for town governments.

[Chodorow et al., *The Mainstream of Civilization,* 6th Ed., 415–16]

(a) _____
(b) _____
(c) _____
(d) _____

4. Abraham Lincoln not only favored a nation-centered definition of federal power, but specifically rejected the idea of the Union as a limited contract between states and a national government. When the electoral college vote cast Lincoln as the winner in 1860, the state of South Carolina saw the (constitutional) writing on the wall and reacted accordingly. This time, South Carolina, in effect, nullified the entire Constitution by **seceding** from the Union. Ten more states that would shortly form the southern Confederacy followed suit. True to their state-power principles, these eleven joined in a weak central government reminiscent of their first national confederation under the articles.
[W. Lance Bennett, *Inside the System*, 119]
   (a) _____
   (b) _____
   (c) _____
   (d) _____

5. Monophonic VCRs lay down the audio track along the tape's edge. The tape's relatively slow speed, even at SP, puts a damper on the sound that can be heard more easily in music than in speech. Sounds can waver, high notes can be muddy, and background noise can come through. Stereo hi-fi VCRs record sound differently. Rotating audio heads lay down **diagonal** audio tracks across the width of the tape, under the video. That process produces sound of near-CD quality. The frequency response (reproduction of sounds from high to low) is excellent, as is stereo separation.
["VCRs," *Consumer Reports*, March 1994, 162–63]
   (a) _____
   (b) _____
   (c) _____
   (d) _____

SECTION 2

List 2
Here are more word parts that are used to signify direction.

WORD PART	MEANING
AD	to; toward
APO	away from; off
DIA	through; across
IL	into
IM	into
IN	into
IR	into
OB	to; toward
OC	to; toward
OF	to; toward
OP	to; toward
PRO	forward; outward
RETRO	(going) back; behind
TRANS	across; through

PRE-EXERCISE ACTIVITY 2
- **List Making**
- **Skill: word parts**

*In the blanks that follow, rewrite List 2. This time, however, reverse the order by writing the **meanings** in the first column. Then gather all the word parts in the list which have that meaning and write them on one line in the second column. This will let you make necessary connections and help you in the process of long-term memorization. The first one has already been done to show you how.*

	MEANING	WORD PARTS	
1.	across	dia, trans	*Note:* This list will be more useful if you write it in alphabetical order.
2.			
3.			
4.			
5.			
6.			
7.			
8.			
9.			
10.			

EXERCISE 3-H
- **Multiple Choice**
- **Skill: word parts**

*A meaning is in boldface for each of the following phrases. From the four choices given, pick the one answer which contains a word part with that meaning. Use both versions of List 2 to help you. **Do not use a dictionary**. Do not focus on the size or difficulty of the words. Look only for the simple word part; it will lead you to the correct answer.*

Copyright © 1996 Harcourt Brace & Company. All rights reserved.

Example: √To turn attention **toward** something
    (A) divert   (C) invert
    (B) revert   (D) advert

Answer: (D) The reason for this answer is that the AD part of *advert* means "toward."

1. **Going back** to the past and seeing it in one's mind
   (A) introspective   (C) perspective
   (B) prospective   (D) retrospective

2. Placed **into** an orbit, trajectory, or stream
   (A) dejected   (C) rejected
   (B) injected   (D) objected

3. To send or pass something **across** from one person, place, or thing to another
   (A) commit   (C) emit
   (B) transmit   (D) permit

4. To present something **to** another person for acceptance or rejection
   (A) defer   (C) refer
   (B) infer   (D) offer

5. Pertaining to changes as they develop **through** time
   (A) synchronic   (C) chronic
   (B) diachronic   (D) isochronic

6. To cause something to move **forward**
   (A) impel   (C) propel
   (B) dispel   (D) repel

7. Making a vivid image or memory **in**
   (A) depressing   (C) oppressing
   (B) impressing   (D) suppressing

8. A military assistant assigned **to** a commanding officer
   (A) proponent   (C) civilian
   (B) renegade   (D) adjutant

9. To turn **toward** a viewer in a way that shows another side
   - (A) convert
   - (B) obvert
   - (C) pervert
   - (D) subvert

10. In geology, a deposit of metal that branches **away from** the main vein
    - (A) apophysis
    - (B) prophylaxis
    - (C) paralysis
    - (D) analysis

EXERCISE 3-I
- Fill in the Blank (one cue)
- Skill: word parts

*Use a **meaning** from List 2 to fill in the blank in each statement. The word part whose meaning you are defining will be found inside the boldfaced word. **Do not use a dictionary**. Do not focus on the size or difficulty of the words. Look only for the simple word part; it will lead you to the correct answer.*

Example: √An **illuminating** remark brings clarity _____ a conversation.

        Answer: *into* [> IL]

1. An **adjunct** is added _____ another thing, but not as an essential part.
2. An **irruption** is a bursting or breaking _____ .
3. **Propitious** signs point _____ to favorable and helpful events.
4. **Transoceanic** means extending _____ the ocean.
5. To **insinuate** is to creep, enter, or flow _____ .
6. To be criminally **implicated** means being tangled up _____ a crime.
7. Something **opportune** works _____ your benefit.
8. **Transmigration** is the belief that the soul goes _____ to another body after death.
9. **Retrogression** is the act of moving _____ .

10. An **apostrophe** can be used to show that a letter has been taken _____ a word.
11. **Retroflexion** refers to the medical condition where an organ is bent _____ upon itself.
12. An **adjuvant** is a substance added _____ a drug to aid the operation of the principal ingredient.
13. **Protrusile** means capable of being thrust _____, as an elephant's trunk.
14. A person can see _____ **diaphanous** material.
15. In astronomy, the point in the orbit of any celestial body at its greatest distance _____ the earth is called its **apogee**.

EXERCISE 3-J
- Fill in the Blank (no cue)
- Skills: word parts, context

*Once again, use a **meaning** from List 2 to fill in the blank in each statement. This time, however, you will have to find the word part yourself in the difficult or technical word. **Do not use a dictionary**. Do not focus on the size or difficulty of the words. Look only for the simple word part; it will lead you to the correct answer.*

Example: √Irradiation treats a cancerous tumor by sending radiation _____ it.

      Answer: *into* [> IR]

1. An offensive joke brings displeasure _____ the listener.
2. An issue that impassions a person brings strong feelings _____ a situation.
3. An admonition is a warning given _____ someone.
4. A transgressor steps _____ the limits of the law.
5. Medical irrigation brings water or another fluid _____ a cavity or wound to cleanse it and flush out debris.
6. A diagonal line runs _____ a figure from corner to corner.

7. The Occident faces _____ the setting of the sun, or the west.
8. Protuberant eyes bulge _____.
9. Apostasy means that an individual goes _____ his or her faith.
10. An adjective is a qualifier given _____ another word.
11. Fibrous tissue that forms _____ the lens of the eye is said to be retrolental.
12. Opprobrious behavior brings shame or disgrace _____ the one performing it.
13. Transpiratory substances, such as skin or leaves, give off vapor or odor _____ the surface.
14. A protractor is a muscle that draws a part _____.
15. The act of gathering ideas _____ a conclusion based on what is suggested rather than actually said is known as illation.

EXERCISE 3-K
- **Matching Columns**
- **Skill: word parts**

Memory check. Do not look back at List 2 or use a dictionary. Special note: Some answers are used more than once.

1. ____ OB   (a) across or through
2. ____ IR   (b) to or toward
3. ____ APO   (c) going back or behind
4. ____ DIA   (d) forward or outward
5. ____ RETRO   (e) into
6. ____ TRANS   (f) away from or off
7. ____ OP
8. ____ PRO
9. ____ AD
10. ____ IN

EXERCISE 3-L
- Fill in (two cues)
- Skills: word parts, dictionary, context

*To finish each word, fill in the blank with one of the **word parts** from your version of List 2. **You must use a college-level dictionary** to make sure that what you write really is a word and that it fits in its sentence. The boldfaced word will give you the meaning of the word part that you must write.*

Example: √Because it has _ _hesive properties, a bandage sticks **to** the skin.

   Answer: *AD* [> to]

1. When comments _ _ritate a listener, they bring annoyance **into** the situation.
2. The Concorde has made _ _ _ _ _oceanic flights much easier for those flying **across** the Atlantic.
3. Difficulty with _ _gestion, taking **in** and swallowing food, is a warning signal.
4. The engine's _ _ _pulsion drove the drag racer **forward** with great thrust.
5. A good way to _ _lustrate a point is to bring **in** a comparison.
6. The _ _ _ _ _spective art exhibit displayed works **going back** over Picasso's entire career.
7. The police informant _ _filtrated the gang by getting **into** its activities and pretending to be just another member.
8. A _ _ _motion moves you **forward** in the corporate power structure.
9. In the late nineteenth century, many _ _migrants entered **into** America.
10. A straight line passing **through** the center of a circle is its _ _ _meter.
11. A person who _ _hales draws air **into** his or her lungs.
12. _ _ _ _ _verse girders are often placed **across** other girders to give more strength to a bridge's structure.
13. To _ _monish is to give a warning or reproof **to** someone.

14. An __sequious person acts **towards** others in a fawning, submissive way.
15. To ____statize is to turn **away from** one's religion, cause, political party, etc.

EXERCISE 3-M
- Fill in (one cue)
- Skills: word parts, dictionary, context

*Continue filling in **word parts** from your version of List 2 as you have been doing, **using a college-level dictionary** to check accuracy. Now, however, there will be no word in boldface. You will have to search the sentence for a clue.*

Example: √To __luminate a room is to bring light into it, often by artificial means.

   Answer: *IL* [> into]

1. An __vocation calls in a higher power for assistance or witness.
2. ___visions are supplies which have been stored by someone looking forward to future needs.
3. __versity is hardship or misfortune directed toward someone.
4. An __plosion is a more or less violent collapse inward.
5. A ___gnosis is the identification of disease through examination.
6. When we __serve something, we turn our attention toward it.
7. To __rupt is to break or to burst in.
8. To look at something in _____spect is to go back and examine the past.
9. An appropriate __lustration will always bring understanding into a discussion.
10. A thought that __curs to you comes to your mind.
11. To _____locate is to move across to another position.

12. The _ _stles were early Christian witnesses sent away from their normal lives to preach the gospel.
13. A _ _ _ _ _ducer is a device that receives energy from one system and carries it across to another system.
14. When the last sound or syllable of a word is taken away or cut off, as in *goin'* for *going*, the process is called _ _ _cope.
15. The forward displacement of an organ, such as the eyeball, is called _ _ _ptosis.

EXERCISE 3-N
- **Paragraph Examples**
- **Skills: word parts, dictionary, context**

Answer these four questions after each paragraph:

(a) *What word part inside the boldfaced word helps you to understand that word? What does that word part mean?*

(b) *Using only the context of the word and the word part that it contains, what do you think the boldfaced word means? (See Chapter 1, Section 2.)*

(c) *Choose one context clue that helped you. (See Chapter 1, Section 2.)*
   1. word signals
   2. punctuation signals
   3. synonyms (substitution)
   4. examples or description
   5. contrast or opposites
   6. prior knowledge; common sense
      If 6, explain: _____

(d) *How does the dictionary define the boldfaced word as it is used in the paragraph?*

1. In 1851 Dover and Calais had been linked by an underwater telegraph cable. The Victorian world was entranced by the novelty of lightning-fast communication between distant places. Though pessimists deemed the idea of spanning the Atlantic a "sink for

capital, and task for lunatics," others argued that a **transatlantic** cable would be a "mighty engine for conveying thought," that it would unite the continents in an instant, create mutual understanding, and render war obsolete.

[Doug Stewart, "The Curse of the Great Eastern," *Smithsonian*, November 1994, 73]

(a) _____
(b) _____
(c) _____
(d) _____

2. When party or issue choices do not offer voters solid prospects for betting on the future, the most reliable form of issue voting is to see in retrospect how well a particular party or candidate has performed. Originally introduced by political scientist V. O. Key, and developed more fully by Morris Fiorina, the term retrospective voting applies when voters cannot trust the promises of candidates, but can judge whether candidates or parties have done a good job in the past. One of the things people can see most clearly in retrospect is how well the economy has performed under a president or a party. Ronald Reagan rose to power in 1980 on the tide of **retrospective** voting when he invited voters to "Ask yourself if you are better off today than you were four years ago."

[W. Lance Bennett, *Inside the System*, 244]

(a) _____
(b) _____
(c) _____
(d) _____

3. Whereas other species adapt to their environment through the long, slow process of evolution and natural selection, culture has allowed humans to adapt relatively quickly to many different habitats and become the most flexible species on earth. Adaptation is the process by which human beings adjust to changes in their environment. **Adaptation** can take two different forms: specialization and generalized adaptability. Specialization involves developing ways of doing things that work extremely well in a particular environment or set of circumstances. Generalized adaptability involves developing more complicated yet more flexible ways of doing things.

[Henry L. Tischler, *Introduction to Sociology*, 4th Ed., 57–58]

(a) _____
(b) _____
(c) _____
(d) _____

4. In one of anthropology's classic works, Arnold Van Gennep analyzed the rites of passage that help individuals through the crucial crises of their lives, such as birth, puberty, marriage, parenthood, advancement to a higher class, occupational specialization, and death. He found it useful to divide ceremonies for all of these life crises into three stages: separation, transition, and **incorporation**. The individual would first be ritually removed from the society as a whole, then isolated for a period, and finally incorporated back into society in his or her new status.

[William A. Haviland, *Cultural Anthropology*, 7th Ed., 358]

(a) _____
(b) _____
(c) _____
(d) _____

5. You may have heard that there is a personality test that asks people what a drawing or inkblot looks like and that people commonly answer "a bat." There are a number of such tests, the best known of which is the Rorschach inkblot test, named after its originator, Swiss psychiatrist Hermann Rorschach (1884–1922). The Rorschach test is a projective test. In projective techniques, there are no clear, specified answers. People are presented with ambiguous stimuli such as inkblots or vague drawings and may be asked to report what these stimuli look like to them or to tell stories about them. Because there is no one proper response, it is assumed that people **project** their own personalities into their responses. The meanings they attribute to these stimuli are assumed to reflect their personalities as well as the drawings or blots themselves.

[Spencer A. Rathus, *Psychology*, 5th Ed., 468]

IL and IM and IN and IR:
Come right in and have no fear;
Ve have pretzels, ve have bier.

(a) _____
(b) _____
(c) _____
(d) _____

SECTION 3: CHAPTER REVIEW (LISTS 1 AND 2 COMBINED)

Review of Word Parts Covered in This Chapter:

WORD PART	MEANING	COMMON EXAMPLE	TEXTBOOK EXAMPLE
AB	away from	*abstain*	*abstraction*
AD	to; toward	*advance*	*adhesion*
ANA	up; going back	*anachronism*	*analeptic*
APO	away from; off	*apostrophe*	*apogee*
CATA	(going) down	*catastrophe*	*catabolism*
DE	away from; down	*departure*	*demythologize*
DIA	through; across	*diameter*	*diapophysis*
E	out of; away from	*eject*	*evaporation*
EC	out of; away from	*eccentric*	*ecclesiology*
EF	out of; away from	*effect*	*effluent*
EM	into	*embrace*	*embolism*
EN	into	*engrave*	*enjambment*
EX	out of; away from	*exit*	*extrication*
IL	into	*illuminate*	*illuviation*
IM	into	*immerse*	*immure*
IN	into	*insert*	*inundate*
IR	into	*irrigation*	*irradiation*
OB	to; toward	*objection*	*obverse*
OC	to; toward	*occur*	*occlusion*
OF	to; toward	*offer*	*offertory*
OP	to; toward	*oppose*	*opprobrium*
PER	through	*permit*	*perfoliate*
PRO	forward; outward	*proclaim*	*proclivity*
RE	going back; again	*return*	*retractile*
RETRO	going back; behind	*retrospect*	*retrograde*
SE	away from	*segregation*	*sedition*
TRANS	across; through	*transmit*	*transducer*
-WARD	in the direction of; toward	*backward*	*doomward*

PRE-EXERCISE ACTIVITY 3
- List Making
- Skill: word parts

*In the blanks that follow, rewrite the combined word parts list. This time, however, reverse the order by writing the **meanings** in the first column. Then gather together all the word parts in the list which have that meaning and write them on one line in the second column. This will let you make necessary connections and help you in the process of long-term memorization. The first one has already been done to show you how. (Note: You do not need to rewrite the examples.)*

	MEANING	WORD PARTS	
1.	across	trans	*Note:* This list will be more useful if you write it in alphabetical order.
2.			
3.			
4.			
5.			
6.			
7.			
8.			
9.			
10.			
11.			
12.			
13.			
14.			
15.			

EXERCISE 3-O
- **Matching Columns**
- **Skill: word parts**

Memory check. Do not look back at the combined list or use a dictionary.

1. ____	CATA	(a)	up
2. ____	-WARD	(b)	through
3. ____	IL	(c)	down
4. ____	PRO	(d)	into
5. ____	TRANS	(e)	toward
6. ____	RETRO	(f)	outward
7. ____	ANA	(g)	out of
8. ____	E	(h)	in the direction
9. ____	OB	(i)	across
10. ____	PER	(j)	going back

EXERCISE 3-P
- **Cross Out**
- **Skills: dictionary, context, word parts**

One word in each set does not contain the word part and meaning that is given, even though it has a set of similar letters. **Use a college-level dictionary** *to find the one that does* **not** *fit.*

	WORD		CROSS OUT THE ONE WORD
Example:	PART	MEANING	THAT DOES NOT FIT
	√EM	in; into	embroil, embryo, emission

Answer: The dictionary reveals that *embroil* and *embryo* involve the meaning *in*. *Emission* does not; cross it out.

WORD PART	MEANING	CROSS OUT THE ONE WORD THAT DOES NOT FIT
1. AB	away from	absolve, aberration, ability

2.	AD	to; toward	advocate, admiral, administer
3.	DE	away from	derringer, devolve, detach
4.	PRO	forward	proposal, promptly, provoke
5.	RE	again; back	revamp, renovation, restless
6.	SE	away from	seclusion, separate, sensible
7.	IM	in; into	immanent, impecunious, importation
8.	DIA	through	diamond, diarrhea, diaphanous
9.	ANA	back; again; up	ananthous, anachronism, anaphora
10.	PER	through	perceive, percolate, perimeter

EXERCISE 3-Q
- **Extended Answer**
- **Skills: word parts, dictionary, context**

Answer the following questions by using a college-level dictionary.

Example: √How is the meaning *into* involved in the word **insert**?

   Answer: To insert is to place something into something else.

1. How is the meaning *down* involved in the word **cataclysm**?

2. How is the meaning *forward* involved in the word **propel**?

3. How is the meaning *out of* involved in the word **excavate**?

4. How is the meaning *through* involved in the word **transpire**?

5. How is the meaning *away from* involved in the word **apogee**?

6. How is the meaning *upward* involved in the word **anabatic**?

7. How is the meaning *into* involved in the word **empowerment**?

8. How is the meaning *away from* involved in the word **degeneration**?

9. How is the meaning *through* involved in the word **perspiration**?

10. How is the meaning *toward* involved in the word **adversary**?

EXERCISE 3-R
- **Fill in the Blanks**
- **Skills: word parts, context**

Answer each statement by filling in the blank. Use the combined lists.

Example: √The opposite of AD is _____ .   Answer: AB (etc.)

√A synonym for *down* is _____ .   Answer: *lower*

What did Roman quarterbacks do? PER and DIA through and through.

1. The opposite of CATA is _____ .   [Write another word part.]
2. The opposite of EC is _____ .   [Write another word part.]
3. The opposite of PRO is _____ .   [Write another word part.]
4. The opposite of SE is _____ .   [Write another word part.]
5. The opposite of OF is _____ .   [Write another word part.]
6. A synonym for *toward* is _____ .   [Write a regular word.]
7. A synonym for *up* is _____ .   [Write a regular word.]
8. A synonym for *away from* is _____ .   [Write a regular word.]
9. A synonym for *into* is _____ .   [Write a regular word.]
10. A synonym for *again* is _____ .   [Write a regular word.]

EXERCISE 3-S
- **Fill in the Blanks**
- **Skill: word parts**

Memory check. Do not look back at the combined list or use a dictionary.

1. Name two word parts that mean *away from*: _____ and _____
2. Name two word parts that mean *going back*: _____ and _____
3. Name two word parts that mean *toward*: _____ and _____
4. Name two word parts that mean *out of*: _____ and _____
5. Name two word parts that mean *into*: _____ and _____
6. Name two word parts that mean *down*: _____ and _____
7. Name two word parts that mean *through*: _____ and _____

EXERCISE 3-T
- **Paragraph Examples**
- **Skills: word parts, dictionary, context**

Answer these four questions after each paragraph:

(a) *What word part inside the boldfaced word helps you to understand that word? What does that word part mean?*

(b) *Using only the context of the word and the word part that it contains, what do you think the boldfaced word means? (See Chapter 1, Section 2.)*

(c) *Choose one context clue that helped you. (See Chapter 1, Section 2.)*
   1. *word signals*
   2. *punctuation signals*
   3. *synonyms (substitution)*
   4. *examples or description*
   5. *contrast or opposites*
   6. *prior knowledge; common sense*
      If 6, explain: _____
      _____

(d) *How does the dictionary define the boldfaced word as it is used in the paragraph?*
   _____

1. A language is a system of verbal and, in many cases, written symbols, with rules for putting them together. It is impossible to overestimate the importance of language in the development, elaboration, and transmission of culture. Language enables people to store meanings and experiences and to pass this heritage on to new generations. In addition, language enables us to **transcend** the here and now, preserving the past and imagining the future; to communicate with others and formulate complex plans; to integrate different kinds of experiences; and to develop abstract ideas.
   [Light & Keller, *Sociology*, 37]
   (a) _____
   (b) _____
   (c) _____
   (d) _____

2. In 1729, J. Bradley attached a telescope rigidly to his chimney and hoped to observe stars passing through its field of view (as the rotating earth carried them through the zenith) in slightly different places during the year because of parallax. What he found, to his surprise, was that all stars shifted back and forth during the year, but by exactly the same amount—20".5. What Bradley had observed was the **aberration** of starlight.
   [George Abell, *Realm of the Universe*, 208]
   (a) _____
   (b) _____
   (c) _____
   (d) _____

3. In **retroactive** interference, new learning interferes with the retrieval of old learning. A medical student may memorize the names of the bones in the leg through rote repetition. Later he or she may find that learning the names of the bones in the arm

makes it more difficult to retrieve the names of the leg bones, especially if the names are similar in sound or in relative location on each limb. In proactive interference, older learning interferes with the capacity to retrieve more recently learned material. High school Spanish may pop in when you are trying to retrieve college French or Italian words. All three are Romance languages, with similar roots and spellings.

[Spencer A. Rathus, *Psychology*, 4th Ed., 247–48]

(a) _____
(b) _____
(c) _____
(d) _____

4. The situations we considered in Chapter 2 were those in which an object moves along a straight-line path, such as the x axis. We now look at some cases in which the object moves in a plane. By this we mean that the object may move in both the x and the y direction simultaneously, corresponding to motion in two dimensions. The particular type of motion we shall concentrate on is called projectile motion. Anyone who has observed a baseball in motion (or for that matter, any object thrown into the air) has observed **projectile** motion.

[Serway & Faughn, *College Physics*, 3rd Ed., 58]

(a) _____
(b) _____
(c) _____
(d) _____

5, 6. Rewards are of two types: intrinsic and extrinsic. Intrinsic rewards are received as a direct consequence of a person's actions. The completion of a complex task may bestow a pleasant feeling of accomplishment. Extrinsic rewards are given by another person, typically a manager, and include promotion and pay increases. For example, Frances Blais sells encyclopedias for the **intrinsic** reward of helping children read well. Bob Michaels, who hates his sales job, nevertheless is motivated by the **extrinsic** reward of high pay.

[Richard L. Daft, *Management*, 2nd Ed., 402–03]

(a) _____
(b) _____
(c) _____
(d) _____

(a) _____
(b) _____
(c) _____
(d) _____

7. Seahorses provide the only known example of monogamy in fishes living in sea grasses or mangroves. As far as we know, our pairs never divorce. Nor do they cheat. This is exceptional: new genetic research techniques are revealing that animals we thought of as firmly paired, including many birds, are often not sexually faithful after all. We can be sure of seahorse fidelity because a female's body visibly **deflates** when she transfers eggs, while the male's pouch inflates; these changes always occur simultaneously. In very few, if any, animals do both sexes make it so obvious they have mated.
   [Amanda Vincent, "The Improbable Seahorse," *National Geographic,* October 1994, 135]

(a) _____
(b) _____
(c) _____
(d) _____

8. The cell membrane is the outermost limit of the cell, but it is more than a simple envelope surrounding the cellular contents. It is an actively functioning part of the living material and many important metabolic reactions take place on its surface. In addition to maintaining the wholeness of the cell, the membrane serves to control the entrance and exit of substances. That is, it allows some substances to pass through the membrane and excludes others. A membrane that functions in this manner is called selectively permeable. A **permeable** membrane, on the other hand, is a membrane that allows all materials to pass through.
   [John W. Hole, Jr., *Human Anatomy and Physiology,* 72]

(a) _____
(b) _____
(c) _____
(d) _____

9, 10. Breaths come in pairs, except at two times in our lives—the beginning and the end. At birth, we inhale for the first time; at death, we exhale for the last. In between, through all the lather

82 CHAPTER 3 DIRECTION

of one's life, each breath passes air over our olfactory sites. Each day we breathe about 23,040 times and move around 438 cubic feet of air. It takes us about five seconds to breathe—two seconds to inhale and three seconds to exhale—and, in that time, molecules of odor flood through our systems. **Inhaling** and **exhaling**, we smell odors.

[Diane Ackerman, *A Natural History of the Senses*, 6–7]

(a) _____
(b) _____
(c) _____
(d) _____

(a) _____
(b) _____
(c) _____
(d) _____

CHAPTER 4 RELATIONSHIP

SECTION 1

List 1
Here are some word parts that are used to signify relationship.

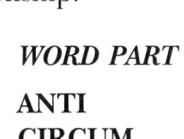

WORD PART	MEANING
ANTI	against; opposed
CIRCUM	around
CO	with; together
COL	with; together
COM	with; together
CON	with; together
CONTRA	against; opposed
COR	with; together
COUNTER	against; opposed
INTRA	inside
INTRO	inside
ISO	same; equal
JUXTA	near; close together
POST	behind; afterward
PRE	earlier; in front of; before
SUB	under; beneath
SUPER	above; over; upper
SUPRA	above; over
ULTRA	above; over; beyond

CHAPTER 4 RELATIONSHIP

PRE-EXERCISE ACTIVITY 1
- **List Making**
- **Skill: word parts**

*In the blanks that follow, rewrite List 1. This time, however, reverse the order by writing the **meanings** in the first column. Then gather all the word parts in the list which have that meaning and write them on one line in the second column. This will let you make necessary connections and help you in the process of long-term memorization. The first one has already been done to show you how.*

	MEANING	WORD PARTS
1.	above	super, supra, ultra
2.		
3.		
4.		
5.		
6.		
7.		
8.		
9.		
10.		
11.		
12.		
13.		
14.		
15.		
16.		
17.		
18.		
19.		
20.		
21.		
22.		

Note: This list will be more useful if you write it in alphabetical order.

Copyright © 1996 Harcourt Brace & Company. All rights reserved.

EXERCISE 4-A
- **Multiple Choice**
- **Skill: word parts**

A meaning is in boldface for each of the following phrases. From the four choices given, pick the one answer which contains a word part with that meaning. Use both versions of List 1 to help you. **Do not use a dictionary**. *Do not focus on the size or difficulty of the words. Look only for the simple word part; it will lead you to the correct answer.*

Example: √To **under**mine a project
        (A) invert   (C) subvert
        (B) convert   (D) revert

        Answer: (C) The reason for this answer is that the SUB part of *subvert* means "under."

1. To place **close together** or situate side by side
   (A) counterpose (C) presuppose
   (B) interpose   (D) juxtapose

2. Sounds **above** the range audible to the human ear
   (A) ultrasonic   (C) subsonic
   (B) infrasonic   (D) hypersonic

3. An agent or device that works **against** pregnancy
   (A) interception (C) conception
   (B) circumception (D) contraception

4. The act of putting oneself **under** the power of another
   (A) submission (C) remission
   (B) commission (D) admission

5. Telling that something will happen **before** it occurs
   (A) interdiction (C) contradiction
   (B) malediction   (D) prediction

6. An organ piece played **after** church services are over
   (A) postlude   (C) interlude
   (B) prelude   (D) etude

86 CHAPTER 4 RELATIONSHIP

7. Located **behind** something
   - (A) interior
   - (B) anterior
   - (C) posterior
   - (D) exterior

8. A flowing **together** of two or more streams
   - (A) influence
   - (B) effluence
   - (C) confluence
   - (D) fluency

9. Unconsciously bringing the characteristics of another person **inside** oneself
   - (A) rejection
   - (B) projection
   - (C) dejection
   - (D) introjection

10. Having an **equal** number of parts
    - (A) heteromerous
    - (B) isomerous
    - (C) numerous
    - (D) exogenous

EXERCISE 4-B
- **Fill in the Blank (one cue)**
- **Skill: word parts**

Use a **meaning** from List 1 to fill in the blank in each statement. The word part whose meaning you are defining will be found inside the boldfaced word. **Do not use a dictionary**. Do not focus on the size or difficulty of the words. Look only for the simple word part; it will lead you to the correct answer.

Example: √Space debris that revolves _____ the moon is called **circumlunar**.

           Answer: *around* [> CIRCUM]

1. **Confederates** work _____ one another.
2. **Introversion** involves directing one's thoughts and interests _____ .
3. **Preventive** measures hinder things _____ they happen.
4. To **countermand** an order is to issue a new directive _____ the original one.

Copyright © 1996 Harcourt Brace & Company. All rights reserved.

5. **Preadolescence** is the period _____ adolescence.
6. Goods or materials imported _____ the law are called **contraband**.
7. **Subglacial** deposits are found _____ a glacier.
8. Objects which are **juxtaposed** have been placed _____ .
9. **Isodynamic** exercise uses the principle of _____ forces working in opposition to one another.
10. To **colligate** ideas is to bring them _____ by an explanation or theory.
11. **Ultramundane** means extending _____ the world or the limits of the universe.
12. An **antipyretic** acts _____ fevers.
13. **Circumlocution** is an evasive way of speaking _____ a subject.
14. To **supererogate** is to go _____ what is required or expected.
15. A **postprandial** drink would be served _____ dinner.

EXERCISE 4-C
- Fill in the Blank (no cue)
- Skills: word parts, context

*Once again, use a **meaning** from List 1 to fill in the blank in each line. This time, however, you will have to find the word part yourself in the difficult or technical word. **Do not use a dictionary**. Do not focus on the size or difficulty of the words. Look only for the simple word part; it will lead you to the correct answer.*

Example: √An antimalarial drug works _____ malaria.

           Answer: *against* [> ANTI]

1. A countermeasure is an action taken _____ another, sometimes in retaliation.
2. The previous day is the day _____ .

3. A superscript is a number written _____ and to the side of another number or letter.
4. Subliminal thoughts exist _____ the level of conscious thought.
5. Postoperative procedures are done _____ surgery.
6. An idea is in contradistinction to another idea when it is _____ it.
7. A correspondent communicates _____ someone by means of letters.
8. Substandard work is _____ what is expected.
9. An isosceles triangle has two _____ sides.
10. Something supraliminal is _____ the threshold of consciousness.
11. Ultraism refers to extreme solutions which go _____ the ordinary.
12. In anatomy, circumvallate means closed _____ by a ridge.
13. An antitussive medicine works _____ coughs.
14. A concatenation is a series of things connected _____ each other.
15. Intravascular blockage occurs _____ the blood vessels.

ULTRAwoman
SUPRAman
SUBman
The Terrific Trio
To The Rescue

EXERCISE 4-D
- **Matching Columns**
- **Skills: word parts, context**

Memory check. Do not look at List 1 or use a dictionary.

1. ____ ISO   (a) before
2. ____ SUB   (b) around
3. ____ ULTRA   (c) near
4. ____ JUXTA   (d) equal

5. ____ INTRO   (e) under
6. ____ CIRCUM   (f) over
7. ____ COUNTER   (g) after
8. ____ POST   (h) with
9. ____ CO   (i) against
10. ____ PRE   (j) inside

EXERCISE 4-E
- Fill in (two cues)
- Skills: word parts, dictionary, context

*To finish each word, fill in the blank with one of the **word parts** from your version of List 1. **You must use a college-level dictionary** to make sure that what you write really is a word and that it fits in the sentence. The word in boldface will give you the meaning of the word part that you must write.*

Example: √Something that is ___mersed is placed **under** water.

  Answer: *SUB* [> under]

1. When Magellan _____navigated the globe, he went **around** the world.
2. Making sure that you have enough food on hand **before** an emergency arises is a good ___caution in winter.
3. Few people realize that there are miles of ___terranean passageways **beneath** the Loop in Chicago.
4. To ___respond is to communicate **with** someone by letter.
5. Your ____erity consists of your descendants, the relatives who come **after** you.
6. An _____spective person looks deep **inside** his or her mind.
7. When a medical treatment is _____indicated, your doctor will advise **against** it.
8. A ___script is written **beneath** another letter or number.
9. Various substances (such as penicillin and streptomycin) that the body produces **against** certain microorganisms are called _____bodies.

10. A _____ intendent is in charge of, or **above**, other workers.
11. A _____ suit is a legal suit filed **against** another lawsuit.
12. ___ tropic means identical or **equal** in all directions.
13. _____ violet rays are just **above** the color violet in the visible color band.
14. Words that connect elements in a sentence **with** each other are called ___ junctions.
15. The area **above** the orbit of the eye is called _____ orbital.

EXERCISE 4-F
- Fill in (one cue)
- Skills: word parts, dictionary, context

*Continue filling in **word parts** from your version of List 1 as you have been doing, **using a college-level dictionary** to check accuracy. Now, however, there will be no word in boldface. You will have to search the sentence for a clue.*

Example: √A _____ lage is a type of art that brings together items normally not associated with one another.

Answer: COL [> together]

1. _____ vail means to act against something in order to offset it.
2. ____ bodies are proteins in the blood that act against toxins.
3. Witnesses who ___ roborate a story agree with it.
4. ___ nuptial financial agreements are made before a marriage takes place.
5. An ___ gon is a polygon whose angles are all equal.
6. A ____ glacial period comes after an ice age.
7. A futuristic style beyond the contemporary is called _____ modern.
8. To _____ scribe something is to draw a line around it.
9. To _____ vene is to act against someone's rights or opinion.

10. ___cutaneous pain is located under the skin.
11. A ___vious statement comes before another statement.
12. The _____duction to a book leads the reader inside the subject to be covered.
13. Something ____ficial merely skims over the surface.
14. To ___miserate is to sympathize with someone.
15. Items that have equal force or strength are ___dynamic.

EXERCISE 4-G
- **Paragraph Examples**
- **Skills: word parts, dictionary, context**

Answer these four questions after each paragraph:

(a) *What word part inside the boldfaced word helps you to understand that word? What does that word part mean?*

(b) *Using only the context of the word and the word part that it contains, what do you think the boldfaced word means? (See Chapter 1, Section 2.)*

(c) *Choose one context clue that helped you. (See Chapter 1, Section 2.)*

    1. *word signals*   4. *examples or description*
    2. *punctuation signals*   5. *contrast or opposites*
    3. *synonyms (substitution)*   6. *prior knowledge; common sense*
        If 6, explain: _____

(d) *How does the dictionary define the boldfaced word as it is used in the paragraph?*

1. On a calm, clear day in February 1977, Jack Corliss and two fellow explorers wedged themselves into the tiny, cramped cabin of the research submarine *Alvin*, said good-bye to the two support ships at the surface, and began a long descent into darkness. About 90 minutes later *Alvin* was gliding along the seafloor a mile and a half below the surface of the Pacific, and Corliss, a

burly Oregon State University marine geologist, was peering out the porthole, searching for a phenomenon that had been suspected but never seen: **submarine** hot springs. Searchlights blazing, *Alvin* cruised through black water above the Galapagos Rift, an undersea volcanic ridge along the equator 200 miles west of Ecuador. It was in just such a place, Corliss and the others surmised, that these so-called hydrothermal vents would be found—if they existed.

[Peter Radetsky, "How Did Life Start?" *Discover*, Special Issue, 1993, 34]

(a) _____
(b) _____
(c) _____
(d) _____

2. A process in which an ideal gas expands (or is compressed) at a constant temperature is of such importance that we shall consider it separately from the processes described earlier. An expansion or compression of a substance at constant temperature is referred to as an isothermal process. The **isothermal** expansion of a gas can be achieved by placing the gas in thermal contact with a heat reservoir at the same temperature.

[Serway & Faughn, *College Physics*, 3rd Ed., 377]

(a) _____
(b) _____
(c) _____
(d) _____

3. The area at the very front of the frontal lobe is called the **prefrontal** area. Whereas it was once believed that this area was the seat of the intellect, it is now apparent that its principal function is sorting out information and ordering stimuli. A few years ago parts of the frontal lobe were surgically removed in efforts to bring the behavior of certain aberrant individuals more into line with the norm. Fortunately, this practice has been largely discontinued.

[Robert Wallace, *Biology: The World of Life*, 318]

(a) _____
(b) _____
(c) _____
(d) _____

4. Many animals are camouflaged—disguised in such a way that they are difficult to perceive even when they are in plain sight. Bulk is nearly always disguised by **countershading**. If an object is the same color all over, its underside appears darker when light falls on it from above and makes it appear rounded. The vast majority of animals have light-colored bellies and dark backs. Light falling from above makes them look uniformly colored and therefore flat. A camouflaged gun or plane is also painted with a pattern that countershades it.
[Arms, et al., *A Journey into Life*, 3rd Ed., 804]
    (a) _____
    (b) _____
    (c) _____
    (d) _____

5. In psychodynamic theory, we tend to introject, or incorporate into our own personalities, elements of the people who are important to us. **Introjection** is more powerful when we are afraid of losing others by death or because of their disapproval of us. (We might fear that people who disapprove of us will leave us.) Thus we might be particularly prone toward bringing inward elements of the people who disapprove of us or who see things differently. Ironically, we take within the harsh parent more so than the generous parent.
[Spencer A. Rathus, *Psychology*, 4th Ed., 526]
    (a) _____
    (b) _____
    (c) _____
    (d) _____

SECTION 2

List 2

Here are more word parts that are used to signify relationship.

WORD PART	MEANING
ANTE	earlier; in front of
CATA	lower; down from
ECTO	outside
ENDO	inside
EPI	upon; outer; near
EXO	outside
EXTRA	outside
EXTRO	outside
HETERO	different; other
HOMO	same; alike
HYPER	excessive; over; above
HYPO	insufficient; under
INFRA	under
INTER	between
META	behind; beyond; later
PARA	beside; beyond; near
PERI	around; near
SYL	with; together
SYM	with; together
SYN	with; together
SYS	with; together
TELE	distant; far

PRE-EXERCISE ACTIVITY 2
- **List Making**
- **Skill: word parts**

*In the blanks that follow, rewrite List 2. This time, however, reverse the order by writing the **meanings** in the first column. Then gather all the word parts in the list which have that meaning and write them on one line in the second column. This will let you make necessary connections and help you in the process of long-term memorization. The first one has already been done to show you how.*

	MEANING	WORD PARTS	
1.	above	hyper	*Note:* This list will be more useful if you write it in alphabetical order.
2.			
3.			
4.			
5.			
6.			
7.			
8.			
9.			
10.			
11.			
12.			
13.			
14.			
15.			
16.			
17.			
18.			
19.			
20.			
21.			

Copyright © 1996 Harcourt Brace & Company. All rights reserved.

	MEANING	WORD PARTS
22.	_____	_____
23.	_____	_____
24.	_____	_____
25.	_____	_____
26.	_____	_____
27.	_____	_____
28.	_____	_____

EXERCISE 4-H
- **Multiple Choice**
- **Skill: word parts**

A meaning is in boldface for each of the following phrases. From the four choices given, pick the one answer which contains a word part with that meaning. Use both versions of List 2 to help you. **Do not use a dictionary.** *Do not focus on the size or difficulty of the words. Look only for the simple word part; it will lead you to the correct answer.*

Example: √**Excessively** or overly active
    (A) hypoactive   (C) interactive
    (B) proactive   (D) hyperactive

    Answer: (D) The reason for this answer is that the HYPER part of hyperactive means excessive or over.

1. The measurement **around** the boundary of a closed area
   (A) diameter   (C) angularity
   (B) perimeter   (D) velocity

2. Words that have identical spelling but **different** meanings and pronunciation
   - (A) antonym
   - (B) synonym
   - (C) heteronym
   - (D) pseudonym

3. Device to transmit data automatically and from a **distance**
   - (A) perimeter
   - (B) telemeter
   - (C) parameter
   - (D) diameter

4. Located **inside** a blood vessel
   - (A) extravascular
   - (B) avascular
   - (C) nonvascular
   - (D) intravascular

5. Existing **between** the sexes
   - (A) asexual
   - (B) intersexual
   - (C) homosexual
   - (D) pansexual

6. **Before** birth
   - (A) antenatal
   - (B) postnatal
   - (C) perinatal
   - (D) neonatal

7. A microorganism able to live and develop **outside** a host
   - (A) endogenous
   - (B) hypogenous
   - (C) ectogenous
   - (D) isogenous

8. The thin membrane that lines the **inside** of the heart
   - (A) pericardium
   - (B) endocardium
   - (C) cardiogram
   - (D) cardiograph

9. The **downward** return or degeneration of cells or tissue
   - (A) cataplasia
   - (B) metaplasia
   - (C) hyperplasia
   - (D) paraplegia

10. Having fingers or toes fused **together**
    - (A) pentadactyl
    - (B) adactyl
    - (C) syndactyl
    - (D) tridactyl

EXERCISE 4-I
- Fill in the Blank (one cue)
- Skill: word parts

Use a **meaning** from List 2 to fill in the blank in each statement. The word part whose meaning you are defining will be found inside the boldfaced word. **Do not use a dictionary.** Do not focus on the size or difficulty of the words. Look only for the simple word part; it will lead you to the correct answer.

Example: √**Interglacial** periods came _____ ice ages.

　　　　Answer: *between* [> INTER]

1. An **interface** is a common boundary _____ adjacent regions.
2. **Exogamy** means marriage _____ one's group or class.
3. In American history, the **antebellum** period is the time _____ the Civil War.
4. **Infrasonic** waves have frequencies _____ those of audible sound.
5. **Periodontal** refers to the tissue and structures _____ the teeth.
6. **Parapsychology** is the branch of psychology that investigates abilities _____ the normal range.
7. **Hypoglossal** means _____ the tongue.
8. **Homocentric** circles have the _____ center.
9. Microorganisms able to live _____ a host are **ectogenous**.
10. An **epiphyte** is a plant that grows _____ another plant.
11. **Syncretism** is the joining _____ of conflicting religious beliefs.
12. **Catadromous** fish go _____ river to spawn.
13. **Endogamy** means marriage _____ one's group.
14. Any person or anything that is _____, in the sense of deviating from the common rule, is a **heteroclite**.
15. **Hyperbaric** refers to pressures _____ normal atmospheric pressure.

EXERCISE 4-J
- **Fill in the Blank (no cue)**
- **Skills: word parts, context**

*Once again, use a **meaning** from List 2 to fill in the blank in each statement. This time, however, you will have to find the word part yourself in the difficult or technical word. **Do not use a dictionary**. Do not focus on the size or difficulty of the words. Look only for the simple word part; it will lead you to the correct answer.*

Example: √Exobiology searches for living organisms _____ the planet Earth.

   Answer: *outside* [> EXO]

1. An interlude is any performance _____ the acts of a play.
2. Homogeneous groups bring together people who are _____.
3. Antemeridian means _____ noon.
4. Extramural activities are carried on _____ the boundaries of a school.
5. An endoparasite, such as a tapeworm, lives _____ animal organs.
6. Hypoacidity refers to an _____ acidity level.
7. An exoenzyme functions _____ a cell.
8. The process known as catabolism breaks _____ complex molecules.
9. In botany, extrorse means turned or facing _____ or away from the axis of growth.
10. Hyperalgesia refers to _____ sensitiveness to pain.
11. A heterophyllous plant has _____ kinds of leaves on the same plant.
12. The parathyroid gland lies _____ the thyroid gland.
13. A perimorph is a mineral that forms _____ another mineral.
14. In geology, epigene means formed or originating _____ the surface of the earth.
15. In anatomy, syssarcosis refers to the joining _____ of two or more bones by muscle.

EXERCISE 4-K
- **Matching Columns**
- **Skill: word parts**

Memory check. Do not look back at List 2 or use a dictionary.

1. ____	PERI	(a)	over
2. ____	EXTRO	(b)	with
3. ____	HOMO	(c)	around
4. ____	HYPO	(d)	in front of
5. ____	TELE	(e)	inside
6. ____	HETERO	(f)	under
7. ____	HYPER	(g)	far away
8. ____	ANTE	(h)	outside
9. ____	SYN	(i)	same
10. ____	ENDO	(j)	different

You name it, they're against it.

EXERCISE 4-L
- **Fill in (two cues)**
- **Skills: word parts, dictionary, context**

To finish each word, fill in the blank with one of the **word parts** from your version of List 2. **You must use a college-level dictionary** to make sure that what you write really is a word and that it fits in the sentence. The word in boldface will give you the meaning of the word part that you must write.

Example: √A _ _ _ _meter measures and transmits information from a **distant** source.

Answer: TELE [> distant]

1. Some students like to have a one-hour _ _ _ _ _val **between** classes.
2. Your _ _ _cedents are the ancestors who came **before** you.
3. The _ _ _taph **upon** his tombstone read, "I told you I was sick."
4. People are at a **low** point after a _ _ _ _strophe.

5. A _ _ _ drome is a group of signs and symptoms that come **together** and indicate an illness or disorder.
6. Humans are _ _ _ _ skeletal; their skeletons are **inside** the body.
7. Lobsters are _ _ skeletal; they have a hard covering **outside**.
8. A _ _ _ _ medic works **beside** or as an emergency assistant to a doctor.
9. A _ _ _ _ nym has the **same** sound (and often the same spelling) as another word, but differs in meaning.
10. A _ _ _ _ _ _ dox person disagrees with his church's beliefs. His religious opinions are **different**.
11. _ _ _ _ _ vehicular activities are performed by an astronaut **outside** a spacecraft.
12. _ _ _ _ tension involves blood pressure way **over** normal.
13. _ _ _ metry involves a relationship in which parts of a figure are identical **with** each other.
14. The _ _ _ thalamus is the part of the brain that lies **below** the thalamus.
15. _ _ _ _ patetic activity is conducted while walking **around**.

EXERCISE 4-M
- Fill in (one cue)
- Skills: word parts, dictionary, context

*Continue filling in **word parts** from your version of List 2 as you have been doing, **using a college-level dictionary** to check accuracy. Now, however, there will be no word in boldface. You will have to search the sentence for a clue.*

Example: √A _ _ _ _ sporous plant produces spores that are all alike.

        Answer: *HOMO* [> alike]

1. When letters are brought together in small units, they form _ _ _ lables.
2. The basic framework that lies under a system or organization is known as its _ _ _ _ structure.

3. A _ _ _ _ _ geneous classroom has students of widely different abilities.
4. _ _ _ _ vascular means located or occurring outside a blood vessel.
5. People who join together to carry out an enterprise form a _ _ _ dicate.
6. An _ _ _ _ _ vert has interests outside himself or herself.
7. The _ _ sphere is the outside portion of the earth's atmosphere.
8. The _ _ _ dermis is the outer, protective layer of skin.
9. An _ _ _ _ _ im is the time period between one event and another.
10. Muscles that are _ _ _ _ tonic have tone or tension below normal.
11. _ _ _ _ physics goes behind or beyond the merely physical and tries to examine ultimate reality.
12. In an _ _ _ _ pic pregnancy, the fertilized ovum develops outside the uterus.
13. The period just before death is known as the _ _ _ _ mortem stage.
14. A plant that grows inside another plant, such as certain fungi, is an _ _ _ _ phyte.
15. _ _ _ _ dromous fish migrate down river to breed.

EXERCISE 4-N
- **Paragraph Examples**
- **Skills: word parts, dictionary, context**

Answer these four questions after each paragraph:

(a) *What word part inside the boldfaced word helps you to understand that word? What does that word part mean?*

(b) *Using only the context of the word and the word part that it contains, what do you think the boldfaced word means? (See Chapter 1, Section 2.)*

(c) *Choose one context clue that helped you. (See Chapter 1, Section 2.)*
   1. *word signals*
   2. *punctuation signals*
   3. *synonyms (substitution)*
   4. *examples or description*
   5. *contrast or opposites*
   6. *prior knowledge; common sense*

   If 6, explain: _____

(d) *How does the dictionary define the boldfaced word as it is used in the paragraph?*

1. Along the seacoasts, many kinds of plants and animals thrive in the intertidal zone, the area between the high and low tide marks, where they are submerged for part of the day. There are three main types of **intertidal** zone: muddy, sandy, and rocky shores, which support very different communities.
   [Arms, et al., *A Journey into Life*, 3rd Ed., 760]
   (a) _____
   (b) _____
   (c) _____
   (d) _____

2, 3. Almost all societies have two kinds of marriage norms or rules. Rules of **endogamy** limit the social categories from within which one can choose a marriage partner. For example, many Americans still attempt to instill in their children the idea that one should marry one's "own kind," that is, someone within the ethnic, religious, or economic group of one's family or origin. Rules of **exogamy**, on the other hand, require an individual to marry someone outside his or her culturally defined group. For example, in many tribal groups, members must marry outside their lineage. In the United States there are laws forbidding the marriage of close relatives, although the rules are variable.
   [Henry L. Tischler, *Introduction to Sociology*, 4th Ed., 247]
   (a) _____
   (b) _____
   (c) _____
   (d) _____

(a) _____
(b) _____
(c) _____
(d) _____

4. I grew up climbing maples and oaks in New England, and I tell you now, treetops were never like they are in a jungle rain forest. For one thing, they weren't as messy. Rain-forest branches look like untended window boxes, a riot of ferns and bromeliads and long, curly mosses. Canopy limbs are cloaked in a layer of settled debris, called "crown soil," which gives rise to a miniature jungle of rain-forest **epiphytes**—plants that grow on other plants. Trees are apparently like the rest of us: the older they are, the hairier.
[Mary Roach, "Aliens in the Treetops," *International Wildlife*, November–December 1994, 9]

(a) _____
(b) _____
(c) _____
(d) _____

5. The reactions of indigenous peoples to the changes that have been thrust upon them by outsiders have varied considerably. Sometimes people have managed to keep faith with their own traditions by inventing creative and ingenious ways of expressing them in the face of powerful foreign domination. This blending of indigenous and foreign elements into a new system is known as **syncretism**, and a fine illustration of it is the game of cricket as played by the Trobriand Islanders. Under British rule, the Trobrianders were introduced by missionaries to the rather staid British game of cricket, to replace the erotic dancing and open sexuality that normally followed the harvest of yams. The Trobrianders made cricket their own by adding battle dress and battle magic, and by incorporating erotic dancing into the festivities.
[William A. Haviland, *Cultural Anthropology*, 7th Ed., 415]

COR
SYS and CON
SYN and COM
SYML and COL
SYL and CO
Together

(a) _____
(b) _____
(c) _____
(d) _____

SECTION 3: CHAPTER REVIEW (LISTS 1 AND 2 COMBINED)

Review of Word Parts Covered in This Chapter:

WORD PART	MEANING	COMMON EXAMPLE	TEXTBOOK EXAMPLE
ANTE	earlier; in front of	*antedate*	*antebellum*
ANTI	against; opposed	*antifreeze*	*anticlimax*
CATA	lower; down from	*catastrophe*	*catarrhine*
CIRCUM	around	*circumstance*	*circumlocution*
CO	with; together	*cooperate*	*cosignatory*
COL	with; together	*collection*	*colligate*
COM	with; together	*commit*	*commissure*
CON	with; together	*contain*	*consummation*
CONTRA	against	*contradict*	*contrapuntal*
COR	with; together	*correspond*	*correlative*
COUNTER	against	*counteract*	*countervail*
ECTO	outside	*ectomorph*	*ectogenous*
ENDO	inside	*endomorph*	*endogenous*
EPI	upon; outer; near	*epitaph*	*epigeal*
EXO	outside	*exotic*	*exothermic*
EXTRA	outside	*extraordinary*	*extrajudicial*
EXTRO	outside	*extrovert*	*extrorse*
HETERO	different; other	*heterosexual*	*heterodox*
HOMO	same; alike	*homosexual*	*homogamous*
HYPER	excessive; over	*hyperactive*	*hyperbole*
HYPO	insufficient; under	*hypodermic*	*hyposensitize*

Continued

WORD PART	MEANING	COMMON EXAMPLE	TEXTBOOK EXAMPLE
INFRA	under	*infrared*	*infrasonic*
INTER	between	*interview*	*interstices*
INTRA	inside	*intramural*	*intravascular*
INTRO	inside	*introduce*	*introjection*
ISO	same; equal	*isogon*	*isochromatic*
JUXTA	near; close together	*juxtapose*	*juxtaposition*
META	behind; beyond; later	*metabolism*	*metamorphosis*
PARA	beside; beyond; near	*parallel*	*paradigm*
PERI	around; near	*perimeter*	*pericardium*
POST	behind; afterward	*postpone*	*postpartum*
PRE	earlier; in front of	*predict*	*prefabricated*
SUB	under; beneath	*subdue*	*subcutaneous*
SUPER	above; over; upper	*Superman*	*superscript*
SUPRA	above; over	*supranational*	*suprarenal*
SYL	with; together	*syllable*	*syllogism*
SYM	with; together	*sympathy*	*symbiosis*
SYN	with; together	*synagogue*	*syndetic*
SYS	with; together	*system*	*syssarcosis*
TELE	distant; far	*television*	*telesthesia*
ULTRA	above; over; beyond	*ultramodern*	*ultramundane*

PRE-EXERCISE ACTIVITY 3
- **List Making**
- **Skill: word parts**

In the blanks that follow, rewrite the combined word parts list. This time, however, reverse the order by writing the **meanings** *in the first column. Then gather all the word parts in the list which have that meaning and write them on one line in the second column. This will let you make necessary connections and help you in the process of long-term memorization. The first one has already been done to show you how. (Note: You do not need to rewrite the examples.)*

	MEANING	WORD PARTS
1.	above	hyper, super, supra, ultra
2.		
3.		
4.		
5.		
6.		
7.		
8.		
9.		
10.		
11.		
12.		
13.		
14.		
15.		
16.		
17.		
18.		
19.		
20.		

Note: This list will be more useful if you write it in alphabetical order.

	MEANING	WORD PARTS
21.	_____	_____
22.	_____	_____
23.	_____	_____
24.	_____	_____
25.	_____	_____
26.	_____	_____
27.	_____	_____
28.	_____	_____
29.	_____	_____
30.	_____	_____
31.	_____	_____
32.	_____	_____
33.	_____	_____
34.	_____	_____
35.	_____	_____
36.	_____	_____
37.	_____	_____

EXERCISE 4-O
- **Matching Columns**
- **Skill: word parts**

Memory check. Do not look back at the combined list or use a dictionary.

1. _____ CONTRA   (a) above
2. _____ PARA   (b) against
3. _____ SUPRA   (c) with
4. _____ INFRA   (d) distant

5. ____ CIRCUM   (e) same
6. ____ SYN   (f) beside
7. ____ INTER   (g) under
8. ____ HOMO   (h) different
9. ____ HETERO   (i) between
10. ____ TELE   (j) around

EXERCISE 4-P
- Cross Out
- Skills: dictionary, context

One word in each set does not contain the word part and meaning that is given, even though it has a set of similar letters. **Use a college-level dictionary** *to find the one that does **not** fit.*

	WORD PART	**MEANING**	**CROSS OUT THE ONE WORD THAT DOES NOT FIT**
Example:	√COR	with; together	correspond, correlate, cortex

Answer: To correspond is to agree *with,* and to correlate is to bring items *together.* The dictionary reveals that *cortex* does not involve the meanings *with* or *together;* cross it out.

WORD PART	MEANING	CROSS OUT THE ONE WORD THAT DOES NOT FIT
1. POST	later; after	postdate, poster, postmortem
2. PRE	before	preview, prepare, pregnant
3. ANTI	against	antique, antibiotic, antimatter
4. COR	with; together	corroborate, corsage, correlation
5. INTER	between	interplanetary, interrelated, internal
6. SUB	under; beneath	subhead, suberic, subjugate
7. EXO	outside	exorbitant, exobiology, exoenzyme
8. ISO	equal; same	isogram, isomerous, isolated

Copyright © 1996 Harcourt Brace & Company. All rights reserved.

110 CHAPTER 4 RELATIONSHIP

| 9. COM | with; together | commix, comedy, communicate |
| 10. EXTRA | outside | extravehicular, extraction, extrasensory |

EXERCISE 4-Q
- **Extended Answer**
- **Skills: word parts, dictionary, context**

Answer the following questions by using a college-level dictionary.

Example: √How is the meaning *around* involved in the word **perimeter?**

      Answer: The perimeter is the distance around an outer boundary.

1. How is the meaning *opposed* involved in the word **antithesis?**

2. How is the meaning *together* involved in the word **symbiosis?**

3. How is the meaning *same* involved in the word **homogeneous?**

4. How is the meaning *lower* involved in the word **catacombs?**

5. How is the meaning *around* involved in the word **circumvent?**

ECTO   ENDO
Visitors from outer and inner space.

Copyright © 1996 Harcourt Brace & Company. All rights reserved.

6. How is the meaning *under* involved in the word **infrared?**

7. How is the meaning *inside* involved in the word **endogenous?**

8. How is the meaning *before* involved in the word **preventive?**

9. How is the meaning *different* involved in the word **heteroplasty?**

10. How is the meaning *above* involved in the word **ultrasonic?**

EXERCISE 4-R
- **Fill in the Blank**
- **Skill: word parts, context**

Answer each question by filling in the blank. Use the combined list.

Examples: √The opposite of ANTI is _____ .   Answer: CO, etc.
  √A synonym for the word *after* is _____ .   Answer: *behind, later,* etc.

1. The opposite of ANTE is _____ . *[Write another word part.]*
2. The opposite of SUB is _____ . *[Write another word part.]*
3. The opposite of CONTRA is _____ . *[Write another word part.]*
4. The opposite of ECTO is _____ . *[Write another word part.]*
5. The opposite of HETERO is _____ . *[Write another word part.]*
6. The opposite of HYPER is _____ . *[Write another word part.]*

7. A synonym for *under* is _____ . *[Write a regular word.]*
8. A synonym for *against* is _____ . *[Write a regular word.]*
9. A synonym for *inside* is _____ . *[Write a regular word.]*
10. A synonym for *same* is _____ . *[Write a regular word.]*

EXERCISE 4-S
- **Fill in the Blanks**
- **Skill: word parts**

Memory check. Do not look back at the combined lists or use a dictionary.

1. Name two word parts that mean *earlier*: _____ and _____
2. Name two word parts that mean *against*: _____ and _____
3. Name two word parts that mean *around*: _____ and _____
4. Name two word parts that mean *with*: _____ and _____
5. Name two word parts that mean *outside*: _____ and _____
6. Name two word parts that mean *inside*: _____ and _____
7. Name two word parts that mean *over*: _____ and _____
8. Name two word parts that mean *under*: _____ and _____
9. Name two word parts that mean *same*: _____ and _____
10. Name two word parts that mean *near*: _____ and _____

EXERCISE 4-T
- **Paragraph Examples**
- **Skills: word parts, dictionary, context**

Answer these four questions after each paragraph:

(a) What word part inside the boldfaced word helps you to understand that word? What does that word part mean?

(b) *Using only the context of the word and the word part that it contains, what do you think the boldfaced word means? (See Chapter 1, Section 2.)*

(c) *Choose one context clue that helped you. (See Chapter 1, Section 2.)*
   1. *word signals*
   2. *punctuation signals*
   3. *synonyms (substitution)*
   4. *examples or description*
   5. *contrast or opposites*
   6. *prior knowledge; common sense*

   If 6, explain: _____

(d) *How does the dictionary define the boldfaced word as it is used in the paragraph?*

1. Jim Trappe and Chris Maser and a small group of colleagues gradually pieced together a textbook case of a tightly linked circular chain of ecological **interdependency**. When a giant fir or hemlock tree dies and crashes to earth, it begins to rot slowly. In a century or more its soft, decayed wood becomes habitat for burrowing voles, who in turn subsist on truffles and distribute reproductive spores throughout the forest in their fecal pellets. The fungi that grow from those spores simultaneously provide more food for the voles and work mutually with the new roots of young trees that will grow to towering size and, centuries hence, crash to earth to begin the cycle anew.
   [Jon R. Luoma, "An Untidy Wonder," *Discover*, Special Issue, 1993, 66]

   (a) _____
   (b) _____
   (c) _____
   (d) _____

2. In this article, we review an array of strategies that should be more widely pursued and elaborated before the AIDS epidemic becomes uncontrollable among drug injectors, their sexual partners and their children. (The familiar phrase "**intravenous** drug user" refers only to people who inject into their veins or arteries. Here we use the terms "drug users who inject" and "injecting drug users" to include individuals who may administer the substance into the muscle or just below the skin surface as well.)
   [Dan C. Des Jarlais and Samuel R. Friedmann, "AIDS and the Use of Injected Drugs," *Scientific American*, February 1994, 82]

(a) _____
(b) _____
(c) _____
(d) _____

3. Vitamin E acts as an **antioxidant**, meaning that it is an agent protecting red cell membranes from being destroyed by oxygen. In premature infants, whose immature lungs are especially vulnerable to oxidation, this effect is especially important. It is only at the very end of pregnancy that the mother's blood concentration of vitamin E rises so that the infant will receive protective amounts; the premature baby is born without this extra vitamin E and so has a deficiency. Without supplemental doses, such a baby will develop anemia from breakage of the red blood cells (hemolytic anemia).

[Hamilton & Whitney, *Nutrition: Concepts and Controversies*, 37]

(a) _____
(b) _____
(c) _____
(d) _____

4. Most of the Earth's oxygen is in the air, but some is dissolved in water. Either water or air may serve as an animal's respiratory medium, the immediate source of oxygen. The respiratory medium gives up oxygen to the body at the body's respiratory surface, which may be the general body surface or a specialized area such as gills or lungs. Most of an animal's cells lie some distance from the respiratory surface and obtain their oxygen from the extracellular fluid, the fluid that bathes every cell. They rely on the blood to bring oxygen from the respiratory surface to the **extracellular** fluid and to remove carbon dioxide by the reverse route.

[Arms, et al., *A Journey into Life*, 3rd Ed., 492]

(a) _____
(b) _____
(c) _____
(d) _____

5, 6. Lobsters, snails, insects, and oysters have **exoskeletons**. Such skeletons serve well in protecting internal parts, but animals with exoskeletons may have a problem with growth. Snails and clams simply secrete extensions to their shells as they grow, so that their shells grow with them. Lobsters, crabs, and crayfish, however, have to discard their old shells and grow new, larger ones. The soft, vulnerable animal crawls out, swells by absorbing quantities of water, grows rapidly for a time, and then secretes a new shell. Vertebrate animals, including man, have an **endoskeleton** that can be observed only by means of X-rays.

        [Robert Wallace, *Biology: The World of Life*, 142]

(a) _____
(b) _____
(c) _____
(d) _____

(a) _____
(b) _____
(c) _____
(d) _____

7. The computer industry launches big ideas the way some people throw beach balls. The biggest and airiest of them all these days is called convergence. The theory goes something like this: the technologies of television, telephone, and computers are all moving along converging trajectories. When they intersect, bang! The world will change. People will make calls from their television sets. Or watch television with their phones. They'll pull out their pocket doodad in the middle of a traffic jam and accomplish what an advanced desktop computer does today. . . . For now, though, the only **convergence** going on is a passel of business mergers among digital wannabes.

        [Laurent Belsie, "Computers for the Rest of Us,"
Christian Science Monitor, 15 Nov. 1994, 13]

(a) _____
(b) _____
(c) _____
(d) _____

8. It is incorrect to call reptiles "cold-blooded." Most maintain a body temperature considerably higher than their surroundings, but they are **ectothermic**, taking most of their heat from the environment. Many reptiles must lie in the sun before they warm up enough to be active. Birds and mammals, on the other hand, are endothermic, generating most of their heat by their metabolism.

Thus, they can be active at any time, which gives them an enormous advantage over reptiles.

[Arms, et al., *A Journey into Life,* 3rd Ed., 459]

(a) _____
(b) _____
(c) _____
(d) _____

9, 10. There are three categories of sound waves covering different ranges of frequencies. Audible waves are longitudinal waves that lie within the range of sensitivity of the human ear, approximately 20 Hz to 20,000 Hz. **Infrasonic** waves are low-frequency waves with frequencies below the audible range. Earthquake waves are an example. **Ultrasonic** waves are longitudinal waves with frequencies above the audible range. For example, certain types of whistles produce ultrasonic waves. Even though the human ear is insensitive to the waves emitted by these whistles, certain animals, such as dogs, are able to hear frequencies in this region.

[Serway & Faughn, *College Physics,* 3rd Ed., 460–61]

(a) _____
(b) _____
(c) _____
(d) _____

(a) _____
(b) _____
(c) _____
(d) _____

CHAPTER 5 DIMENSION

SECTION 1

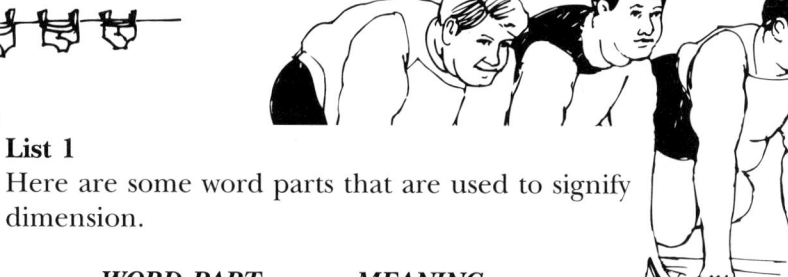

List 1
Here are some word parts that are used to signify dimension.

WORD PART	MEANING
ALTI	high
ALTO	high
BATHO	deep
EURY	wide
LATI	wide
MACRO	large/long
MAGNI	large
MAXI	large/long
MICRO	small/short
PACHY	thick
STRICT	thin; narrow
TENU	thin; narrow

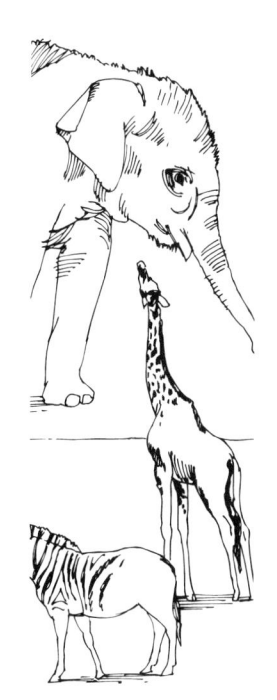

PRE-EXERCISE ACTIVITY 1
- **List Making**
- **Skill: word parts**

*In the blanks that follow, rewrite List 1. This time, however, reverse the order by writing the **meanings** in the first column. Then gather all the word parts in the list that have that meaning and write them on one line in the second column. This will let you make necessary connections and help you in the process of long-term memorization. The first one has already been done to show you how.*

	MEANING	WORD PARTS	
1.	deep	batho	*Note:* This list will be more useful if you write it in alphabetical order.
2.	_____	_____	
3.	_____	_____	
4.	_____	_____	
5.	_____	_____	
6.	_____	_____	
7.	_____	_____	
8.	_____	_____	
9.	_____	_____	
10.	_____	_____	

EXERCISE 5-A
- **Multiple Choice**
- **Skill: word parts**

A meaning is in boldface for each of the following phrases. From the four choices given, pick the one answer that contains a word part with that meaning. Use both versions of List 1 to help you. **Do not use a dictionary.** *Do not focus on the size or difficulty of the words. Look only for the simple word part; it will lead you to the correct answer.*

Example: √Freedom from restrictions; **wide** possibilities for
opinion or action
(A) gratitude   (C) latitude
(B) attitude   (D) magnitude

Answer: (C) The reason for this answer is that the LATI part of *latitude* means "wide."

1. With the **largest** or greatest amount possible
   (A) medium   (C) abbreviated
   (B) minimum   (D) maximum

2. An instrument used to determine **height**, especially in an aircraft
   (A) barometer   (C) altimeter
   (B) thermometer   (D) bathometer

3. **Narrow** or tight enough to form a blockage
   (A) compunction   (C) connection
   (B) constriction   (D) convection

4. An instrument used to measure the **depth** of water
   (A) barometer   (C) altimeter
   (B) thermometer   (D) bathometer

5. Having a **thin** consistency
   (A) ingenuous   (C) perilous
   (B) magnanimous   (D) tenuous

6. The physics of **large**-scale phenomena
   (A) microphysics   (C) macrophysics
   (B) metaphysics   (D) astrophysics

7. A **thick**-skinned, hoofed mammal, such as the elephant
   (A) endoderm   (C) pachyderm
   (B) echinoderm   (D) ectoderm

8. An abnormally **small** red blood cell
   (A) erythrocyte   (C) microcyte
   (B) macrocyte   (D) leucocyte

9. Able to stay alive on a **wide** variety of foods
   - (A) stenophagous
   - (B) coprophagous
   - (C) euryphagous
   - (D) hylophagous

10. An abnormally **large** red blood cell
    - (A) erythrocyte
    - (B) macrocyte
    - (C) microcyte
    - (D) leucocyte

EXERCISE 5-B
- **Fill in the Blank (one cue)**
- **Skill: word parts**

*Use a **meaning** from List 1 to fill in the blank in each statement. The word part whose meaning you are defining will be found inside the boldfaced word. **Do not use a dictionary.** Do not focus on the size or difficulty of the words. Look only for the simple word part; it will lead you to the correct answer.*

Example: √**Altostratus** clouds are characterized by a generally uniform gray sheet or layer, and they float _____ over the earth.

   Answer: *high* [> ALTO]

1. **Restrictions** _____ a person's choices.
2. When we have **latitude** of action, we have a _____ range of choices.
3. To **maximize** something is to make it as _____ as possible.
4. An argument that is _____ and unsubstantial is **tenuous**.
5. A **magnum** is a _____ wine bottle having a capacity of 1.5 liters.
6. A **microbe** is a germ so _____ that it can be seen only with a microscope.
7. **Altissimo** is a musical notation that means very _____ .

8. A **macron** is a symbol placed over a vowel to show that it has a _____ sound.
9. An **altiplane** is a _____ plateau sculpted by glacial processes.
10. Sea creatures that can tolerate a _____ range of depths are **eurybathic**.
11. Rock believed to have crystallized at a considerable _____ below the earth's surface is classified as **batholith**.
12. A **microtome** is an instrument for cutting very _____ sections of tissue.
13. **Macrodontia** means having abnormally _____ teeth.
14. The instrument used to measure the _____ of water is the **bathometer**.
15. **Pachysandra** is an evergreen plant with _____ stamens.

EXERCISE 5-C
- Fill in the Blank (no cue)
- Skills: word parts, context

*Once again, use a **meaning** from List 1 to fill in the blank in each statement. This time, however, you will have to find the word part yourself in the difficult or technical word. **Do not use a dictionary.** Do not focus on the size or difficulty of the words. Look only for the simple word part; it will lead you to the correct answer.*

Example: √A microvillus is a _____, fingerlike projection of the surface of a cell.

Answer: *small* [> MICRO]

1. A magnifier is a lens that makes objects appear _____.
2. Altitude sickness affects mountain climbers who venture too _____ too fast.
3. A maxim is a statement about conduct that tries to pack the _____est amount of wisdom into a small amount of space.

4. In medicine, a stricture is a _____ing of a hollow structure.
5. Altimetry measures how _____ a given object is.
6. A magnate is a person of _____ importance, especially in business.
7. A microseism is a _____ earthquake.
8. A wire that is very _____ is said to have tenuity.
9. A macrocyte is an abnormally _____ red blood cell.
10. A microcyte is an abnormally _____ red blood cell.
11. Alto-relievo is a sculpturing technique that is also called _____ relief.
12. A latifoliate plant has _____ leaves.
13. Eurythermal animals can tolerate _____ variations in temperature.
14. A batholith is a mass of rock found at a great _____.
15. A pachydermatous person is hard to upset since he or she is so _____-skinned.

EXERCISE 5-D
- **Matching Columns**
- **Skills: word parts, context**

Memory check. Do not look at List 1 or use a dictionary. Special note: This time, some answers are used more than once.

1. _____ MAGNI   (a) thin; narrow
2. _____ STRICT   (b) high
3. _____ BATHO   (c) thick
4. _____ ALTO   (d) deep
5. _____ EURY   (e) small; short
6. _____ PACHY   (f) large
7. _____ MACRO   (g) wide
8. _____ LATI
9. _____ TENU
10. _____ MICRO

Deep-cleaning action

EXERCISE 5-E
- Fill in (two cues)
- Skills: word parts, dictionary, context

*To finish each word, fill in the blank with one of the **word parts** from your version of List 1. **You must use a college-level dictionary** to make sure that what you write really is a word and that it fits in the sentence. The word in boldface will give you the meaning of the word part that you must write.*

Example: √_ _ _ _thermal animals can tolerate **wide** variations in temperature.

        Answer: *EURY*   [> wide]

1. A re_ _ _ _ _ion is a rule that **narrows** one's possibilities.
2. To _ _ _ _mize your profits is to make them **larger**.
3. A **wide**-ranging freedom from limitations and rules is called _ _ _ _tude.
4. _ _ _ _ous means having a **thin** or slender form.
5. The **thick**-skinned hippopotamus is a _ _ _ _ _derm.
6. The film used to photograph documents in a very **small** format is _ _ _ _ _film.
7. _ _ _ _lith is igneous rock believed to have crystallized at a considerable **depth**.
8. _ _ _ _tude tells how **high** an airplane is above the earth's surface.
9. A _ _ _ _ _ficent building, such as a cathedral, seems **larger** and more stately than other buildings.
10. A _ _ _ _ _climate is the climate of a **large** geographical area.
11. Re_ _ _ _ _ _ive covenants, which are clauses that **narrow** the ability of a property owner to sell to minorities, are illegal.
12. _ _ _ _ _tude is a measure of how **large** an object is.
13. To at_ _ _ _ate is to make **thin**, fine, or weak.
14. _ _ _ _ _physics is the branch of physics that studies **small**, invisible systems.
15. The _ _ _ _ _cosm is the **large** world or universe considered as a whole.

EXERCISE 5-F
- Fill in (one cue)
- Skills: word parts, dictionary, context

Use the following word parts to fill in the blanks. **Use a college-level dictionary** *to make sure that you have formed an actual word. Since there is no meaning in boldface, you will have to search each sentence for a clue. Each item should be used only once.*

| ALTO | EURY | MAGN | STRICT |
| BATHO | MACRO | PACHY | |

1. Unre_____ed access to files means that there are no narrow limitations on your ability to get at them.
2. A _____um is a very large wine bottle.
3. Organisms that are adaptable to a wide range of temperatures are _____thermal.
4. A _____cyte is an abnormally large red blood cell.
5. The ground cover known as _____sandra gets its name from its thick stamens.
6. _____cumulus clouds, rounded and fleecy in appearance, float high above the earth.
7. A _____meter is an instrument used to measure the depth of water.

| ALTI | LATI | MICRO | TENU |
| BATHO | MAGNI | PACHY | |

8. A _____tudinarian favors a wide and generous interpretation of religious rules.
9. Because of its thick skin, the elephant falls into the category of _____derms.
10. _____ity refers to thinness of consistency, as with a gas.
11. The use of low, sentimentalized emotion is called _____s.
12. A _____volt is a very small unit of electromotive force equal to one millionth of a volt.
13. An _____plane is a high plateau formed by glaciers; Bolivia has many examples.
14. _____fication is a process of enlargement.

EXERCISE 5-G
- **Paragraph Examples**
- **Skills: word parts, dictionary, context**

Answer these four questions after each paragraph:

(a) *What word part inside the boldfaced word helps you to understand that word? What does that word part mean?*

(b) *Using only the context of the word and the word part that it contains, what do you think the boldfaced word means? (See Chapter 1, Section 2.)*

(c) *Choose one context clue that helped you. (See Chapter 1, Section 2.)*
   1. *word signals*
   2. *punctuation signals*
   3. *synonyms (substitution)*
   4. *examples or description*
   5. *contrast or opposites*
   6. *prior knowledge; common sense*

   If 6, explain: _____

(d) *How does the dictionary define the boldfaced word as it is used in the paragraph?*

1. A person with tuberculosis carries TB bacteria in his or her lungs. If that person coughs near you, you may breathe in microscopic TB bacteria. Your normal breathing carries the bacteria to your lungs, where a type of large white blood cell, called a macrophage, engulfs the bacteria. This cell's job is to fight infection. If your immune system is healthy, the macrophage usually will disable the TB bacteria and you'll remain healthy. If your immunity is weakened, due to aging or chronic disease, TB bacteria can multiply in the **macrophage** until they break out and spread to other regions of your lung or body.
   ["Tuberculosis," *Mayo Clinic Health Letter*, April 1993, 3]
   (a) _____
   (b) _____
   (c) _____
   (d) _____

2. A total solar eclipse is one of the most spectacular of natural phenomena. The very beginning of a solar eclipse is called first contact, when the moon just begins to silhouette itself against the

edge of the sun's disk. As the minutes tick by, more and more of the sun is covered by the moon in partial phases. Second contact occurs about an hour after first contact, at the instant when the sun becomes completely hidden behind the moon. It is then that the corona flashes into view. The corona is the sun's outer **tenuous** atmosphere, consisting of sparse gases that extend for millions of miles in all directions from the apparent surface of the sun. The total phase of the eclipse ends, as abruptly as it began, with third contact, when the moon begins to uncover the sun. Gradually the partial phases of the eclipse repeat themselves, in reverse order. Finally, during last contact, the moon has completely uncovered the sun.

[adapted from George Abell, *Realm of the Universe*, 79]

(a) _____
(b) _____
(c) _____
(d) _____

3. **Altitude** and latitude have similar effects on vegetation. As you go up a mountain, the vegetation changes much as it does when you travel north or south from the equator. This is because similar temperatures favor similar types of plants. Vegetation type is also influenced by moisture.

[Arms, et al., *A Journey into Life,* 3rd Ed., 750]

(a) _____
(b) _____
(c) _____
(d) _____

4. Microwaves are short-wavelength radio waves that have wavelengths between about 1 mm and 30 cm and are generated by electronic devices. Microwaves are used in communication, particularly in the transmission of long-distance telephone messages. In this process, the information to be transmitted is encoded on microwaves by either amplitude or frequency modulation and carried from point to point via **microwave** relay towers.

[Serway & Faughn, *College Physics,* 3rd Ed., 733]

(a) _____
(b) _____
(c) _____
(d) _____

5. A new, easy-to-use asthma inhalant called salmeterol is available that may be more effective than other medications. In asthma, your lung's airways become inflamed and **constricted**, making it difficult for air to pass through. Like many other inhalants, salmeterol relaxes muscles surrounding the larger air passages in your lungs. But the new inhalant gives longer relief. You use salmeterol in the morning and evening for relief lasting 12 hours. Most inhalers relieve symptoms for up to six hours and are taken 3 to 4 times daily.

["Update '94," *Mayo Clinic Health Letter,* November 1994, 3]

(a) _____
(b) _____
(c) _____
(d) _____

SECTION 2

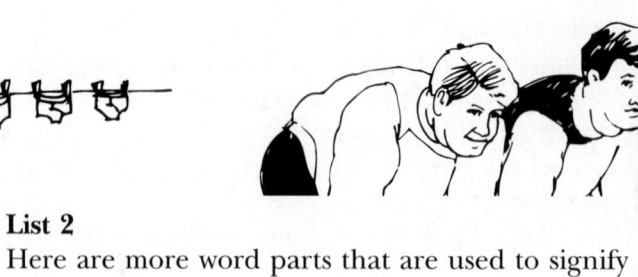

List 2
Here are more word parts that are used to signify dimension.

WORD PART	MEANING
AMPL	large
BATHY	deep
BREV	small/short
-ETTE	small/short
MAJ	large; great
MEGA	large
MEGALO	large
-MEGALY	large
MINI	small/short
PLATY	flat; wide
STENO	narrow; thin
-ULE	small

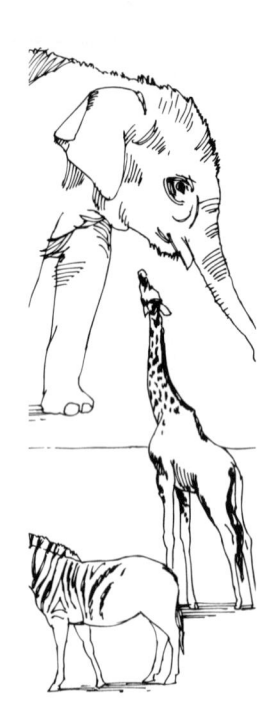

PRE-EXERCISE ACTIVITY 2
- **List Making**
- **Skill: word parts**

*In the blanks that follow, rewrite List 2. This time, however, reverse the order by writing the **meanings** in the first column. Then gather all the word parts in the list that have that meaning and write them on one line in the second column. This will let you make necessary connections and help you in the process of long-term memorization. The first one has already been done to show you how.*

	MEANING	WORD PARTS	
1.	deep	bathy	*Note:* This list will be more useful if you write it in alphabetical order.
2.			
3.			
4.			
5.			
6.			
7.			
8.			
9.			

EXERCISE 5-H
- **Multiple Choice**
- **Skill: word parts**

*A meaning is in boldface for each of the following phrases. From the four choices given, pick the one answer that contains a word part with that meaning. Use both versions of List 2 to help you. **Do not use a dictionary.** Do not focus on the size or difficulty of the words. Look only for the simple word part; it will lead you to the correct answer.*

Example: √A very **large** stone used in prehistoric monuments
    (A) otolith   (C) paleolith
    (B) eolith   (D) megalith

Answer: (D) The reason for this answer is that the MEGA part of *megalith* means "large."

1. **Greatness** or stateliness
   (A) travesty   (C) majesty
   (B) amnesty   (D) tapestry

2. **Shortness** of duration or expression
   (A) longevity   (C) levity
   (B) brevity   (D) civility

3. To make **larger** or more powerful
   (A) amplify   (C) simplify
   (B) classify   (D) verify

4. A **small**, slender tube used for measuring or transferring liquids
   (A) pipit   (C) pipette
   (B) piperine   (D) piping

5. To make **smaller** or less significant
   (A) magnify   (C) glorify
   (B) minify   (D) calcify

6. A **small**, sealed glass container for one sterile dose of medicine
   (A) ampere   (C) amplitude
   (B) amplifier   (D) ampule

7. A diving apparatus, suspended by a cable, used to study **deep-sea** life
   (A) hemisphere   (C) atmosphere
   (B) stratosphere   (D) bathysphere

8. Abnormal **enlargement** of the heart
   (A) tachycardia   (C) bradycardia
   (B) megalocardia   (D) dextrocardia

Copyright © 1996 Harcourt Brace & Company. All rights reserved.

9. Feeding on a **narrow** range of foods
   - (A) stenophagous
   - (B) euryphagous
   - (C) xylophagous
   - (D) omnivorous

10. Having a broad or **flat** skull
    - (A) megacephalic
    - (B) microcephalic
    - (C) platycephalic
    - (D) macrocephalic

EXERCISE 5-I
- Fill in the Blank (one cue)
- Skill: word parts

*Use a **meaning** from List 2 to fill in the blank in each statement. The word part whose meaning you are defining will be found inside the boldfaced word. **Do not use a dictionary.** Do not focus on the size or difficulty of the words. Look only for the simple word part; it will lead you to the correct answer.*

Example: √A **kitchenette** is a very _____, compact kitchen.

   Answer: *small* [> -ETTE]

1. A **barrette** is a _____ bar or clasp for holding one's hair in place.
2. A **miniseries** is a _____ series of events or presentations.
3. The **majority** party in an election is the party that gets the _____ number of votes.
4. To **miniaturize** a device, such as a television, is to make it _____.
5. The _____ metal cap found on the tip end of an umbrella is called a **ferrule**.
6. The **amplitude** of an object is a measurement of how _____ it is.
7. A **megalopolis** is a very _____ city.

8. A **breve** is a symbol placed over a vowel to show that it has a _____ sound.
9. Veins that are abnormally _____ are said to have **stenosis**.
10. A **bathyscape** is a vessel capable of exploring _____ parts of the ocean.
11. Something **megascopic** is _____ enough to be seen with the naked eye.
12. An **amplidyne** is a direct-current generator that takes a small amount of power and makes it _____ .
13. **Cardiomegaly** is a condition in that the heart is abnormally _____ .
14. A **platyhelminth** is a _____ worm.
15. **Brevirostrates** are birds with _____ beaks.

EXERCISE 5-J
- Fill in the Blank (no cue)
- Skills: word parts, context

*Once again, use a **meaning** from List 2 to fill in the blank in each statement. This time, however, you will have to find the word part yourself in the difficult or technical word. **Do not use a dictionary**. Do not focus on the size or difficulty of the words. Look only for the simple word part; it will lead you to the correct answer.*

Example: √The platypus has a _____ bill, feet, and tail.

        Answer: *flat* [> PLATY]

1. A major earthquake is a _____ tremor with serious consequences.
2. Amplifiers make a radio signal _____ .
3. When a number of companies are joined into one _____ company, it may be referred to as a megacorporation.
4. A miniaturist is an artist who paints _____ paintings.

5. A capsule is a _____, soluble gelatin container for enclosing a dose of medicine.
6. A pipette is a _____ tube used in a lab for measuring or transferring liquids.
7. A major-domo is a man in charge of a _____, royal, or noble household.
8. A vignette is a _____ literary sketch.
9. Megaliths were _____ stones used to construct monuments.
10. The _____ parts of the ocean are referred to as bathyal.
11. The megalosaur was a _____ meat-eating dinosaur of the Jurassic period.
12. A stenothermal animal can live only in a _____ range of temperature.
13. Platyrrhine monkeys have _____ noses.
14. Brevipennate birds have _____ wings.
15. Stenophagous animals feed on a _____ variety of foods.

EXERCISE 5-K
- **Matching Columns**
- **Skills: word parts, context**

Memory check. Do not look at List 2 or use a dictionary. Special note: This time, some answers are used more than once.

1. ____	BREV	(a)	narrow
2. ____	-ETTE	(b)	flat
3. ____	AMPL	(c)	deep
4. ____	STENO	(d)	small; short
5. ____	BATHY	(e)	large
6. ____	MAJ	(f)	high
7. ____	MINI		
8. ____	PLATY		
9. ____	MEGA		
10. ____	-ULE		

EURY
The wide, wide, wide world of sports.

EXERCISE 5-L
- **Fill in (two cues)**
- **Skills: word parts, dictionary, context**

*To finish each word, fill in the blank with one of the **word parts** from your version of List 2. **You must use a college-level dictionary** to make sure that what you write really is a word and that it fits in the sentence. The word in boldface will give you the meaning of the word part that you must write.*

Example: √A _ _ _ _ lith was a very **large** stone used in prehistoric monuments.

Answer: *MEGA* [> large]

1. A nod_ _ _ is a **small**, knotlike protuberance or lump.
2. A kitchen_ _ _ _ is a very **small**, compact cooking area.
3. A reinforced, spherical **deep**-diving chamber, manned and lowered by cable, is called a _ _ _ _ _ sphere.
4. An ab_ _ _ _ iation is a **shortened** version of a word.
5. _ _ _ _ ification is the state of being made **larger**.
6. A **small** case containing magnetic tape used for audio or video recording is called a cass_ _ _ _ .
7. The funnel-shaped device used by cheerleaders to make a voice seem **larger** and louder is called a _ _ _ _ phone.
8. An air of _ _ _ esty is characterized by **greatness**, stateliness, and power.
9. _ _ _ _ ity refers to **shortness** of time.
10. A _ _ _ _ computer is a **small**, compact personal computer.
11. A _ _ _ _ vitamin is taken in doses much **larger** than the recommended levels
12. _ _ _ _ _ sis is the contraction or **narrowing** of a passage, duct, or canal.
13. The _ _ _ _ _ pus has several **flat** features, including its tail, its bill, and its feet.
14. A din_ _ _ is a nook or **small** alcove used for informal meals.
15. _ _ _ _ pod means **large**-footed.

EXERCISE 5-M
- Fill in (one cue)
- Skills: word parts, dictionary, context

Use the following word parts to fill in the blanks. **Use a college-level dictionary** *to make sure that you have formed an actual word. Since there is no meaning in boldface, you will have to search each sentence for a clue. Each item should be used only once.*

| AMPL | ETTE | MEGALY | PLATY |
| BATHY | MAJ | MINI | |

1. A _____ helminth is a worm with a flattened body.
2. A small carved, sculpted, or cast figure is called a statu_____.
3. To be called _____estic, a piece of music must have a greatness and dignity to it.
4. In physics, _____ification makes a variable quantity such as voltage or current larger without altering any other quality.
5. The _____mum is the smallest quantity, number, or degree possible.
6. Cardio_____ is an abnormal enlargement of the heart.
7. _____metry is the science of measuring the depths of the sea.

| BATHY | MEGA | PLATY | ULE |
| BREV | MINI | STENO | |

8. Australian and South Pacific birds with large feet are classified as _____podes.
9. _____thermal organisms can survive only within a narrow range of temperature.
10. A bird with a short beak or bill is a _____irostrate.
11. _____seism is a term used to describe an earthquake occurring at great depths.
12. _____cephalic is a term used to describe a flat head.
13. A small, grainlike particle or spot is called a gran_____.
14. A _____series is a program or film broadcast in smaller parts rather than all at once.

136 CHAPTER 5 DIMENSION

EXERCISE 5-N
- **Paragraph Examples**
- **Skills: word parts, dictionary, context**

Answer these four questions after each paragraph:

(a) *What word part inside the boldfaced word helps you to understand that word? What does that word part mean?*

(b) *Using only the context of the word and the word part that it contains, what do you think the boldfaced word means? (See Chapter 1, Section 2.)*

(c) *Choose one context clue that helped you. (See Chapter 1, Section 2.)*
   1. *word signals*   4. *examples or description*
   2. *punctuation signals*   5. *contrast or opposites*
   3. *synonyms (substitution)* 6. *prior knowledge; common sense*
        If 6, explain: _____

(d) *How does the dictionary define the boldfaced word as it is used in the paragraph?*

1. I grew up climbing maples and oaks in New England, and I tell you now, treetops were never like they are in a jungle rain forest. For one thing, they weren't as messy. Rain-forest branches look like untended window boxes, a riot of ferns and bromeliads and long, curly mosses. Canopy limbs are cloaked in a layer of settled debris, called "crown soil," that gives rise to a **miniature** jungle of rain-forest epiphytes—plants that grow on other plants. Trees are apparently like the rest of us: the older they are, the hairier.
    [Mary Roach, "Aliens in the Treetops," *International Wildlife*, November–December 1994, 9]

   (a) _____
   (b) _____
   (c) _____
   (d) _____

2. It is the invisible world of microbes that has given us more than 3,000 antibiotics, including the penicillin that has saved countless lives. Viruses and bacteria comprise the backbone of the biotechnology industry. No life-saving products have been derived from

such attractive **megafauna** as snow leopards and bald eagles, although they may symbolize conservation.
[Carol Kaesuk Yoon, "Drugs from Bugs," *Garbage*, Summer 1994, 26]

(a) _____
(b) _____
(c) _____
(d) _____

3. A hormone delivers its "message" to the target cell by changing the shape of the receptor that binds it. Other molecules in the cell are already set up in such a way that the receptor's new shape initiates certain changes in the cell, such as changes in permeability, enzyme activity, or gene transcription. All of these changes involve large numbers of ions or molecules, compared to the number of messenger molecules the cell received. In effect, the altered receptor **amplifies** the signal of a tiny amount of hormone into a much larger response by the cell.
[Arms, et al., *A Journey into Life*, 3rd Ed., 633]

(a) _____
(b) _____
(c) _____
(d) _____

4. The sun's chromosphere contains many small jetlike spikes of gas rising vertically through it. These features, called spicules, occur at the edges of supergranule cells; when viewed near the limb of the sun, so many are seen in projection that they give the effect of a forest. They consist of gas jets moving upward at about 30 km/s and rising to heights of from 5,000 to 20,000 km above the photosphere. Individual **spicules** last only ten minutes or so.
[George O. Abell, *Realm of the Universe*, 280]

(a) _____
(b) _____
(c) _____
(d) _____

5. The flatworms, or platyhelminthes, are the most primitive group of animals with bilateral symmetry, the beginnings of cephalization, the development of true organs, and three fully developed body layers. The middle layer contains the reproductive organs, an excretory system, and distinct layers of muscles. However, the

138 CHAPTER 5 DIMENSION

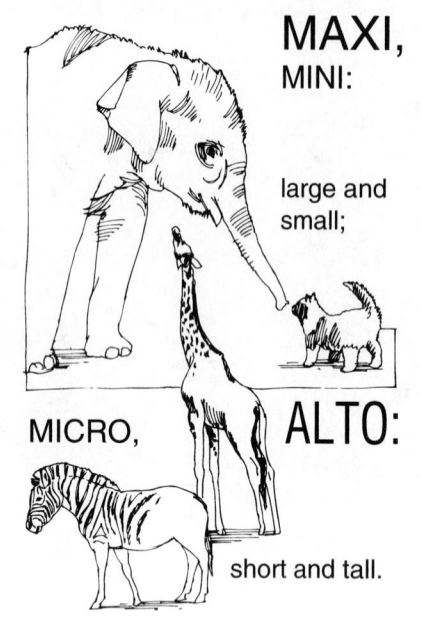

MAXI, MINI: large and small;

MICRO, ALTO: short and tall.

digestive tract still has only one opening. There is no coelum, circulatory system, or blood to transport food around the body. Hence food is distributed by the digestive system, which branches throughout the body of **platyhelminthes**. Gas exchange and waste excretion occur over the entire surface of the extremely flat body.

[Arms, et al., *A Journey into Life,* 3rd Ed., 633]

(a) _____

(b) _____

(c) _____

(d) _____

Copyright © 1996 Harcourt Brace & Company. All rights reserved.

SECTION 3: CHAPTER REVIEW (LISTS 1 AND 2 COMBINED)

Review of Word Parts Covered in This Chapter:

WORD PART	MEANING	COMMON EXAMPLE	TEXTBOOK EXAMPLE
ALTI	high	*altitude*	*altimeter*
ALTO	high	*altostratus*	*alto-relievo*
AMPL	large	*amplifier*	*amplitude*
BATHO	deep	*bathometer*	*batholith*
BATHY	deep	*bathysphere*	*bathyal*
BREV	small/short	*abbreviate*	*brevipennate*
-ETTE	small/short	*dinette*	*pipette*
EURY	wide	*eurythmics*	*eurythermal*
LATI	wide	*latitude*	*latitudinarian*
MACRO	large/long	*macrocosm*	*macrophage*
MAGNI	large	*magnify*	*magniloquent*
MAJ	large; great	*majority*	*majuscule*
MAXI	large/long	*maximum*	*maximalist*
MEGA	large	*megabucks*	*megacycle*
MEGALO	large	*megalopolis*	*megalomania*
-MEGALY	large	*cardiomegaly*	*dactylomegaly*
MICRO	small/short	*microscope*	*microbiology*
MINI	small/short	*miniskirt*	*minim*
PACHY	thick	*pachyderm*	*pachytene*
PLATY	flat; wide	*platypus*	*platyhelminth*
STENO	thin; narrow	*stenography*	*stenosis*
STRICT	thin; narrow	*restrict*	*stricture*
TENU	thin; narrow	*tenuous*	*attenuated*
-ULE	small	*capsule*	*spicule*

PRE-EXERCISE ACTIVITY 3
- **List Making**
- **Skill: word parts**

*In the blanks that follow, rewrite the combined word parts list. This time, however, reverse the order by writing the **meanings** in the first column. Then gather all the word parts in the list that have that meaning and write them on one line in the second column. This will let you make necessary connections and help you in the process of long-term memorization. The first one has already been done to show you how. (Note: You do not need to rewrite the examples.)*

	MEANING	WORD PARTS	
1.	deep	batho, bathy	*Note:* This list will be more useful if you write it in alphabetical order.
2.	_____	_____	
3.	_____	_____	
4.	_____	_____	
5.	_____	_____	
6.	_____	_____	
7.	_____	_____	
8.	_____	_____	
9.	_____	_____	
10.	_____	_____	
11.	_____	_____	

EXERCISE 5-O
- **Matching Columns**
- **Skill: word parts**

Memory check. Do not look at the list or use a dictionary. Special note: This time, some answers are used more than once.

1. _____ ALTO   (a) thick
2. _____ TENU   (b) wide
3. _____ AMPL   (c) high
4. _____ BATHY   (d) small
5. _____ MAXI   (e) deep
6. _____ -ETTE   (f) large
7. _____ LATI   (g) narrow
8. _____ PACHY
9. _____ MINI
10. _____ MAGNI

EXERCISE 5-P

- **Cross Out**
- **Skills: dictionary, word parts, context**

One word in each set does not contain the word part and meaning that is given, even though it has a set of similar letters. **Use a college-level dictionary** *to find the one that does **not** fit.*

Example:

	WORD PART	MEANING	CROSS OUT THE ONE WORD THAT DOES NOT FIT
	√LATI	wide	latinate, latitudinous, latifundium

Answer: *Latitudinous* means having width, and *latifundium* is an estate with wide, expansive holdings of land. The dictionary reveals that the word *latinate* does not involve the meaning "wide;" cross it out.

WORD PART	MEANING	CROSS OUT THE ONE WORD THAT DOES NOT FIT
1. MAXI	large; long	maxivan, maxilla, maximize
2. TENU	thin; narrow	tenure, tenuous, attenuated
3. MAJ	large; great	majuscule, majority, majolica
4. ALTO	high	altocumulus, altostratus, altogether

5.	MINI	small	diminish, mining, minibus
6.	AMPL	large	example, amplitude, ampleness
7.	MAGN	large	magnificent, magniloquent, magnolia
8.	MEGA	large	megalosaur, Megara, megadose
9.	LATI	wide	laticiferous, latitude, latifundium
10.	BATH	deep	bathos, bathrobe, bathymetry

EXERCISE 5-Q
- **Extended Answer**
- **Skills: word parts, dictionary, context**

Answer the following questions by using a college-level dictionary.

Example: √How is the meaning *large* involved in the word **macroform?**

Answer: A macroform is a reproduction of a document in a size large enough to be read by the unaided eye.

BREV ETTE ULE

1. How is the meaning *large* involved in the word **megaspore?**

2. How is the meaning *narrow* involved in the word **stenopetalous?**

3. How is the meaning *wide* involved in the word **euryphagous?**

4. How is the meaning *deep* involved in the word **batholith?**

5. How is the meaning *short* involved in the word **abbreviate?**

6. How is the meaning *small* involved in the word **spicule?**

A very brief interlude

7. How is the meaning *narrow* involved in the word **constriction?**

8. How is the meaning *small* involved in the word **microcircuit?**

9. How is the meaning *high* involved in the word **alto-relievo?**

10. How is the meaning *thick* involved in the word **pachyderm?**

EXERCISE 5-R
- **Fill in the Blank**
- **Skills: word parts, context**

Answer each question below by filling in the blank. Use the combined list.

Example: √The opposite of micro is _____ .   Answer: MACRO (etc.)

√A synonym for *wide* is _____ .   Answer: *broad*

1. The opposite of BATHY is _____ .   [Write another word part.]
2. The opposite of EURY is _____ .   [Write another word part.]
3. The opposite of MEGA is _____ .   [Write another word part.]
4. The opposite of PACHY is _____ .   [Write another word part.]
5. The opposite of MINI is _____ .   [Write another word part.]
6. A synonym for *small* is _____ .   [Write a regular word.]
7. A synonym for *large* is _____ .   [Write a regular word.]
8. A synonym for *thick* is _____ .   [Write a regular word.]
9. A synonym for *narrow* is _____ .   [Write a regular word.]
10. A synonym for *high* is _____ .   [Write a regular word.]

Copyright © 1996 Harcourt Brace & Company. All rights reserved.

EXERCISE 5-S
- **Fill in the Blanks**
- **Skill: word parts**

Memory check. Do not look back at the combined list or use a dictionary.

1. Name two word parts that mean *thin*: _____ and _____
2. Name two word parts that mean *large*: _____ and _____
3. Name two word parts that mean *small*: _____ and _____
4. Name two word parts that mean *wide*: _____ and _____
5. Name two word parts that mean *high*: _____ and _____
6. Name two word parts that mean *deep*: _____ and _____

EXERCISE 5-T
- **Paragraph Examples**
- **Skills: word parts, dictionary, context**

Answer these four questions after each paragraph:

(a) What word part inside the boldfaced word helps you to understand that word? What does that word part mean?

(b) Using only the context of the word and the word part that it contains, what do you think the boldfaced word means? (See Chapter 1, Section 2.)

(c) Choose one context clue that helped you. (See Chapter 1, Section 2.)

    1. word signals   4. examples or description
    2. punctuation signals   5. contrast or opposites
    3. synonyms (substitution)   6. prior knowledge; common sense
        If 6, explain: _____

(d) *How does the dictionary define the boldfaced word as it is used in the paragraph?*
_____

1. In America, the most dramatic examples of the trend for expanding metropolitan areas to draw on surrounding areas for their labor pool and other resources are the Los Angeles metropolitan area, the Dallas-Fort Worth area, and the so-called 500 mile northeast corridor from Washington, D.C., to Boston, Massachusetts, which is forming one enormous metropolis including 60 million people—sometimes called a megalopolis—with New York City as its hub. A megalopolis is a metropolitan area with a population of one million or more that consists of two or more smaller metropolitan areas. Despite the much-heralded flow of population to nonmetropolitan areas, more than one-third of all Americans live in the country's 23 **megalopolises**.
    [Henry L. Tischler, *Introduction to Sociology*, 4th Ed., 359]
    (a) _____
    (b) _____
    (c) _____
    (d) _____

2. One of the causes of poor indoor air quality is dust and moisture. Dust mites (**microscopic** insects found in household dust) aren't technically pollutants. Yet, along with mold, they can cause severe allergy. Damp conditions increase levels. To keep dust mites at bay, vacuum and dust often. Have your heating and cooling ductwork cleaned regularly. Frequently clean drain pans under your refrigerator or air conditioner.
    ["Indoor Air Pollution," *Mayo Clinic Health Letter*, November 1993, 5]
    (a) _____
    (b) _____
    (c) _____
    (d) _____

3. The nutrients that any animal must ingest as food may be divided, for convenience, into macronutrients—nutrients needed in large quantities—and micronutrients—nutrients required only in small amounts. The macronutrients are proteins, fats, and carbohydrates. **Macronutrients** can be stored until the body needs them for energy. Micronutrients are the

substances an organism must have in its diet in small quantities because it cannot make them for itself or because it cannot make them as fast as it needs them. Micronutrients can be divided into vitamins, which are organic compounds, and minerals, which are inorganic.

[Arms, et al., *A Journey into Life*, 3rd Ed., 474]

(a) _____
(b) _____
(c) _____
(d) _____

4. The loudness of a sound is determined by the height, or amplitude, of sound waves. The higher the amplitude of the wave, the louder the sound. Frequency and **amplitude** are independent dimensions. Sounds both high and low in pitch can be either high or low in loudness. The loudness of a sound is usually expressed in the unit decibel, abbreviated dB, which is named after the inventor of the telephone, Alexander Graham Bell.

[Spencer A. Rathus, *Psychology*, 5th Ed., 136]

(a) _____
(b) _____
(c) _____
(d) _____

5. In reproducing, a pine tree forms two kinds of cones, in which meiosis produces two kinds of spores (small microspores in the pollen cones and larger megaspores in the seed cones). **Megaspores** remain in the seed cones, and develop into female gametophytes, each containing two to several eggs. Microspores develop into immature male gametophytes, otherwise known as pollen grains.

[Arms, et al., *A Journey into Life*, 3rd Ed., 421]

(a) _____
(b) _____
(c) _____
(d) _____

6. Stricture of the esophagus is a rare disorder that usually occurs in elderly people. It is the result of accumulation of scar tissue in the esophagus, often caused by persistent acid reflux. Because the scarred portions of the esophagus gradually become enlarged, the passageway for food becomes increasingly

constricted. The result is difficulty in swallowing. The usual treatment for **stricture** is to enlarge the passageway with either a water-filled rubber bag or a flexible metal rod. This procedure, done under a general anesthetic, must be repeated every few weeks or so to be effective. Surgery to remove the scar tissue may be necessary.
   [*The American Medical Association Family Medical Guide*, 458]
   (a) _____
   (b) _____
   (c) _____
   (d) _____

7. A disorder of the sebaceous glands is responsible for the condition called acne, which is common in adolescents. In this condition, the glands become overactive and inflamed in some body regions. At the same time, their ducts may become plugged, and the inflamed glands may be surrounded by small red elevations containing blackheads (comedones) or pimples (**pustules**).
   [John W. Hole, Jr., *Human Anatomy and Physiology*, 4th Ed., 165]
   (a) _____
   (b) _____
   (c) _____
   (d) _____

8. A basic feature of democracy is that it is rooted in representative government, which means that the authority to govern is achieved through, and legitimized by, popular elections. Representative institutions can operate freely only if certain other conditions prevail. First, there must be what sociologist Edward Shils (1968) calls civilian rule. That is, every qualified citizen has the legal right to run for and hold an office of government. In addition, majority rule must be maintained. Because of the complexity of a modern democracy it is not possible for "the people" to rule. Democracy also assumes that minority rights must be protected. The majority may not always act wisely and may be unjust. The minority abides by the laws as determined by the **majority**, but the minority must be free to try to change these laws.
   [Henry L. Tischler, *Introduction to Sociology*, 4th Ed., 318]
   (a) _____
   (b) _____
   (c) _____
   (d) _____

148 CHAPTER 5 DIMENSION

9. The anterior and posterior (back) lobes of the pituitary gland produce or secrete many hormones. . . . Growth hormone regulates the growth of muscles, bones, and glands. Children who are naturally deficient in growth hormone may not grow taller than 3 or 4 feet unless they receive injections of the hormone. On the other hand, an excess of growth hormone can lead to **acromegaly**, a condition in which people may grow two to three feet taller than they normally would. Wrestler "Andre the Giant," who is over 7 feet tall and weighs in at nearly 500 pounds, secreted extremely high levels of growth hormone as a child.

   [Spencer A. Rathus, *Psychology*, 5th Ed., 83–84]

   (a) _____
   (b) _____
   (c) _____
   (d) _____

10. A less common cause of back pain in older adults is spinal or lumbar **stenosis**. Stenosis means a narrowing of the spinal canal. Narrowing compresses nerves in your lower back and can cause numbness, pain, and weakness in your back and legs. Symptoms often worsen when you walk and subside when you sit or bend forward.

    ["Back Care," *Supplement to Mayo Clinic Health Letter*, February 1994, 1]

    (a) _____
    (b) _____
    (c) _____
    (d) _____

CHAPTER 6 SHAPE

SECTION 1

List 1

Here are some word parts that are used to signify shape.

WORD PART	MEANING
ACRO	pointed; tip end
ANGUL	angled; bent
BACILL	rod-shaped
CINCT	round or girdle-shaped
CLIN	bent; sloped; leaning
-FORM	shaped like
GYR	spiral; rotating
-HEDRAL	faceted
-HEDRON	faceted
ORTHO	straight
PUNCT	pointed
ROT	round; circular
SPHER	round; globe-shaped

149

150 CHAPTER 6 SHAPE

PRE-EXERCISE ACTIVITY 1
- **List Making**
- **Skill: word parts**

*In the blanks that follow, rewrite List 1. This time, however, reverse the order by writing the **meanings** in the first column. Then gather all the word parts in the list that have that meaning and write them on one line in the second column. This will let you make necessary connections and help you in the process of long-term memorization. The first one has already been done to show you how.*

	MEANING	WORD PARTS	
1.	angled	angul	*Note:* This list will be more useful if you write it in alphabetical order.
2.	_____	_____	
3.	_____	_____	
4.	_____	_____	
5.	_____	_____	
6.	_____	_____	
7.	_____	_____	
8.	_____	_____	
9.	_____	_____	
10.	_____	_____	
11.	_____	_____	
12.	_____	_____	
13.	_____	_____	
14.	_____	_____	
15.	_____	_____	
16.	_____	_____	

Copyright © 1996 Harcourt Brace & Company. All rights reserved.

EXERCISE 6-A
- **Multiple Choice**
- **Skill: word parts**

A meaning is in boldface for each of the following phrases. From the four choices given, pick the one answer that contains a word part with that meaning. Use both versions of List 1 to help you. **Do not use a dictionary.** *Do not focus on the size or difficulty of the words. Look only for the simple word part; it will lead you to the correct answer.*

Example: √**Round** in shape, like a ball
      (A) lyrical   (C) spherical
      (B) satirical   (D) empirical

    Answer: (C) The reason for this answer is that the SPHER part of *spherical* means "round."

1. **Shaped like** a tooth
   (A) dental   (C) dentured
   (B) dentition   (D) dentiform

2. An administrative division of a city encircled or **girdled** by boundaries
   (A) precursor   (C) prefect
   (B) precinct   (D) premise

3. To turn with a **circular** motion
   (A) perorate   (C) obliterate
   (B) captivate   (D) rotate

4. Featuring markings like dots or spots that look like they were made with a **pointed** object
   (A) celibate   (C) foliolate
   (B) punctate   (D) proportionate

5. **Rod-shaped**
   (A) bacillary   (C) planetary
   (B) tertiary   (D) legendary

6. A plant whose growing point is at the **tip end**
   (A) endogen   (C) acrogen
   (B) cyanogen   (D) oxygen

7. Stratified rock **bent** downward in opposite directions
   (A) anticline (C) antithesis
   (B) antiphon (D) anticlimax

8. A figure with six **facets**
   (A) hexameter (C) hexahedron
   (B) hexachord (D) hexapod

9. **Spiral** or rotating motion
   (A) evocation (C) saltation
   (B) gyration (D) permutation

10. The branch of dentistry that specializes in **straightening** crooked teeth
    (A) pedodontics (C) orthodontics
    (B) endodontics (D) gerodontics

EXERCISE 6-B
- **Fill in the Blank (one cue)**
- **Skill: word parts**

Use a **meaning** from List 1 to fill in the blank in each statement. The word part whose meaning you are defining will be found inside the boldfaced word. **Do not use a dictionary.** Do not focus on the size or difficulty of the words. Look only for the simple word part; it will lead you to the correct answer.

Example: √To **gyrate** is to move in a _____ around an axis.

   Answer: *spiral* [> GYR]

1. A tree **inclined** by the wind is _____ in the direction it is blowing.
2. A **hemisphere** is half of a _____ figure.
3. **Rotund** objects, such as oranges, are _____ .
4. An abnormal _____ in an organ is termed **angulation**.
5. **Precincts** are the parts or regions _____ about a place.

6. Anything that is **punctate** has _____ or spotted markings.
7. **Dendriform** objects are _____ a tree.
8. A **decahedron** is a solid figure with ten _____ .
9. A fern is called an **acrogen** because it has its reproductive structures only at the _____ .
10. **Gyroidal** means having a _____ arrangement.
11. Something that is **bacilliform** is shaped like a _____ .
12. **Orthotropous** means growing in a _____ line.
13. **Spherics** is the geometry and trigonometry of figures that are formed on the surface of a _____ .
14. **Acrocephaly** is a malformation of the skull that makes it slightly _____ .
15. An **orthognathous** jaw is _____ .

EXERCISE 6-C
- **Fill in the Blank (no cue)**
- **Skills: word parts, context**

*Once again, use a **meaning** from List 1 to fill in the blank in each statement. This time, however, you will have to find the word part yourself in the difficult or technical word. **Do not use a dictionary.** Do not focus on the size or difficulty of the words. Look only for the simple word part; it will lead you to the correct answer.*

Example: √A bacillus is any of several _____ bacteria.

　　　　　Answer: *rod-shaped* [> BACILL]

1. A puncture is caused by a _____ instrument or object.
2. A rotor is a machine component that turns in a _____ motion.
3. A spherical object is shaped like a _____ .
4. A punctilious person is concerned about every detail and _____ of conduct.

5. A polyhedron is a figure with many _____ .
6. Angulate means having _____ or corners.
7. A rotary tiller has blades that turn with a _____ motion.
8. A cruciform decoration is _____ a cross.
9. Orthograde means walking with the body _____ or upright.
10. Bacillary means consisting of little _____ .
11. An acrogen is a plant that has a stem with the growing _____ at its extremity.
12. Synclinal means _____ downward in opposite directions.
13. Gyroidal planes in certain crystalline forms have a _____ arrangement.
14. The acromion is the _____ of the spine of the shoulder blade.
15. Crickets are orthopterous; they have _____ wings.

Guardian Anguls

EXERCISE 6-D
- **Matching Columns**
- **Skills: word parts, context**

Memory check. Do not look at List 1 or use a dictionary. Special note: This time, one answer is used twice.

1. _____ -FORM   (a) rod-shaped
2. _____ ACRO   (b) bent
3. _____ GYR   (c) straight
4. _____ BACILL   (d) round
5. _____ ROT   (e) spiral
6. _____ ORTHO   (f) faceted

7. ____ ANGUL   (g) angled
8. ____ CLIN   (h) pointed
9. ____ -HEDRAL   (i) shaped like
10. ____ PUNCT

EXERCISE 6-E
- **Fill in (two cues)**
- **Skills: word parts, dictionary, context**

*To finish each word, fill in the blank with one of the **word parts** from your version of List 1.* **You must use a college-level dictionary** *to make sure that what you write really is a word and that it fits in the sentence. The word in boldface will give you the meaning of the word part that you must write.*

Example: √A ___ oidal arrangement has a **spiral** shape.

    Answer: *GYR-* [> spiral]

1. A ___ator is a muscle that allows a part of the body to move in a **round** or circular motion.
2. To de___e a job is to refuse it—to turn or **bend** away from the offer.
3. A hexa_____ is a solid figure with six **facets** or faces, as a cube.
4. _____ureless tires will not go flat instantly if they are pierced by **pointed** or sharp objects.
5. Tri_____ation is a surveying technique that establishes the distance between points by measuring **angles**.
6. A _____ure is a rope or belt that goes **around** a clergyperson's waist and holds an alb (a long, flowing vestment) in place.
7. An octa_____ is a solid figure having eight **facets**.
8. ___ation is **spiral** motion and whirling.
9. The medical specialty concerned with **straightening** or correcting deformities of the skeletal system is _____pedics.
10. ___ini is pasta that is **round** or wheel-like in shape.

Copyright © 1996 Harcourt Brace & Company. All rights reserved.

11. In botany, ____carpous means having the reproductive organ at the **tip end** of the primary axis.
12. The characters in ancient cunei____ writing were **shaped like** a wedge.
13. A _____ometer is an instrument for measuring the curvature of a **sphere** or cylinder.
14. A _____us is a **rod-shaped** bacterium.
15. In math, _____gonal measurements focus on **straight** angles, also called right angles.

EXERCISE 6-F
- **Fill in (one cue)**
- **Skills: word parts, dictionary, context**

Use the following word parts to fill in the blanks. **Use a college-level dictionary** *to make sure that you have formed an actual word. Since there is no meaning in boldface, you will have to search each sentence for a clue. Each item should be used only once.*

| ACRO | BACILL | GYR | ORTHO |
| ANGUL | CLIN | -HEDRON | ROT |

1. De_____ation is a sloping or bending downwards.
2. Leaves that come to a point and have the veins come to a halt at the tip end are said to be ____drome.
3. A _____us gets its name from its rodlike shape.
4. _____genesis is evolution that proceeds in a straight path without branching out into other patterns.
5. A tetra_____ is a solid figure having four faces.
6. _____arity refers to angled corners or outlines.
7. The device used in an oven or over a barbecue grill to turn meat around with a constant circular motion to roast it slowly and evenly is called a ____isserie.
8. A single whorl of a spiral shell is called a ____ation.

CINCT	-FORM	ORTHO	ROT
CLIN	-HEDRAL	PUNCT	

9. A de_____ate flower has a downward bend or slope.
10. A _____iform mark is shaped like a point or dot.
11. An ovi_____ object is shaped like an egg.
12. A suc_____ statement is compressed—drawn into a tight circle, as it were.
13. A hepta_____ figure has seven facets.
14. _____gnathous means straight-jawed.
15. The ___ifera are a class of microscopic creatures with organs that move in a circular motion to allow them to swim.

EXERCISE 6-G
- **Paragraph Examples**
- **Skills: word parts, dictionary, context**

Answer these four questions after each paragraph:

(a) *What word part inside the boldfaced word helps you to understand that word? What does that word part mean?*

(b) *Using only the context of the word and the word part that it contains, what do you think the boldfaced word means? (See Chapter 1, Section 2.)*

(c) *Choose one context clue that helped you. (See Chapter 1, Section 2.)*
    1. *word signals*   4. *examples or description*
    2. *punctuation signals*   5. *contrast or opposites*
    3. *synonyms (substitution)* 6. *prior knowledge; common sense*
        If 6, explain: _____

(d) *How does the dictionary define the boldfaced word as it is used in the paragraph?*

1. In his controversial work *The Decline of the West* (1932), German historian Oswald Spengler theorized that every society moves through four stages of development: childhood, youth, mature adulthood, and old age. Spengler felt that Western society had reached the "golden age" of maturity during the Enlightenment of the eighteenth century, and since then had begun the inevitable crumbling and decline that go along with old age. Nothing, he believed, could stop this process. Just as the great civilizations of Babylon, Egypt, Greece, and Rome had **declined** and died, so too would the West.
   [Henry L. Tischler, *Introduction to Sociology,* 4th Ed., 418]
   (a) _____
   (b) _____
   (c) _____
   (d) _____

2. Here are the orthodontic devices most commonly used today to straighten malaligned teeth. The conventional form of orthodontic treatment, metal braces, gave rise to all those schoolyard nicknames: "metal mouth," "tin grin," and the like. Jokes aside, they remain a highly effective treatment. Orthodontists now offer a newer style of braces made of a clear ceramic or plastic. The major advantage of these models is that from a few feet away, they are virtually invisible. Another form, lingual braces, sometimes referred to as "inside" or "invisible" braces, are metal brackets affixed to the back of your teeth. Although they are less noticeable than traditional metal braces, they are more difficult for an orthodontist to fit in place. Also, these types of braces generally can't be used when your **orthodontic** treatment includes jaw surgery.
   ["Orthodontics for Adults," *Mayo Clinic Health Letter*, Volume 7, Number 11, 2]
   (a) _____
   (b) _____
   (c) _____
   (d) _____

3. Everyone has a surprisingly large repertoire of familiar faces that they quickly recognize, despite radical changes due to age, facial hair, expression or other details. In fact, there is no known upper limit to the number of faces a person can accurately identify. Many neurologists agree that prosopagnosia—difficulty recog-

nizing familiar faces—is associated primarily with damage to the right **hemisphere** of the brain. And psychologists have shown in studies of individuals without brain damage that, compared with the left hemisphere, the right hemisphere is superior at perceiving faces, as it is for processing certain other kinds of complex visual patterns.

[Diana Van Lanker, "Old Familiar Voices," *Psychology Today*, November 1987, 12]

(a) _____
(b) _____
(c) _____
(d) _____

4. For a long time it's been thought that the rotation of Earth was just something that happened naturally as it formed from smaller bodies. But according to a computer model developed by scientists Luke Dones and Scott Tremaine, the many small collisions Earth experienced wouldn't impart much spin to the planet. ... The researchers reported last January that only a collision with something the size of Mars or larger could explain the Earth's rapid **rotation**.

[Tim Folger, "This Battered Earth," *Discover*, January 1994, 33]

(a) _____
(b) _____
(c) _____
(d) _____

5. If all three sides of a triangle are congruent, the triangle is called equilateral. If all three angles of a triangle are congruent, the triangle is called equiangular. If no two sides of a triangle are congruent, the triangle is called scalene.

　　Theorem: The base angles of an isosceles triangle are congruent.
　　Corollary: Every equilateral triangle is **equiangular**.

[Richard D. Anderson, et al., *School Mathematics Geometry*, 174]

(a) _____
(b) _____
(c) _____
(d) _____

SECTION 2

REMARK

List 2

Here are more word parts that are used to signify shape.

WORD PART	MEANING
ACU	pointed; sharp
CIRCUL	round; circular
CURV	bent; curved
CYCL	round; circular
FLECT	bent
FLEX	bent
GON	angled
-OID	shaped like; resembling
ORB	round; circular
RECT	straight
SINU	bent
TORT	bent

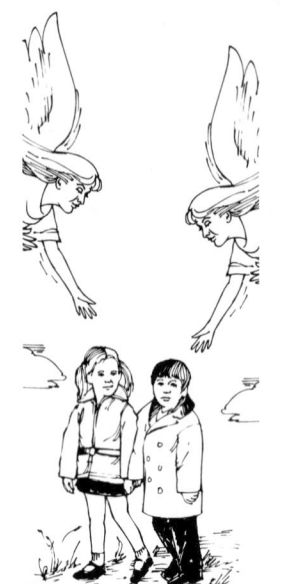

PRE-EXERCISE ACTIVITY 2
- **List Making**
- **Skill: word parts**

*In the blanks that follow, rewrite List 2. This time, however, reverse the order by writing the **meanings** in the first column. Then gather all the word parts in the list that have that meaning and write them on one line in the second column. This will let you make necessary connections and help you in the process of long-term memorization. The first one has already been done to show you how.*

MEANING	WORD PARTS	
1. angled	gon	*Note:* This list will be more useful if you write it in alphabetical order.
2.		
3.		
4.		
5.		
6.		
7.		
8.		
9.		

EXERCISE 6-H
- **Multiple Choice**
- **Skill: word parts**

A meaning is in boldface for each of the following phrases. From the four choices given, pick the one answer that contains a word part with that meaning. Use both versions of List 2 to help you. **Do not use a dictionary.** *Do not focus on the size or difficulty of the words. Look only for the simple word part; it will lead you to the correct answer.*

CHAPTER 6 SHAPE

Example: √**Roundness** in shape, like a ball
    (A) polarity   (C) austerity
    (B) angularity   (D) circularity

Answer: (D) The reason for this answer is that the CIRCUL part of *circularity* means "round."

1. Twisted or **bent** out of shape
   (A) converted   (C) orthotic
   (B) distorted   (D) rectified

2. To **straighten** out or correct something
   (A) rectify   (C) fortify
   (B) mystify   (D) putrefy

3. An abnormal **bending** of the spine
   (A) posture   (C) composure
   (B) curvature   (D) sinecure

4. Tapering to a **point**
   (A) laureate   (C) acuminate
   (B) angulate   (D) desolate

5. A **bend** or turn
   (A) acuity   (C) bellicosity
   (B) viscosity   (D) sinuosity

6. **Circular** or spherical
   (A) oracular   (C) orbicular
   (B) ocular   (D) jocular

7. **Bent** backward
   (A) retrograde   (C) retrospective
   (B) retrogressive   (D) retroflex

8. An instrument that measures **circular** line segments or arcs
   (A) barometer   (C) pedometer
   (B) cyclometer   (D) tachometer

9. A figure with six **angles** and six sides
   - (A) hexachord
   - (B) hexapod
   - (C) hexameter
   - (D) hexagon

10. **Shaped like** or resembling a heart
    - (A) cardinal
    - (B) cardioid
    - (C) cardiac
    - (D) cardiovascular

EXERCISE 6-I
- **Fill in the Blank (two cues)**
- **Skill: word parts**

*Use a **meaning** from List 2 to fill in the blank in each statement. The word part whose meaning you are defining will be found inside the boldfaced word.* **Do not use a dictionary.** *Do not focus on the size or difficulty of the words. Look only for the simple word part; it will lead you to the correct answer.*

Example: √A **circular** tower is _____ .

   Answer: *round* [> CIRCUL]

1. A **correction** sets wrong things _____ .
2. **Contortionists** in a circus are able to _____ their bodies into seemingly impossible positions.
3. **Curvature** is a property of space near massive bodies in that their gravitational field causes light to _____ .
4. The **circulatory** system sends blood _____ the body.
5. An **inflection** is a turning, _____, or curving.
6. A **sinuous** path has many _____ or turns.
7. A **polygon** is a closed plane figure with many _____ .
8. A **tortuous** road is full of _____, turnings, and windings.
9. A **curvilinear** figure is bounded by _____ lines.
10. A **flexor** muscle _____ a part of the body.

164 CHAPTER 6 SHAPE

11. An **anthropoid**, such as a chimpanzee, _____ a human being.
12. A leaf that is **acuminate** tapers to a _____ .
13. Something **orbicular**, such as a disc, is _____ .
14. **Cyclosis** is the regular _____ movement of protoplasm within a cell.
15. A bird with a _____ bill is classified as **rectirostral**.

EXERCISE 6-J
- **Fill in the Blank (no cue)**
- **Skills: word parts, context**

*Once again, use a **meaning** from List 2 to fill in the blank in each statement. This time, however, you will have to find the word part yourself in the difficult or technical word. **Do not use a dictionary.** Do not focus on the size or difficulty of the words. Look only for the simple word part; it will lead you to the correct answer.*

Example: √Flection is the act of _____ .

       Answer: *bending* [> FLECT]

1. An orbiting spacecraft moves in a _____ path.
2. Something curvaceous has _____ lines.
3. A circumflex accent is a _____ line or mark placed over certain long vowels.
4. Rectification consists in setting things _____ .
5. A polygon is a closed figure, especially one that has more than four _____ .
6. To circularize is to make something _____ .
7. A genuflection is a _____ of the knee done as a gesture of reverence or worship.
8. Curvature is a necessary feature of a rocking chair. The rockers must be _____ .

9. A heptagon is a plane figure with seven _____ and seven sides.
10. Sinuated leaves have _____ and segmented edges.
11. An aculeate animal is furnished with a _____ sting or prickle.
12. An orbicular leaf is _____ in shape.
13. A cyclometer is an instrument designed to measure the arcs of _____.
14. Helicoid means _____ a spiral, as is the shell of a snail.
15. Torticollis is an affliction of the muscles of the neck in that the head is _____ to one side.

Punct Rock

EXERCISE 6-K
- **Matching Columns**
- **Skills: word parts, context**

Memory check. Do not look at List 2 or use a dictionary. Special note: This time, some answers are used more than once.

1. ____	TORT	(a)	bent
2. ____	ACU	(b)	straight
3. ____	-OID	(c)	round
4. ____	CYCL	(d)	shaped like
5. ____	ORB	(e)	angled
6. ____	RECT	(f)	pointed
7. ____	GON		
8. ____	FLECT		
9. ____	CIRCUL		
10. ____	SINU		

EXERCISE 6-L
- **Fill in (two cues)**
- **Skills: word parts, dictionary, context**

*To finish each word, fill in the blank with one of the **word parts** from your version of List 2. **You must use a college-level dictionary** to make sure that what you write really is a word and that it fits in the sentence. The word in boldface will give you the meaning of the word part that you must write.*

Example: √To dis_ _ _ _ something is to **twist** it out of its normal shape.

Answer: TORT [> twist]

1. The Penta_ _ _ in Washington, D.C., gets its name from the fact that it is a five-sided and five-**angled** building.
2. _ _ _ _ _ _ation is the continuous movement of blood **around** the body.
3. A cor_ _ _ _ion **straightens** out something that is wrong.
4. A person who is in_ _ _ _ible will not be turned or **bent** away from a certain belief or course of action.
5. A large-scale wind storm that moves in a circular or **round** path is a _ _ _ _one.
6. A _ _ _ _angle is a parallelogram with four right (**straight** or 90-degree) angles.
7. To de_ _ _ _ is to **bend** or turn aside.
8. A re_ _ _ _ is a sharp reply that **bends** an accusation or insult back upon the person saying it.
9. A crystall_ _ _ is a substance that **resembles** a crystal.
10. To in_ _ _ _ate is to **bend** or manipulate an idea so that it is slyly hinted rather than directly said.
11. The **round** or elliptical path followed by a planet is its _ _ _it.
12. In geometry, _ _ _ _ature is the derivative of the **bending** of the tangent with respect to arc length.
13. In anatomy, re_ _ _ion refers to a **bending** or folding back of a part upon itself.
14. _ _ _ity is **sharpness** of mind and keenness of perception.
15. An ennea_ _ _ has nine **angles** and nine sides.

EXERCISE 6-M
- **Fill in (one cue)**
- **Skills: word parts, dictionary, context**

Use the following word parts to fill in the blanks. **Use a college-level dictionary** *to make sure that you have formed an actual word. Since there is no meaning in boldface, you will have to search each sentence for a clue. Each item should be used only once.*

ACU	FLEX	-OID	RECT
CYCL	GON	ORB	

1. The term ____ilinear refers to anything characterized by straight lines.
2. The ____ops was a mythical giant who had a single round eye in the middle of his forehead.
3. An iso____ is a figure that has all angles equal.
4. The petals of a flower that are bent sharply downwards are said to be de____ed.
5. The mouths of some insects are ____leated in order to draw blood.
6. The starfish is aster____. That is, it is shaped like a star.
7. ____ital velocity is the speed at which a spacecraft must move in order to stay on a controlled circular course.

CIRCUL	FLECT	RECT	TORT
CURV	GON	SINU	

8. A re____ion bends light back to the eye of the viewer.
9. ____itude is rightness of conduct and moral virtue.
10. A refrigerator re____ates its coolant by sending it around a closed system in a circular path.
11. ____iometry is the theory or science of measuring angles.
12. ____ile means bent or twisted.
13. A ____ate leaf has a bending, wavy margin.
14. A ____aceous figure is curved and well shaped.

EXERCISE 6-N
- Paragraph Examples
- Skills: word parts, dictionary, context

Answer these four questions after each paragraph:

(a) *What word part inside the boldfaced word helps you to understand that word? What does that word part mean?*

(b) *Using only the context of the word and the word part that it contains, what do you think the boldfaced word means? (See Chapter 1, Section 2.)*

(c) *Choose one context clue that helped you. (See Chapter 1, Section 2.)*
   1. *word signals*
   2. *punctuation signals*
   3. *synonyms (substitution)*
   4. *examples or description*
   5. *contrast or opposites*
   6. *prior knowledge; common sense*
      If 6, explain: _____

(d) *How does the dictionary define the boldfaced word as it is used in the paragraph?*

1. The fingers of a bat are all very long with extended shanks between the knuckles; the index and middle fingers are close together at the leading edge of the wing, but the ring and little fingers fan out behind to support the main wing surface. This whole arrangement gives fine control of the wing shape since all the joints can be **flexed** by tendons operated by muscles in the arm. Thus bats are by far the most maneuverable of aerial animals.
   ["Bat," *World Encyclopedia of Animals*, 13]

   (a) _____
   (b) _____
   (c) _____
   (d) _____

2. Class Agnatha: Jawless Fishes
   The most primitive vertebrates were ostracoderms. Known only as fossils, these agnathan fish were covered with heavy bony plates. Their modern relatives are the jawless **cyclostomes** ("round mouths"), the lampreys and the hagfishes. Adult lampreys and

hagfishes are long, cylindrical creatures without paired fins. The adult lamprey is a semiparasite, and hagfishes are scavengers.

[Arms, et al., *A Journey into Life*, 3rd Ed., 453]

(a) _____
(b) _____
(c) _____
(d) _____

3. That the specific heat of water is higher than that of land is responsible for the pattern of air flow at a beach. During the day, the sun adds roughly equal amounts of heat to beach and water, but the lower specific heat of sand causes the beach to reach a higher temperature than the water. Because of this, the air above the land reaches a higher temperature than that over the water. Consequently, cooler air from above the water is drawn in to displace this rising hot air, resulting in a breeze from ocean to land during the day. The hot air gradually cools as it rises and thus sinks, setting up [a] circulating pattern. . . . During the night, the land cools more quickly than the water and the **circulating** pattern reverses itself because the hotter air is now over the water. . . .

[Serway & Faughn, *College Physics*, 3rd Ed., 347]

(a) _____
(b) _____
(c) _____
(d) _____

4. The bright stars in x-ray binaries show periodic changes in the frequency of dark lines, or absorption lines, in their spectra. These changes, known as Doppler shifts, result from the **orbital** motion of the visible star around the x-ray source. Radiation from an approaching object appears compressed, or bluer; likewise, radiation from a receding object looks stretched, or redder. The degree of the Doppler shift indicates the star's rate of motion.

[Edward P. J. van den Hueval and Jan van Paradijs, "X-Ray Binaries," *Scientific American*, November 1993, 66]

(a) _____
(b) _____
(c) _____
(d) _____

170 CHAPTER 6 SHAPE

      Cinct   Sankt   Sunkt

5. Distortion is an aberration of a lens or mirror in which the image has a **distorted** shape as a result of nonuniform lateral magnification over the field of view. There are two common forms of lens distortion. In barrel distortion, the magnification decreases towards the edge of the field. In pincushion distortion, there is greater magnification at the edge.
    [Valerie Illingworth, *The Anchor Dictionary of Astronomy*, 119]

(a) _____
(b) _____
(c) _____
(d) _____

SECTION 3: CHAPTER REVIEW (LISTS 1 AND 2 COMBINED)

Review of Word Parts Covered in This Chapter:

WORD PART	MEANING	COMMON EXAMPLE	TEXTBOOK EXAMPLE
ACRO	pointed; tip end	acrobat	acrocarpous
ACU	pointed; sharp	acute	acuminate
ANGUL	angled	angular	hexangular
BACILL	rod-shaped	bacillus	bacilliform
CINCT	round; girdle-shaped	precinct	cincture
CIRCUL	round; circular	circulate	circularize
CLIN	bent; sloped; leaning	inclined	declination
CURV	bent; curved	curved	curvilinear
CYCL	round; circular	cyclone	cyclometer
FLECT	bent	reflect	inflection
FLEX	bent	flexible	flexion
-FORM	shaped like	cruciform	dentiform
GON	angled	polygon	heptagon
GYR	spiral	gyrate	gyrostatics
-HEDRAL	faceted	polyhedral	hexahedral
-HEDRON	faceted	polyhedron	enneahedron
-OID	shaped like; resembling	humanoid	ovoid
ORB	round; circular	orbit	orbicular
ORTHO	straight	orthopedics	orthognathous
PUNCT	pointed	puncture	punctilious
RECT	straight	rectangle	rectilinear
ROT	round; circular	rotate	rotund
SINU	bent	sinus	sinuosity
SPHER	round	hemisphere	spherometer
TORT	bent	torture	tortuosity

172 CHAPTER 6 SHAPE

PRE-EXERCISE ACTIVITY 3
- List Making
- Skill: word parts

*In the blanks that follow, rewrite the combined word parts list. This time, however, reverse the order by writing the **meanings** in the first column. Then gather all the word parts in the list that have that meaning and write them on one line in the second column. This will let you make necessary connections and help you in the process of long-term memorization. The first one has already been done to show you how.*

	MEANING	WORD PARTS
1.	angled	angul, gon
2.		
3.		
4.		
5.		
6.		
7.		
8.		
9.		
10.		
11.		
12.		
13.		
14.		
15.		
16.		
17.		

Note: This list will be more useful if you write it in alphabetical order.

EXERCISE 6-O
- **Matching Columns**
- **Skill: word parts**

Memory check. Do not look back at the combined list or use a dictionary.
Special note: This time, one answer is used twice.

1. ____	ANGUL	(a)	bent
2. ____	ACRO	(b)	straight
3. ____	BACILL	(c)	pointed
4. ____	CYCL	(d)	angled
5. ____	-OID	(e)	faceted
6. ____	SINU	(f)	shaped like
7. ____	-HEDRON	(g)	rod-shaped
8. ____	RECT	(h)	round
9. ____	CINCT	(i)	spiral
10. ____	GYR		

EXERCISE 6-P
- **Cross Out**
- **Skills: dictionary, word parts, context**

One word in each set does not contain the word part and meaning that is given, even though it has a set of similar letters. **Use a college-level dictionary** *to find the one that does* **not** *fit.*

	WORD		CROSS OUT THE ONE WORD
Example:	**PART**	**MEANING**	**THAT DOES NOT FIT**
	√TORT	twisted	tortoni, torture, torticollis

Answer: *Torture* involves twisting and torment, and *torticollis* is a painful twisting of the head. The dessert called *tortoni* comes from the name of its creator; cross it out.

WORD PART	MEANING	CROSS OUT THE ONE WORD THAT DOES NOT FIT
1. ACRO	pointed	acrogen, across, acrocarpous
2. CLIN	bent	incline, clinometer, clingstone
3. GON	angled	gondola, polygon, goniometer
4. GYRO	spiral	gyromagnetic, gyrose, gyron
5. ORB	round	suborbital, absorbent, orbicular
6. ROT	round	rottenness, rotisserie, rotunda
7. CURV	bent; curved	incurvate, curvilinear, scurvy
8. FORM	shaped like	ensiform, formulation, cruciform
9. ACU	pointed	acuminate, aculeate, immaculate
10. -OID	resembling	avoid, ovoid, anthropoid

EXERCISE 6-Q

- **Extended Answer**
- **Skills: word parts, dictionary, context**

Answer the following questions by using a college-level dictionary.

Example: √How is the meaning *round* involved in the word **rotiform?**

Answer: Rotiform means shaped like a wheel, which is round.

1. How is the meaning *bent* involved in the word **contortion?**

2. How is the meaning *round* involved in the word **orbicular?**

3. How is the meaning *pointed* or *sharp* involved in the word **acumen?**

4. How is the meaning *round* involved in the word **uncirculated?**

5. How is the meaning *straight* involved in the word **orthopedics?**

6. How is the meaning *bent* involved in the word **genuflection?**

_____

7. How is the meaning *shaped like* involved in the word **ramiform?**

_____

8. How is the meaning *bent* involved in the word **declination?**

_____

9. How is the meaning *angle* involved in the word **isogonic?**

_____

10. How is the meaning *rod-shaped* involved in the word **bacillary?**

_____

A pointed remark

EXERCISE 6-R
- **Fill in the Blanks**
- **Skill: word parts**

Memory check. Do not look back at the combined list or use a dictionary.

1. Name two word parts that mean *straight*: _____ and _____ .
2. Name two word parts that mean *faceted*: _____ and _____ .
3. Name two word parts that mean *bent*: _____ and _____ .
4. Name two word parts that mean *shaped like:* _____ and _____ .
5. Name two word parts that mean *round*: _____ and _____ .
6. Name two word parts that mean *angled*: _____ and _____ .
7. Name two word parts that mean *pointed*: _____ and _____ .

Copyright © 1996 Harcourt Brace & Company. All rights reserved.

EXERCISE 6-S
- **Paragraph Examples**
- **Skills: word parts, dictionary, context**

Answer these four questions after each paragraph.

(a) *What word part inside the boldfaced word helps you to understand that word? What does that word part mean?*

(b) *Using only the context of the word and the word part that it contains, what do you think the boldfaced word means? (See Chapter 1, Section 2.)*

(c) *Choose one context clue that helped you. (See Chapter 1, Section 2.)*
   1. *word signals*
   2. *punctuation signals*
   3. *synonyms (substitution)*
   4. *examples or description*
   5. *contrast or opposites*
   6. *prior knowledge; common sense*
      If 6, explain: _____

(d) *How does the dictionary define the boldfaced word as it is used in the paragraph?*

1. The piston moves up and down in the cylinder. This up-and-down motion is called reciprocating motion. The piston moves in a straight line. This straight-line motion must be changed to a turning motion in order for it to turn the car wheels. A crank and a connecting rod change reciprocating to **rotary** motion.
   [William Crouse, *Automotive Mechanics*, 213]
   (a) _____
   (b) _____
   (c) _____
   (d) _____

2. Earlier this year, water-management executives in San Diego and Tampa gave the go-ahead to projects that will take the drinking water these cities now pipe into homes for showering, flushing toilets, and washing clothes, and they will collect it, purify it, and **circulate** it back to homes for reuse as drinking water. Seeking to avoid the dreaded term "waste water," acolytes of water treatment

call the process "potable reuse." It may well be the ultimate example of closing the loop.
[David Clarke, "Let Them Drink Waste Water," *Garbage*, Summer 1994, 10]

(a) _____
(b) _____
(c) _____
(d) _____

3. Jews can be divided into three groups, based on the manner in which they approach traditional religious precepts. **Orthodox** Jews observe traditional religious laws very closely. They maintain strict dietary laws and do not work, drive, or engage in other everyday practices on the Sabbath. Women are not permitted to be ordained as rabbis. Reform Jews, on the other hand, allow for major reinterpretations of religious practices and customs, often in response to changes in society. Conservative Jews represent a compromise between the two extremes. They are less traditional than the Orthodox Jews, but not as willing to make major modifications in religious observance as the Reform Jews. Both Reform and Conservative Jews have permitted women to become rabbis.
[Henry L. Tischler, *Introduction to Sociology*, 4th Ed., 285]

(a) _____
(b) _____
(c) _____
(d) _____

4. We use the expression n-gon for a polygon of exactly n vertices and n sides. Thus every polygon is an n-gon, for some n. By that definition, a triangle is a 3-gon and a quadrilateral is a 4-gon; however, the terms 3-gon and 4-gon are rarely used. For certain n-gons there are special names, which are derived from the corresponding Greek names. For instance, a 5-gon is a pentagon, a 6-gon is a hexagon, a 7-gon is a heptagon, an 8-gon is an octagon, and a 10-gon is a **decagon**.
[Richard D. Anderson, et al., *School Mathematics Geometry*, 590]

(a) _____
(b) _____
(c) _____
(d) _____

5. A heat engine carries some working substance through a cyclic process, defined as one in which the substance eventually returns to its initial state. As an example of a **cyclic** process, consider the operation of a steam engine in which the working substance is water. The water is carried through a cycle in which it first evaporates into steam in a boiler and then expands against a piston. After the steam is condensed with cooling water, it is returned to the boiler and the process is repeated.

[Serway & Faughn, *College Physics*, 3rd Ed., 378]

(a) _____
(b) _____
(c) _____
(d) _____

6. One simple phobia is fear of elevators. Some people will not enter elevators, despite the hardships they suffer (such as walking six flights of steps) as a result. Yes, the cable could break. The ventilation could fail. One could be stuck waiting in midair for repairs. But these problems are uncommon, and it does not make sense for most of us to repeatedly walk flights of stairs to elude them. Similarly, some people with simple phobias for hypodermic needles will not receive injections, even when they are the advised remedy for profound illness. Injections can be painful, but most people with phobias for needles would gladly suffer an excruciating pinch if it would help them fight illness. Other simple phobias include claustrophobia (fear of tight or enclosed places), **acrophobia** (fear of heights), and fear of mice, snakes, and other creepy-crawlies.

[Spencer A. Rathus, *Psychology*, 4th Ed., 483]

(a) _____
(b) _____
(c) _____
(d) _____

7. *Demodex folliculorum*, a tiny, eight-legged relative of the spider, makes its home at the base of our eyelashes. There, the creatures hatch, defecate, copulate, and die, sometimes a half dozen mites to a lash, though we wouldn't know it. They don't hurt a bit, and as far as anyone knows, they're perfectly benign. Never much longer than a hair is wide, follicle mites feed by **puncturing** the

cells of our eyelash follicles with two tiny needles, then pumping out cellular fluid as needed.

[Doug Stewart, "Do Fish Sleep?" *National Wildlife*, April–May 1994, 58]

(a) _____
(b) _____
(c) _____
(d) _____

8. The most recent development in manufacturing technology is called **flexible** manufacturing, which uses computers to automate and integrate manufacturing such components as robots, machines, product design, and engineering analysis. Companies such as Deere, General Motors, Intel, and Illinois Tool Works use flexible manufacturing in a single manufacturing plant to do small batch and mass production operations at the same time. Bar codes enable machines to make instantaneous changes—such as putting a larger screw in a different location—as different batches flow down the automated assembly line. The structures associated with the new technology tend to have few rules, decentralization, a small ratio of administrators to workers, face-to-face lateral communication, and a team-oriented, organic approach.

[Richard L. Daft, *Management*, 2nd Ed., 294]

(a) _____
(b) _____
(c) _____
(d) _____

9, 10. Two of the cervical vertebrae are of special interest. The first vertebra, or atlas, supports and balances the head. It has practically no body or spine and appears as a bony ring with two transverse processes (bony projections). On its upper surface, the atlas has two **reniform**, or kidney-shaped, facets that join with the occipital condyles of the skull. The second cervical vertebra, or axis, bears a toothlike odontoid process on its body. This tooth-shaped process projects upward and lies in the ring of the atlas. As the head is turned from side to side, the atlas pivots around the **odontoid** process.

[John W. Hole, Jr., *Human Anatomy and Physiology*, 4th Ed., 212]

(a) _____
(b) _____

(c)
(d)

(a)
(b)
(c)
(d)

CHAPTER 7 TIME

SECTION 1

List 1
Here are some word parts that are used to signify time.

WORD PART	MEANING
ANN	year
ANTE	earlier; before
ANTIQ	ancient
CO	at the same time; with
NEO	new
NOCT	evening; night
POST	later; after
PRE	earlier; before
SEN	old
SIMUL	at the same time
TEMPO	time
VET	old; experienced

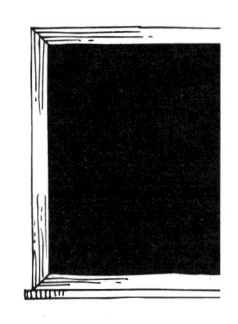

181

Copyright © 1996 Harcourt Brace & Company. All rights reserved.

PRE-EXERCISE ACTIVITY 1
- **List Making**
- **Skill: word parts**

*In the blanks that follow, rewrite List 1. This time, however, reverse the order by writing the **meanings** in the first column. Then gather all the word parts in the list which have that meaning and write them on one line in the second column. This will let you make necessary connections and help you in the process of long-term memorization. The first one has already been done to show you how.*

	MEANING	WORD PARTS	
1.	after	post	*Note:* This list will be more useful if you write it in alphabetical order.
2.	_____	_____	
3.	_____	_____	
4.	_____	_____	
5.	_____	_____	
6.	_____	_____	
7.	_____	_____	
8.	_____	_____	
9.	_____	_____	
10.	_____	_____	
11.	_____	_____	
12.	_____	_____	
13.	_____	_____	
14.	_____	_____	

EXERCISE 7-A
- **Multiple Choice**
- **Skill: word parts**

A meaning is in boldface for each of the following phrases. From the four choices given, pick the one answer which contains a word part with that meaning. Use both versions of List 1 to help you. **Do not use a dictionary.** *Do not focus on the size or difficulty of the words. Look only for the simple word part; it will lead you to the correct answer.*

Example: √To happen **earlier** in time
        (A) intercede   (C) antecede
        (B) concede   (D) recede

        Answer: (C) The reason for this answer is that the ANTE part of *antecede* means "earlier."

1. In music, the **time** or rate at which a piece is to be played
   (A) texture   (C) volume
   (B) tempo   (D) key

2. A person or thing that comes **earlier** and indicates the approach of someone or something else
   (A) postulant   (C) precursor
   (B) anticline   (D) simulacrum

3. Decline or deterioration of powers due to **old** age
   (A) juvenescence   (C) luminescence
   (B) senescence   (D) inflorescence

4. Music appropriate for **night** listening because of its dreamy or restful character
   (A) sonata   (C) nocturne
   (B) symphony   (D) passacaglia

5. A **new** growth of abnormal tissue
   (A) protoplasm   (C) endoplasm
   (B) cytoplasm   (D) neoplasm

6. A program produced **at the same time** on radio and television
   (A) theatrical cast   (C) broadcast
   (B) simulcast   (D) telecast

7. Happening twice a **year**
   - (A) biannual
   - (B) binaural
   - (C) bicephalus
   - (D) binary

8. Person with **experience**
   - (A) neophyte
   - (B) veteran
   - (C) tyro
   - (D) novice

9. Coming **later** in time
   - (A) anterior
   - (B) prior
   - (C) interior
   - (D) posterior

10. Pertaining to the **evening**
    - (A) nocturnal
    - (B) temporal
    - (C) diurnal
    - (D) hebdomadal

EXERCISE 7-B
- Fill in the Blank (one cue)
- Skill: word parts

*Use a **meaning** from List 1 to fill in the blank in each statement. The word part whose meaning you are defining will be found inside the boldfaced word. **Do not use a dictionary**. Do not focus on the size or difficulty of the words. Look only for the simple word part; it will lead you to the correct answer.*

Example: √**Noctuids** are moths that are usually active by _____ .

Answer: *night*   [> NOCT]

1. When two men bear the same name in an immediate family, **senior** is used after the name of the _____ one.
2. To **presuppose** is to assume something _____ hand.
3. **Simultaneous** operations occur _____ .
4. To **antecede** someone is to come _____ .

5. An **antiquary** is an expert on _____ monuments, relics, and customs.
6. An **inveterate** gambler has an _____ habit and history of placing bets.
7. The period _____ adolescence is known as **pre-adolescence**.
8. **Temporizing** is the attempt to gain _____ by evasive action.
9. A **neologism** is a _____ word or phrase.
10. **Anno** Domini means in the _____ of our Lord and is abbreviated as A.D.
11. **Postdiluvian** refers to the period _____ the biblical Flood.
12. Two people or items that exist _____ are called **coeval**.
13. **Superannuated** ideas have been around for too many _____ to be useful or workable.
14. **Neoteric** means modern or _____ .
15. The clouds that are visible during the short _____ of summer are called **noctilucent**.

EXERCISE 7-C
- **Fill in the Blank (no cue)**
- **Skills: word parts, context**

*Once again, use a **meaning** from List 1 to fill in the blank in each statement. This time, however, you will have to find the word part yourself in the difficult or technical word. **Do not use a dictionary**. Do not focus on the size or difficulty of the words. Look only for the simple word part; it will lead you to the correct answer.*

Example: √An anniversary is the _____ly remembrance of a past event.

Answer: *yearly* [> ANN]

186 CHAPTER 7 TIME

1. In a coincidence, events happen _____ with no apparent connection.
2. Temporal means pertaining to _____.
3. An antiquated law is _____ and no longer relevant.
4. A postdated check has a date _____ the actual date of writing.
5. Annals are a _____ly record of events.
6. A precedent is an _____ legal decision which guides lawyers and judges.
7. When they were first invented, senates were governing assemblies or councils composed of the _____.
8. A simulcast is broadcast on radio and television _____.
9. An annuity is a _____ly grant, allowance, or income.
10. Senescent means growing _____.
11. The postpartum period is the time _____ childbirth.
12. Cotidal areas on a map show points that have tides _____.
13. The antepartum period is the time _____ childbirth.
14. A neoteric writer is a _____ writer.
15. A noctuid is a _____-flying moth.

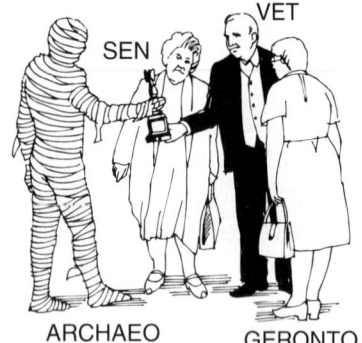

VET and SEN have been around,
And GERONTO's old and wise;
But when you seek longevity,
ARCHAEO takes the prize.

EXERCISE 7-D
- **Matching Columns**
- **Skill: word parts**

Memory check. Do not look back at List 1 or use a dictionary. Special note: This time, one answer is used twice.

1. _____ TEMPO   (a) new
2. _____ SIMUL   (b) night
3. _____ NEO   (c) ancient

Copyright © 1996 Harcourt Brace & Company. All rights reserved.

4. _____ SEN   (d) time
5. _____ ANN   (e) year
6. _____ NOCT   (f) at the same time
7. _____ ANTIQ   (g) earlier
8. _____ CO   (h) later
9. _____ POST   (i) old
10. _____ ANTE

EXERCISE 7-E
- Fill in (two cues)
- Skills: word parts, dictionary, context

*To finish each word, fill in the blank with one of the **word parts** from your version of List 1. **You must use a college-level dictionary** to make sure that what you write really is a word and that it fits in the sentence. The word in boldface will give you the meaning of the word part that you must write.*

Example: √The abbreviation A.M. means _____ meridian or **before** noon.

           Answer: *ANTE* [> before]

1. A person with long **experience** in a position is a _____eran.
2. A _____plasm is a **new** growth of abnormal tissue.
3. Something that lasts for a short period of **time** is _____rary.
4. _____ual events happen every **year**.
5. Works published **after** a writer's death are called _____humous.
6. A collector of **ancient** artifacts is called an _____uary.
7. The Peruvian empire _____dates the Mexican empire. That is, it came **earlier**.
8. The last stage of life, **old** age, is called _____ectitude.
9. A _____phyte is someone **new** at what he or she is doing.
10. Animals which are active in the **evening** are called _____urnal.
11. _____taneous events happen **at the same time**.

12. When you make a ___diction, you tell what you think is going to happen **before** it actually does.
13. A __-anchor on a news broadcast appears **at the same time** with another anchorperson and works jointly with him or her.
14. An **old**, long-established practice is an in___erate habit.
15. Something con___orary happens during your life**time**.

EXERCISE 7-F
- Fill in (one cue)
- Skills: word parts, dictionary, context

*Continue filling in **word parts** from your version of List 1, as you have been doing, **using a college-level dictionary** to check accuracy. This time, however, there will be no word in boldface. You will have to search the sentence for a clue.*

Example: √__ tenants are renters who hold the lease at the same time and are equally responsible for the rent.

Answer: *CO* [> at the same time]

1. The yearly recurrence of the date of a past event is its ___iversary.
2. Your ___cedents are those relatives who came before you and from whom you are descended.
3. Your con___oraries are the people who live in your time.
4. A ___logism is a new word, meaning, usage, or phrase.
5. Legislative ___ sponsors introduce a bill at the same time in a joint effort.
6. ___uity refers to ancient eras.
7. A person who shows significant deterioration in memory and alertness because of old age is said to be ___ile.
8. Your ___erity are the relatives who come after you, your descendants.
9. A ___caution is a measure taken earlier to avert dangerous or evil results.

10. The term equi_____ial refers to that period when night equals the period of daylight.
11. To _____pone something is to put it off until later.
12. A semi_____ual meeting takes place twice a year.
13. A _____eran officer is experienced in military theory and practice.
14. Any _____classic approach to the arts produces a new version of a classic style.
15. In American history, the _____-bellum period was the time before the Civil War.

EXERCISE 7-G
- **Paragraph Examples**
- **Skills: word parts, dictionary, context**

Answer these four questions after each paragraph:

(a) *What word part inside the boldfaced word helps you to understand that word? What does that word part mean?*

(b) *Using only the context of the word and the word part that it contains, what do you think the boldfaced word means? (See Chapter 1, Section 2.)*

(c) *Choose one context clue that helped you. (See Chapter 1, Section 2.)*
   1. *word signals*   4. *examples or description*
   2. *punctuation signals* 5. *contrast or opposites*
   3. *synonyms (substitution)* 6. *prior knowledge; common sense*
      If 6, explain: _____

(d) *How does the dictionary define the boldfaced word as it is used in the paragraph?*

1. **Post-traumatic** stress disorder (PTSD) is defined as intense and persistent feelings of anxiety and helplessness that are caused by a traumatic experience, such as a physical threat to oneself or

one's family, destruction of one's community, or the witnessing of the death of another person. PTSD has troubled many Vietnam War veterans, victims of rape, and persons who have seen their homes and communities inundated by floods or swept away by tornadoes. In some cases, PTSD occurs six months or more after the event.

[Spencer A. Rathus, *Psychology*, 4th Ed., 485]

(a) _____
(b) _____
(c) _____
(d) _____

2. A cooperative interaction occurs when people act together to promote common interests or achieve shared goals. The members of a basketball team pass to one another, block opponents, rebound, and assist one another to achieve a common goal—winning the game. Likewise, family members cooperate to promote their interests as a family—husband and wife both may hold jobs as well as share in household duties, and children may help out by mowing the lawn and washing the dishes. College students often **cooperate** by studying together for tests.

[Henry L. Tischler, *Introduction to Sociology*, 4th Ed., 98]

(a) _____
(b) _____
(c) _____
(d) _____

3. Once senators or representatives are appointed to committees, they usually remain at their own pleasure until they move to a better committee, die, retire, or are defeated in an election. In rare cases, senior committee or subcommittee chairs may be removed by a vote from the party conference or caucus, which may be spearheaded by a rebellion from unhappy committee members. As old members leave, however, it is still customary (although not as automatic as it once was) for committee members to rise through the **seniority** ranks (measured by length of service on a particular committee) to become chair if they are from the majority party, or ranking minority member if they are from the minority party.

[W. Lance Bennett, *Inside the System*, 488]

(a) _____
(b) _____

(c) _____
(d) _____

4. Height and weight are two of the most obvious dimensions of physical growth. The most dramatic gains in height and weight occur during prenatal development. Within nine months, a child develops from a nearly microscopic cell to a neonate about 20 inches in length. Weight increases by the billions. During infancy, dramatic gains continue. Babies usually double their birth weight in about five months and triple it by the first birthday. Their height increases by about 10 inches in the first year. Children grow another four to six inches during the second year and gain about four to seven pounds. Because newborn children do not "know" that it is necessary to eat in order to live or to reduce feelings of hunger, it is fortunate that they have rooting and sucking reflexes. **Neonates** will turn their heads (root) toward stimuli that prod or stroke the cheek, chin, or corners of the mouth. They will suck objects that touch their lips.
[Spencer A. Rathus, *Psychology,* 4th Ed., 350]

(a) _____
(b) _____
(c) _____
(d) _____

5. Today, at least 50 genetic tests for hereditary diseases are available; by the turn of the century, DNA tests are almost certain to be a standard part of medical exams. From a single sample of a patient's blood, doctors will be able to spot genetic mutations that signal the approach not only of rare hereditary diseases but also the common killers, including breast cancer, heart disease, and diabetes—and defeat them. For all its promise, the ability to glimpse the future will not come without costs. Knowing a patient's genetic **predispositions** will be central to preventive medicine, a keystone of health care reform.
[Shannon Brownlee, et al., "Genes and Cancer," *U.S. News & World Report,* 22 Aug. 1994, 94]

(a) _____
(b) _____
(c) _____
(d) _____

SECTION 2

List 2

Here are more word parts that are used to signify time.

WORD PART	MEANING
ARCHAEO	ancient; primitive
CHRON	time
ENN	year
FORE	earlier; before
GER	old; elderly
GERONTO	old; elderly
HORO	hour; time
JOURN	day
JUVEN	young
NOV	new
RETRO	earlier; past
SYNCHRO	at the same time

PRE-EXERCISE ACTIVITY 2
- **List Making**
- **Skill: word parts**

*In the blanks that follow, rewrite List 2. This time, however, reverse the order by writing the **meanings** in the first column. Then gather all the word parts in the list which have that meaning and write them on one line in the second column. This will let you make necessary connections and help you in the process of long-term memorization. The first one has already been done to show you how.*

	MEANING	WORD PARTS	
1.	ancient	archaeo	*Note:* This list will be more useful if you write it in alphabetical order.
2.			
3.			
4.			
5.			
6.			
7.			
8.			
9.			
10.			
11.			
12.			
13.			
14.			

EXERCISE 7-H
- **Multiple Choice**
- **Skill: word parts**

A meaning is in boldface for each of the following phrases. From the four choices given, pick the one answer which contains a word part with that meaning. Use both versions of List 2 to help you. **Do not use a dictionary.** *Do not focus on the size or difficulty of the words. Look only for the simple word part; it will lead you to the correct answer.*

Example: √Something brand **new**
    (A) malformation   (C) lamentation
    (B) consternation   (D) innovation

    Answer: (D) The reason for this answer is that the NOV part of *innovation* means "new."

1. The study of **ancient** people and their cultures through excavated remains
   (A) horology   (C) archaeology
   (B) zoology   (D) geology

2. Effective as of a **past** date, as a pay raise
   (A) inactive   (C) hypoactive
   (B) retroactive   (D) proactive

3. Our ancestors—the relatives who lived at an **earlier** time
   (A) progeny   (C) descendants
   (B) forebears   (D) offspring

4. A **daily** record of events and observations
   (A) novel   (C) chronicle
   (B) journal   (D) periodical

5. Occurring **at the same time**
   (A) synchronous   (C) monotonous
   (B) sonorous   (D) glutinous

6. Government by a council of **old** people
   (A) gerontocracy   (C) oligarchy
   (B) democracy   (D) aristocracy

Copyright © 1996 Harcourt Brace & Company. All rights reserved.

7. The science of making timepieces or measuring **time**
   - (A) horology
   - (B) zoology
   - (C) archaeology
   - (D) odontology

8. Happening every two **years**
   - (A) bicephalous
   - (B) bijugate
   - (C) bisected
   - (D) biennial

9. Reading material designed for the **young**
   - (A) memorabilia
   - (B) necrophilia
   - (C) hemophilia
   - (D) juvenilia

10. The technique of measuring **time** accurately
    - (A) hypsometry
    - (B) psychometry
    - (C) chronometry
    - (D) geometry

EXERCISE 7-I
- **Fill in the Blank (one cue)**
- **Skill: word parts**

Use a **meaning** from List 2 to fill in the blank in each statement. The word part whose meaning you are defining will be found inside the boldfaced word. **Do not use a dictionary**. Do not focus on the size or difficulty of the words. Look only for the simple word part; it will lead you to the correct answer.

Example: √In olden times, a **journey** was a _____'s worth of travel.

Answer: *day* [> JOURN]

1. A strong inner certainty that comes _____ than an actual event is a **foreboding**.
2. The qualities or acts of the _____ are called **juvenilities**.
3. A **tricentennial** celebration marks a 300-_____ anniversary.

4. A **chronometer** is a device for measuring _____ precisely.
5. In photography, **synchroflash** refers to a device that makes the shutter and the artificial light source operate _____.
6. In legal terms, **novation** is the substitution of a _____ obligation for an old one.
7. Originally, the word **journeyman** referred to a worker trained enough to deserve a _____'s pay.
8. **Synchromesh** refers to a mechanism that allows gears to work together _____.
9. **Gerontocracy** means government by the _____.
10. Malice **aforethought** is a decision made _____ a crime to commit the unlawful act without just cause.
11. An **innovation** is a _____ way of doing something.
12. A **decennial** reunion takes place every ten _____.
13. A **horologe** is any instrument for indicating _____.
14. The branch of dentistry dealing with the problems of the _____ is called **gerodontology**.
15. **Archaeopteryx** is the name of an _____ reptilelike bird.

EXERCISE 7-J
- **Fill in the Blank (no cue)**
- **Skills: word parts, context**

*Once again, use a **meaning** from List 2 to fill in the blank in each statement. This time, however, you will have to find the word part yourself in the difficult or technical word. **Do not use a dictionary**. Do not focus on the size or difficulty of the words. Look only for the simple word part; it will lead you to the correct answer.*

Example: √Fear of the _____ is called gerontophobia.

Answer: *elderly* [> GERONTO]

1. Retrospection is the act of looking at the _____.
2. Synchronized events are meant to occur _____.
3. A chronic illness lasts for a long _____.
4. Gerontology is the branch of medicine that studies and treats the _____.
5. A journal is a _____ record of occurrences, experiences, or observations.
6. Foreknowledge comes _____ something happens.
7. Returning to an _____ condition is called retrogression.
8. A novice is _____ at whatever he or she is doing.
9. A juvenile court has jurisdiction over _____ offenders.
10. A foretaste is an _____ partial experience of what is to come.
11. A sesquicentennial marks the completion of 150 _____.
12. Horology is the art of making _____ pieces.
13. Diachrony is a change in a language over _____.
14. The Archaeozoic period refers to the period when the most _____ datable rocks were formed.
15. Nova Scotia, a province in Canada, means _____ Scotland.

PRE   ANTE   POST

When it comes to being early, PRE and ANTE lead the pack,
And there's never any question that POST will be in back.
But in spite of what your mother said about which course to take,
Would you rather hold the back end or the front end of a snake?

EXERCISE 7-K
- **Matching Columns**
- **Skill: word parts**

Memory check. Do not look back at List 2 or use a dictionary. Special note: This time, one answer is used twice.

1. _____ ENN   (a) new
2. _____ SYNCHRO   (b) ancient
3. _____ NOV   (c) earlier
4. _____ RETRO   (d) time
5. _____ ARCHAEO   (e) old
6. _____ CHRON   (f) year
7. _____ JOURN   (g) young
8. _____ FORE   (h) at the same time
9. _____ JUVEN   (i) day
10. _____ GERONTO

EXERCISE 7-L
- **Fill in (two cues)**
- **Skills: word parts, dictionary, context**

*To finish each word, fill in the blank with one of the **word parts** from your version of List 2. **You must use a college-level dictionary** to make sure that what you write really is a word and that it fits in the sentence. The word in boldface will give you the meaning of the word part that you must write.*

1. **Young** offenders are sent to _____ile court for trial.
2. A new law that applies to **past** occurrences is called _____active.
3. _____nous events happen **at the same time**.
4. A _____oscope is an instrument for measuring very brief intervals of **time**.
5. A bicent_____ial occurs every 200 **years**.

6. A _____cast is a conjecture about what will happen **before** the actual event.
7. The branch of medicine that deals with the problems and diseases of **old** age is called _____iatrics.
8. An _____logical dig tries to learn more about **ancient** people, their dwellings, and their artifacts.
9. An in_____ation is a **new** way of doing something.
10. A _____icle is a record of the **time** sequence of events, a history.
11. A person who makes clocks or **timepieces** is called a _____logist.
12. To ad_____ a meeting literally means to end it until another **day**.
13. Restoring **youthful** vigor or appearance is called re_____ation.
14. To _____warn a person is to issue an alert **before** a dangerous event.
15. Re_____ating an old building results in making it look **new**.

EXERCISE 7-M
- Fill in (one cue)
- Skills: word parts, dictionary, context

*Continue filling in **word parts** from your version of List 2 as you have been doing, **using a college-level dictionary** to check the accuracy. This time, however, there will be no word in boldface. You will have to search each sentence for a clue.*

Example: √A _____cast is issued before an event happens.

   Answer: *FORE* [> before]

1. To go back to an earlier and usually worse condition is to _____gress.
2. Movies are careful to _____nize the sound track and the picture so that they run at the same time.

3. A diagram of the heavens as they were at the hour of a person's birth is called a _ _ _ _scope.
4. _ _ _ _ _ological order is an arrangement of events according to the time order in which they occurred.
5. Per_ _ _ial problems continue to show up year after year.
6. The scientific study of aging and the problems of old age is called _ _ _ _ _ _ _logy.
7. To prevent something by taking earlier measures is to _ _ _ _stall it.
8. _ _ _ _ _ _ _logy is the scientific study of ancient peoples and their cultures.
9. A _ _ _el solution to a problem is new and unusual.
10. _ _ _ _gone conclusions are reached even before an event occurs.
11. To _ _ _ _ _alize is to make daily entries in a record book.
12. An ana_ _ _ _ism is something that is not placed in its correct historical time.
13. Someone who is young in appearance is said to be _ _ _ _ _escent.
14. Presidential elections are quadr_ _ _ial; they occur every four years.
15. In botany, the term _ _ _ _logic refers to flowers that open and close at certain hours.

EXERCISE 7-N
- **Paragraph Examples**
- **Skills: word parts, dictionary, context**

Answer these four questions after each paragraph:

(a) *What word part inside the boldfaced word helps you to understand that word? What does that word part mean?*

(b) *Using only the context of the word and the word part that it contains, what do you think the boldfaced word means? (See Chapter 1, Section 2.)*

(c) *Choose one context clue that helped you. (See Chapter 1, Section 2.)*
   1. *word signals*
   2. *punctuation signals*
   3. *synonyms (substitution)*
   4. *examples or description*
   5. *contrast or opposites*
   6. *prior knowledge; common sense*
      If 6, explain: _____

(d) *How does the dictionary define the boldfaced word as it is used in the paragraph?*

_____

1. Thousands of immense logs are continually decaying on the floor of a natural old-growth forest. Like any decaying organic matter, they recycle nutrients into the soil. Yet foresters have long assumed that the rotting logs made a rather small ecological contribution, because compared with the twigs, leaves, and extensive root systems, the logs' wood and bark are weak in nutrients. . . . No one had considered that, ecologically, the logs might be doing a great deal. In **retrospect**, it's almost unbelievable that we could have been that stupid.
   [Jon R. Luoma, "An Untidy Wonder," *Discover*, Special Issue, 1993, 62]

   (a) _____
   (b) _____
   (c) _____
   (d) _____

2. The cemetery at Hierakonpolis, which dates back to about 3800 B.C., already contained artifacts that archaeologists consider characteristic of Egyptian civilization. For example, the arrangement of the cemetery as a necropolis, with wooden or reed houses built over many of the tombs, represented an early stage of the cult of the dead that later came to dominate Egyptian religion. In addition, some Hierakonpolis tombs from this early period contained pots bearing writing-like symbols that may actually be primitive writing, though **archaeologists** have not yet deciphered them.
   [Chodorow, et al., *The Mainstream of Civilization*, 6th Ed., 18]

   (a) _____
   (b) _____
   (c) _____
   (d) _____

3. Managers rely on sales forecasts to predict future company sales. Sales forecasting is critical because it defines customers' demands for products or services. Sales forecasts determine production levels for three months, six months, or one year into the future. Managers use them to hire necessary personnel, buy needed raw materials, make plans to finance an expansion, and arrange needed transportation services. Medium- and large-size companies such as Sound Warehouse, Paychex, Wallace Computer Services, and Monsanto use sales **forecasts** to plan production activities.

     [Richard L. Daft, *Management*, 2nd Ed., 212]

   (a) _____
   (b) _____
   (c) _____
   (d) _____

4. Once they are familiar with the environment, lower animals and people appear to be motivated to seek **novel** stimulation. For example, when they have not been deprived of food for a great deal of time, rats will often explore unfamiliar arms of mazes rather than head straight for the section of the maze in which they have learned to expect food. Animals who have just copulated and thereby reduced their sex drives will often show renewed interest in sexual behavior when presented with a novel sex partner. Monkeys will learn how to manipulate gadgets for the incentive of being able to observe novel stimulation through a window. Children will spend hour after hour manipulating the controls of video games for no apparent external reward.

     [Spencer A. Rathus, *Psychology*, 4th Ed., 314–15]

   (a) _____
   (b) _____
   (c) _____
   (d) _____

5. Thucydides (ca. 460–400 B.C.) is considered the father of history. His reference to the lack of romance in his history may be a swipe at Herodotus, who provided romance aplenty and who was quick to believe whatever his informants told him. Thucydides observed the rule of chronography, the precise determination of the dates of past events, a discipline first practiced in the sixth century B.C. **Chronography** was based on the regular four-year

cycle of the Olympiad, the athletic contest in honor of Zeus, held for the first time in 776 B.C. Fragments of the works of the chronographers preserved in later writings have enabled modern historians to establish the chronology of many ancient events.

[Chodorow, et al., *The Mainstream of Civilization*, 6th Ed., 18]

(a) _____

(b) _____

(c) _____

(d) _____

Synchro

SECTION 3: CHAPTER REVIEW (LISTS 1 AND 2 COMBINED)

Word Parts Covered in This Chapter:

WORD PART	MEANING	COMMON EXAMPLE	TEXTBOOK EXAMPLE
ANN	year	*annual*	*superannuated*
ANTE	earlier; before	*antedate*	*antediluvian*
ANTIQ	ancient; primitive	*antique*	*antiquarian*
ARCHAEO	ancient	*archaeology*	*archaeopteryx*
CHRON	time	*chronic*	*chronoscope*
CO	at the same time; with	*co-anchor*	*coadjutor*
ENN	year	*bicentennial*	*decennial*
FORE	earlier; before	*forecast*	*forenamed*
GER	old	*geriatrics*	*gerodontics*
GERONTO	old	*gerontology*	*gerontocracy*
HORO	hour; time	*horoscope*	*horologe*
JOURN	day	*journey*	*journalize*
JUVEN	young	*juvenile*	*juvenescent*
NEO	new	*neophyte*	*neoteric*
NOCT	evening	*nocturnal*	*nocturne*
NOV	new	*novel*	*novitiate*
POST	later; after	*postdate*	*postdiluvian*
PRE	earlier; before	*predate*	*preformation*
RETRO	earlier; past	*retroactive*	*retrogressive*
SEN	old	*senior*	*senescent*
SIMUL	at the same time	*simulcast*	*simultaneity*
SYNCHRO	at the same time	*synchronize*	*synchroscope*
TEMPO	time	*temporary*	*temporize*
VET	old; experienced	*veteran*	*inveterate*

PRE-EXERCISE ACTIVITY 3
- **List Making**
- **Skill: word parts**

*In the blanks that follow, rewrite the combined word parts list. This time, however, reverse the order by writing the **meanings** in the first column. Then gather all the word parts in the list which have that meaning and write them on one line in the second column. This will let you make necessary connections and help you in the process of long-term memorization. The first one has already been done to show you how.*

	MEANING	WORD PARTS	
1.	after	post	*Note:* This list will be more useful if you write it in alphabetical order.
2.			
3.			
4.			
5.			
6.			
7.			
8.			
9.			
10.			
11.			
12.			
13.			
14.			
15.			
16.			
17.			
18.			

EXERCISE 7-O
- **Matching Columns**
- **Skill: word parts**

Memory check. Do not look back at the combined list or use a dictionary.

1. ____	GERONTO	(a)	new
2. ____	PRE	(b)	time
3. ____	NOCT	(c)	old
4. ____	ENN	(d)	young
5. ____	POST	(e)	at the same time
6. ____	CHRON	(f)	before
7. ____	JOURN	(g)	after
8. ____	SYNCHRO	(h)	year
9. ____	NEO	(i)	day
10. ____	JUVEN	(j)	evening

EXERCISE 7-P
- **Cross Out**
- **Skills: dictionary, word parts, context**

One word in each set does not contain the word part and meaning that is given, even though it has a set of similar letters. **Use a college-level dictionary** to find the one that does **not** fit.

	WORD		**CROSS OUT THE ONE WORD**
Example:	**PART**	**MEANING**	**THAT DOES NOT FIT.**
	√NEO	new	neonatal, neophyte, Borneo

Answer: The dictionary shows that *neonatal* and *neophyte* have the word *new* in their definitions. *Borneo* does not; cross it out.

WORD PART	MEANING	CROSS OUT THE ONE WORD THAT DOES NOT FIT.
1. SEN	old	sentiment, seniority, senescent
2. ANN	year	annual, annalist, annex
3. VET	experienced	veteran, veto, inveterate
4. NOV	new	novena, novelty, renovate
5. CO	at the same time	coexistence, coeval, covet
6. PRE	earlier	prediction, pressure, predate
7. ANTE	earlier	anteater, antedate, antecedents
8. TEMP	time	temporary, contemporary, temptation
9. POST	later	postage, postpone, posthumous
10. FORE	earlier	foreknowledge, forecaster, forested

EXERCISE 7-Q
- **Extended Answer**
- **Skills: word parts, dictionary, context**

Answer the following questions by using a college-level dictionary.

Example: √How is the meaning *year* involved in the word **annual?**

Answer: Annual means "yearly."

1. How is the meaning *at the same time* involved in the word **simultaneous?**

2. How is the meaning *year* involved in the word **tricentennial?**

3. How is the meaning *old* involved in the word **gerontologist?**

4. How is the meaning *earlier* involved in the word **foresight?**

5. How is the meaning *ancient* involved in the word **archaeological?**

6. How is the meaning *later* involved in the word **postexilic?**

7. How is the meaning *past* involved in the word **retrospect?**

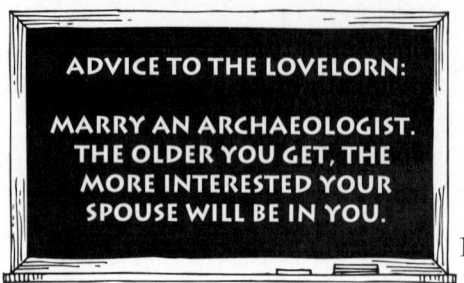

8. How is the meaning *evening* involved in the word **nocturnal?**

9. How is the meaning *time* involved in the word **horologe?**

10. How is the meaning *new* involved in the word **innovative?**

> ADVICE TO THE LOVELORN:
>
> MARRY AN ARCHAEOLOGIST. THE OLDER YOU GET, THE MORE INTERESTED YOUR SPOUSE WILL BE IN YOU.

EXERCISE 7-R
- **Fill in the Blank**
- **Skills: word parts, context**

Answer each question by filling in the blank. Use the combined list.

Example: √The opposite of FORE is _____.   Answer: POST
         √A synonym for *evening* is _____.   Answer: *night*

1. The opposite of ANTE is _____.   [Write another word part.]

2. The opposite of JUVEN is _____.   [Write another word part.]

3. The opposite of POST is _____.   [Write another word part.]

4. The opposite of NOV is _____.   [Write another word part.]

5. The opposite of GERONTO is _____. [Write another word part.]

6. A synonym for *earlier* is _____. [Write a regular word.]
7. A synonym for *old* is _____. [Write a regular word.]
8. A synonym for *new* is _____. [Write a regular word.]
9. A synonym for *at the same time* is _____. [Write a regular word.]
10. A synonym for *young* is _____. [Write a regular word.]

EXERCISE 7-S
- **Fill in the Blanks**
- **Skill: word parts**

Memory check. Do not look back at the combined list or use a dictionary.

1. Name two word parts that mean *year*: _____ and _____.
2. Name two word parts that mean *old*: _____ and _____.
3. Name two word parts that mean *earlier*: _____ and _____.
4. Name two word parts that mean *at the same time*: _____ and _____.
5. Name two word parts that mean *ancient*: _____ and _____.
6. Name two word parts that mean *time*: _____ and _____.
7. Name two word parts that mean *new*: _____ and _____.

EXERCISE 7-T
- **Paragraph Examples**
- **Skills: word parts, dictionary, context**

Answer these four questions after each paragraph:

(a) *What word part inside the boldfaced word helps you to understand that word? What does that word part mean?*

(b) *Using only the context of the word and the word part that it contains, what do you think the boldfaced word means? (See Chapter 1, Section 2.)*

(c) *Choose one context clue that helped you. (See Chapter 1, Section 2.)*
  1. *word signals*
  2. *punctuation signals*
  3. *synonyms (substitution)*
  4. *examples or description*
  5. *contrast or opposites*
  6. *prior knowledge; common sense*
     If 6, explain: _____

(d) *How does the dictionary define the boldfaced word as it is used in the paragraph?*

1. A revolution in surgery stemming mainly from **innovative** technology has changed what you may expect from your next operation. The key development: endoscopic surgery. Endoscopic surgery relies on the endoscope, a pencil-thin, hollow tube with its own lighting system and miniature video camera. It allows a surgeon to see inside your body without "cutting you open." Your surgeon inserts the endoscope through a tiny incision less than an inch long. Then while viewing the procedure on a video screen, your surgeon operates with miniature instruments inserted through one or more other small incisions.
   ["Endoscopic Surgery," *The Mayo Clinic Health Letter*, September 1994, 6]

   (a) _____
   (b) _____
   (c) _____
   (d) _____

2. In addition to circadian rhythms, some animals have yearly cycles. Many mammals continue to hibernate at roughly the same

time even if they are deprived of environmental cues that could tell them the time of year. Deer kept under constant conditions grow, and later shed, their antlers at the same time every year. Several species of birds start migratory behavior at the same time of year even if they are deprived of environmental cues. In this last case, the adaptive advantage of the **annual** rhythm is probably that it permits a bird to return north for the breeding season even though it receives few cues of seasonal change in the relatively constant tropical environment where it winters.

[Arms, et al., *A Journey into Life*, 3rd Ed., 638]

(a) _____
(b) _____
(c) _____
(d) _____

3. Children appear to develop language in an invariant sequence of steps. . . . We begin with the prelinguistic vocalizations of crying, cooing, and babbling. Remember that true language has semanticity; that is, sounds (or signs, in the case of sign language) are symbols. Cries and coos do not represent objects and events, so they are **prelinguistic**. By about 8 months, cooing decreases markedly. By about the fifth or sixth month, children have already begun to babble.

[Spencer A. Rathus, *Psychology*, 4th Ed., 264–65]

(a) _____
(b) _____
(c) _____
(d) _____

4. Polar bears begin the breeding process in April or May when they take time out from hunting seals on the sea ice of Hudson Bay to mate. Shortly after conception, the female's pregnancy grinds to a halt. The embryo, nothing more than a hollow ball of cells the size of a pinhead, floats inside the mother for four months or more. This process, known as delayed implantation, works in **synchrony** with the food supply. It allows a female polar bear to wait until after the important spring and summer seal-hunting periods before committing to the energetic demands of pregnancy.

[Wayne Lynch, "Den Mothers and Their Cubs," *International Wildlife*, November–December 1994, 12]

(a) _____

(b) _____
(c) _____
(d) _____

5. Insomnia—trouble falling asleep or trouble remaining asleep—is not an illness to be cured by a sleeping pill, but a symptom or complaint which can have many causes. . . . Purely medical conditions that may make it difficult to fall asleep include anything that produces pain or discomfort, as well as certain glandular conditions. Other physical disorders are associated with difficulty in remaining asleep. For example, in sleep apnea the breathing apparatus fails to function normally during sleep and the sleeper has to awaken repeatedly in order to breathe; in **nocturnal** myoclonus (muscle spasms), repeated muscle jerks cause the sleeper to awaken.
   [Ernest Hartmann, "Approaches to Insomnia," *The Harvard Medical School Mental Health Letter*, Volume 1, Number 8, 8]
   (a) _____
   (b) _____
   (c) _____
   (d) _____

6. Senescence is the process of growing old, and it culminates in the death of the individual. The process involves a continuation of the degenerative changes that began during adulthood. As a result, the body becomes less and less able to cope with the demands placed on it by the individual and the environment. The cause of **senescence** is not well understood. However, the degenerative changes that occur seem to involve a variety of factors.
   [John W. Hole, Jr., *Human Anatomy and Physiology*, 4th Ed., 879]
   (a) _____
   (b) _____
   (c) _____
   (d) _____

7. Juvenile crime refers to the breaking of criminal laws by individuals under the age of eighteen. Regardless of the specific statistics reliability, one thing is clear: serious crime among our nation's youth is a matter of great concern. Hard-core youthful offenders—perhaps 10 percent of all juvenile criminals—are responsible, by some estimates, for two-thirds of all serious

crimes. Although the vast majority of **juvenile** delinquents commit only minor violations, the juvenile justice system is overwhelmed by these hard-core criminals.

[Henry L. Tischler, *Introduction to Sociology*, 4th Ed., 135]

(a) _____
(b) _____
(c) _____
(d) _____

8. Seahorses provide the only known example of monogamy in fishes living in sea grasses or mangroves. As far as we know, our pairs never divorce. Nor do they cheat. This is exceptional: new genetic research techniques are revealing that animals we thought of as firmly paired, including many birds, are often not sexually faithful after all. We can be sure of seahorse fidelity because a female's body visibly deflates when she transfers eggs, while the male's pouch inflates; these changes always occur **simultaneously**. In very few, if any, animals do both sexes make it so obvious they have mated.

[Amanda Vincent, "The Improbable Seahorse," *National Geographic*, October 1994, 135]

(a) _____
(b) _____
(c) _____
(d) _____

9. Where some form of conjugal or extended family is the norm, family exogamy requires that either the husband or wife, if not both, must move to a new household upon marriage. There are five common patterns of residence that a newly married couple may adopt. As among the Maya, a woman may go to live with her husband in the household in which he grew up; this is known as patrilocal residence. As among the Hopi, the man may leave the family in which he grew up to go live with his wife in her parents' household; this is called matrilocal residence. As in the case of extended families on the coast of Maine, a marrried couple may have the option of choosing whether to live matrilocally or patrilocally, an arrangement that is labelled ambilocal residence. As in most of modern North America, a married couple may form a household in an independent location, an arrangement referred to as **neolocal** residence. . . .

[William A. Haviland, *Cultural Anthropology*, 7th Ed., 249]

(a) _____
(b) _____
(c) _____
(d) _____

10. Aging is the process of growing old, regardless of chronological age. In an attempt to standardize terms, the World Health Organization classifies persons who are between 60 and 75 years of age as elderly. Those between 76 and 90 are classified as old, and those over 90 years of age are referred to as very old. **Gerontology** is the scientific study of the process of aging, and all aspects—biological, sociological, and historical—of the problems associated with aging.

[Alexander P. Spence, *Biology of Human Aging*, 9–10]

(a) _____
(b) _____
(c) _____
(d) _____

CHAPTER 8 THE SENSES

SECTION 1

List 1
Here are some word parts that are used to signify the senses.

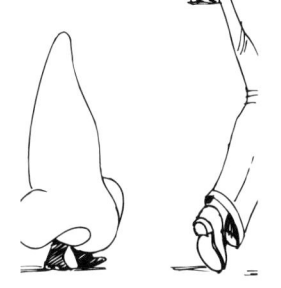

WORD PART	MEANING
ACOUST	sound; hearing
AUR	ear; hearing
CUT	skin
GUST	taste
NAS	nose
OCUL	eye
ODOR	smell
OPSY	see
OR	mouth
PHON	sound
SENS	senses
SPEC	see; look
SPIC	see; look
TACT	touch; feel
TANG	touch; feel

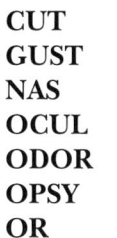

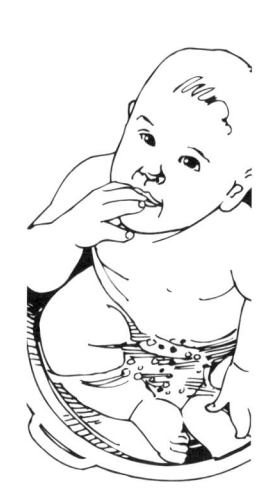

PRE-EXERCISE ACTIVITY 1
- **List Making**
- **Skill: word parts**

*In the blanks that follow, rewrite List 1. This time, however, reverse the order by writing the **meanings** in the first column. Then gather all the word parts in the list which have that meaning and write them on one line in the second column. This will let you make necessary connections and help you in the process of long-term memorization. The first one has already been done to show you how.*

	MEANING	WORD PARTS	
1.	ear	aur	*Note:* This list will be more useful if you write it in alphabetical order.
2.			
3.			
4.			
5.			
6.			
7.			
8.			
9.			
10.			
11.			
12.			
13.			
14.			

EXERCISE 8-A
- **Multiple Choice**
- **Skill: word parts**

A meaning is in boldface for each of the following phrases. From the four choices given, pick the one answer which contains a word part with that meaning. Use both versions of List 1 to help you. **Do not use a dictionary.** *Do not focus on the size or difficulty of the words. Look only for the simple word part; it will lead you to the correct answer.*

Example: √The outer layer of **skin**
 (A) epicure (C) epigram
 (B) epidermis (D) epithet

   Answer: (B) The reason for this answer is that the DERM part of *epidermis* means "skin."

1. Pertaining to the **nose**
   (A) tactile (C) nasal
   (B) aural (D) oral

2. Perceived by or affecting the **senses**
   (A) sedulous (C) sensuous
   (B) serious (D) stannous

3. In physics, a unit of **sound**
   (A) photon (C) proton
   (B) phonon (D) neuron

4. Pertaining to the sense of **hearing**
   (A) tactile (C) nasal
   (B) aural (D) oral

5. The official act of **seeing** and examining a body after death
   (A) autoplasty (C) autopsy
   (B) autolysis (D) autoclave

6. Pertaining to the **mouth**
   (A) tactile (C) nasal
   (B) aural (D) oral

7. Having or using only one **eye**
   - (A) monocular
   - (B) monochromatic
   - (C) monaural
   - (D) monolithic

8. To **taste** carefully and appreciatively
   - (A) dehisce
   - (B) demit
   - (C) depute
   - (D) degust

9. Pertaining to the sense of **touch**
   - (A) tactile
   - (B) aural
   - (C) nasal
   - (D) oral

10. The **skin**, including both of its layers
    - (A) lapis
    - (B) cutis
    - (C) verdigris
    - (D) hubris

EXERCISE 8-B
- Fill in the Blank (one cue)
- Skill: word parts

Use a **meaning** *from List 1 to fill in the blank in each statement. The word part whose meaning you are defining will be found inside the boldfaced word.* **Do not use a dictionary.** *Do not focus on the size or difficulty of the words. Look only for the simple word part; it will lead you to the correct answer.*

Example: √A **telephone** transmits _____ over a distance.

Answer: *sound* [> PHON]

1. In **nasalized** speech, the voice issues through the _____ .
2. **Acoustical** tile helps to deaden the _____ in a room.
3. A ghost that can be _____ is called a **specter**.
4. Something that **disgusts** us leaves a bad _____ .
5. Natural gas used in the home is given an **odorant** to make it _____ .
6. In a **biopsy**, living tissue is removed and _____ under a microscope.

7. In ancient Greece, an **oracle** was a divine pronouncement made through the _____ of a priest or priestess.
8. **Phonetics** is the study of speech _____ .
9. In geometry, a **tangent** is a line that _____ a curve or a surface.
10. A **conspicuous** object is easy to _____ .
11. **Sensory** data comes through the _____ .
12. The **cuticle** is the nonliving _____ that surrounds the edge of fingernails or toenails.
13. Something which is **auriform** is shaped like the human _____ .
14. **Taction** means contact or _____ .
15. The **oculomotor** muscles help to move the _____ .

EXERCISE 8-C
- **Fill in the Blank (no cue)**
- **Skills: word parts, context**

*Once again, use a **meaning** from List 1 to fill in the blank in each statement. This time, however, you will have to find the word part yourself in the difficult or technical word. **Do not use a dictionary**. Do not focus on the size or difficulty of the words. Look only for the simple word part; it will lead you to the correct answer.*

Example: √An oral dose of medicine is administered by _____ .

Answer: *mouth* [> OR]

1. Tactile toys appeal to a baby's sense of _____ .
2. Sensation is the awareness of stimuli through the _____ .
3. Our gustatory sense is our sense of _____ .
4. Spectacles allow the user to _____ better.
5. We tend to _____ down on things that are despicable.

6. A tangential remark merely _____ on the subject under discussion.
7. An odoriferous object _____ .
8. Phonology studies the patterns of speech _____ in a language.
9. An acoustician is a _____ expert.
10. Orinasal sounds come through the nose and _____ simultaneously.
11. During a necropsy, the doctor _____ and examines a body after death.
12. Something auriculate has _____ like parts.
13. Intraocular pain occurs inside the _____ .
14. The nasopharynx is where the mouth and _____ passages meet.
15. Auricular evidence is detected by the _____ .

Waiting aur after aur after aur . . .

EXERCISE 8-D
- **Matching Columns**
- **Skill: word parts**

Memory check. Do not look back at List 1 or use a dictionary.

1. ____	SPEC	(a)	hear
2. ____	ACOUST	(b)	smell
3. ____	TACT	(c)	ear
4. ____	OCUL	(d)	see
5. ____	ODOR	(e)	nose
6. ____	OR	(f)	taste
7. ____	NAS	(g)	skin
8. ____	CUT	(h)	mouth
9. ____	AUR	(i)	touch
10. ____	GUST	(j)	eye

Copyright © 1996 Harcourt Brace & Company. All rights reserved.

EXERCISE 8-E
- Fill in (two cues)
- Skills: word parts, dictionary, context

*To finish each word, fill in the blank with one of the **word parts** from your version of List 1. **You must use a college-level dictionary** to make sure that what you write really is a word and that it fits in the sentence. The word in boldface will give you the meaning of the word part that you must write.*

Example: √_ _ _ _atorial delights please the sense of **taste**.

   Answer: GUST [> taste]

1. Humans have bin_ _ _ _ar vision; they use two **eyes**.
2. Something which is _ _ _ _ible can be **touched**.
3. When you start to su_ _ _ _t someone, you begin to **see** beneath mere appearances.
4. _ _ _ _ual means arising from or due to **touch**.
5. _ _ _al passages can become congested, and then we find it difficult to breathe through the **nose**.
6. The act of **tasting** is called _ _ _ _ation.
7. The projecting outer portion of the **ear** is called the _ _ _icle.
8. The _ _ _ _etic alphabet tells us how to **sound** out words.
9. De_ _ _ _ants are meant to disguise bodily **smells**.
10. Sub_ _ _aneous pain is felt beneath the surface of the **skin**.
11. Medicines that de_ _ _ _itize a person make his or her **senses** react less to substances that cause allergies.
12. When you deliver an _ _ation, you open your **mouth** and let the speech come forth.
13. In a bi_ _ _ _, the medical staff **looks** at tissue to discover evidence of disease.
14. Something in_ _ _ _ has not been **touched**; it is unchanged.
15. A _ _ _aneous rash affects the **skin**.

EXERCISE 8-F
- Fill in (one cue)
- Skills: word parts, dictionary, context

*Continue filling in **word parts** from your version of List 1 as you have been doing, **using a college-level dictionary** to check accuracy. This time, however, there will be no word in boldface. You will have to search the sentence for a clue.*

Example:　　√The _ _al cavity is found in the mouth.

　　　　　　Answer: *OR* [> mouth]

1. _ _ _ _ar movements are made by the eyes.
2. The _ _ _icle is the skin that surrounds the edges of the fingernail or toenail.
3. _ _otund speech is full and rich, the result of shaping the mouth correctly when speaking.
4. The _ _ _oscope is an instrument for viewing the inside of the nose.
5. Something which is in_ _ _ible cannot be touched.
6. When you re_ _ _ _t someone, you look on that person as a role model.
7. _ _ _ _ory input comes through the senses.
8. Electro_ _ _ _ _ics is the branch of electronics that deals with the conversion of electricity into sound.
9. Mal_ _ _ _ous materials smell bad.
10. To get in con_ _ _ _ with someone is to get in touch.
11. Eu_ _ _ _y is pleasing or agreeable sound.
12. When we in_ _ _ _t something, we look at it very closely.
13. _ _ _ _atory delights please our sense of taste.
14. Stones are in_ _ _ _ate; they have no feeling.
15. A _ _ _ _ometer measures the intensity of sound.

EXERCISE 8-G
- **Paragraph Examples**
- **Skills: word parts, dictionary, context**

Answer these four questions after each paragraph:

(a) *What word part inside the boldfaced word helps you to understand that word? What does that word part mean?*

(b) *Using only the context of the word and the word part that it contains, what do you think the boldfaced word means? (See Chapter 1, Section 2.)*

(c) *Choose one context clue that helped you. (See Chapter 1, Section 2.)*
   1. *word signals*
   2. *punctuation signals*
   3. *synonyms (substitution)*
   4. *examples or description*
   5. *contrast or opposites*
   6. *prior knowledge; common sense*
      If 6, explain: _____

(d) *How does the dictionary define the boldfaced word as it is used in the paragraph?*

1. If a split-brain patient handles a key with his left hand behind a screen, **tactile** impressions of the key are projected into the right hemisphere, which has little or no language ability. Thus he will not be able to describe the key. If he holds it in his right hand, he will have no trouble describing it because sensory impressions are projected into the left hemisphere of the cortex, which contains language functions.
   [Spencer A. Rathus, *Psychology*, 4th Ed., 69]
   (a) _____
   (b) _____
   (c) _____
   (d) _____

2. In Johnstone Strait I was no longer peering down at whales in a tank, I was among them. They swirled the water beneath me and rose beside me. I was the visitor; they were at home. I lowered my **hydrophone**, an underwater microphone, placed the headset over my ears and pressed the "record" button. Echoing in the

vastness of the deep, numbing water were the familiar calls of whale dialect.

[Alexandra Morton, "Life Among the Whales," *Smithsonian*, November 1994, 48]

(a) _____
(b) _____
(c) _____
(d) _____

3. Pitirim A. Sorokin (1889–1968) theorized that cultures are divided into two groups: ideational cultures, which emphasize spiritual values, and sensate cultures, which are based on what is immediately apparent through the senses. In an ideational culture, progress is achieved through self-control and adherence to a strong moral code. In a **sensate** culture, people are dedicated to self-expression and the gratification of their immediate physical needs.

[Henry L. Tischler, *Introduction to Sociology*, 4th Ed., 418]

(a) _____
(b) _____
(c) _____
(d) _____

4. Thousands of immense logs are continually decaying on the floor of a natural old-growth forest. Like any decaying organic matter, they recycle nutrients into the soil. Yet foresters have long assumed that the rotting logs made a rather small ecological contribution, because compared with the twigs, leaves, and extensive root systems, the logs' wood and bark are weak in nutrients. . . . No one had considered that, ecologically, the logs might be doing a great deal. In **retrospect**, it's almost unbelievable that we could have been that stupid.

[Jon R. Luoma, "An Untidy Wonder," *Discover*, Special Issue, 1993, 62]

(a) _____
(b) _____
(c) _____
(d) _____

5. When today's amphibious fishes come on land, they generally use their gills to breathe air. Wooly sculpins, when on land, obtain 71 percent of their oxygen through their gills and oral membranes

and 29 percent by breathing through their skin, called **cutaneous** respiration. Sculpins ventilate their gills at a slower, more irregular rate in air than in water. Because air contains about 20 times more oxygen per unit volume than water, the fish still absorb the same amount of oxygen.

[Caroline Harding, "Fish Out of Water," *National Wildlife*, October–November 1994, 12]

(a) _____
(b) _____
(c) _____
(d) _____

SECTION 2

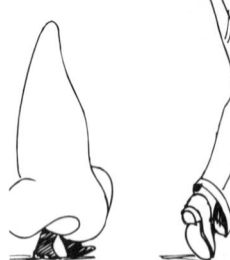

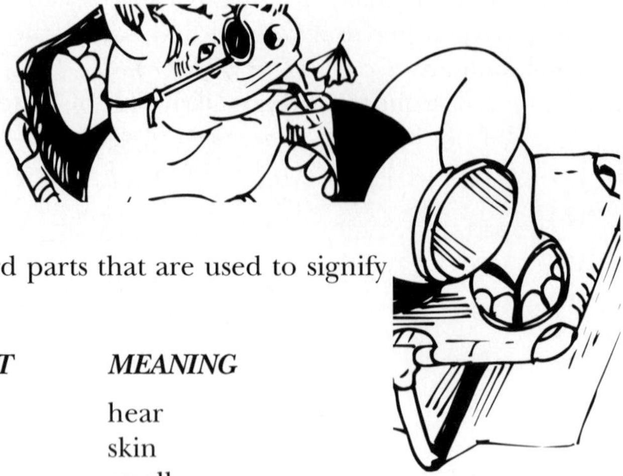

List 2
Here are more word parts that are used to signify the senses.

WORD PART	MEANING
AUD	hear
DERM	skin
OLFACT	smell
OP	eye
OPTO	eye
OSM	smell
OT	ear
PALP	touch
RHIN	nose
SAP	taste
SAV	taste
SCOPE	see
SON	sound
VID	see
VIS	see

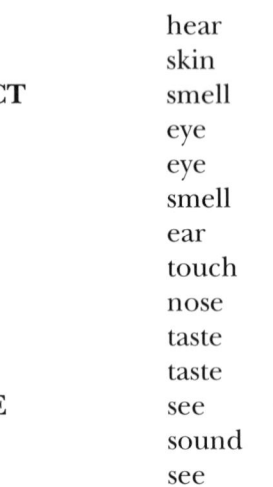

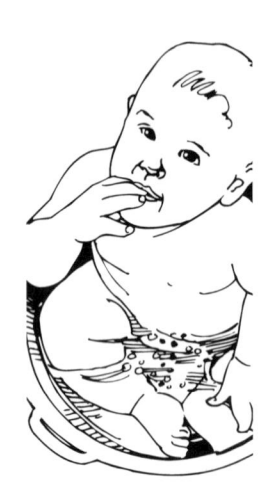

PRE-EXERCISE ACTIVITY 2
- **List Making**
- **Skill: word parts**

*In the blanks that follow, rewrite List 2. This time, however, reverse the order by writing the **meanings** in the first column. Then gather all the word parts in the list which have that meaning and write them on one line in the second column. This will let you make necessary connections and help you in the process of long-term memorization. The first one has already been done to show you how.*

	MEANING	**WORD PARTS**	
1.	ear	ot	*Note:* This list will be more useful if you write it in alphabetical order.
2.	_____	_____	
3.	_____	_____	
4.	_____	_____	
5.	_____	_____	
6.	_____	_____	
7.	_____	_____	
8.	_____	_____	
9.	_____	_____	
10.	_____	_____	

EXERCISE 8-H
- **Multiple Choice**
- **Skill: word parts**

A meaning is in boldface for each of the following phrases. From the four choices given, pick the one answer which contains a word part with that meaning. Use both versions of List 2 to help you. **Do not use a dictionary.** *Do not focus on the size or difficulty of the words. Look only for the simple word part; it will lead you to the correct answer.*

Example: √Pertaining to **sound**
    (A) cosmic   (C) frenetic
    (B) antic   (D) sonic

Answer: (D) The reason for this answer is that the SON part of *sonic* means "sound."

1. Able to be **seen**
   (A) audible
   (B) tangible
   (C) visible
   (D) palpable

2. Relating to the sense of **smell**
   (A) olfactory
   (B) refractory
   (C) cursory
   (D) hortatory

3. Able to be **heard**
   (A) audible
   (B) tangible
   (C) visible
   (D) palpable

4. Having **taste** or flavor
   (A) morbid
   (B) vapid
   (C) sapid
   (D) rabid

5. Able to be **touched**
   (A) audible
   (B) risible
   (C) visible
   (D) palpable

6. Giving out a deep, vibrating **sound**
   (A) resonant
   (B) flagrant
   (C) dormant
   (D) gallant

7. Reconstructive surgery of the **ear**
   (A) rhinoplasty
   (B) otoplasty
   (C) dermatoplasty
   (D) thoracoplasty

8. Characterized by a sense of **smell**
   (A) photographic
   (B) phlegmatic
   (C) osmatic
   (D) Socratic

Copyright © 1996 Harcourt Brace & Company. All rights reserved.

9. Reconstructive surgery of the **nose**
   - (A) rhinoplasty
   - (B) otoplasty
   - (C) dermatoplasty
   - (D) thoracoplasty

10. Full of flavor or **taste**
    - (A) cursory
    - (B) auditory
    - (C) savory
    - (D) advisory

EXERCISE 8-I
- Fill in the Blank (one cue)
- Skill: word parts

*Use a **meaning** from List 2 to fill in the blank in each statement. The word part whose meaning you are defining will be found inside the boldfaced word. **Do not use a dictionary**. Do not focus on the size or difficulty of the words. Look only for the simple word part; it will lead you to the correct answer.*

Example: √An **optometrist** examines a patient's _____ .

   Answer: *eyes* [> OPTO]

1. Something **inaudible** cannot be _____ .
2. The **auditory** nerves transmit _____ to the brain.
3. A person who has a _____ problem should see a **dermatologist**.
4. **Supersonic** aircraft fly faster than the speed of _____ .
5. The **otic** nerve is located in the _____ .
6. A **telescope** is an instrument for _____ distant objects.
7. To **revise** is to _____ corrections that you would like to make and then do them.
8. The **olfactory** nerve is connected from the brain to the _____ .
9. **Myopia** refers to a condition of the _____ .
10. **Dermabrasion** removes scars by scraping off _____ .

11. **Sapid** means agreeable to the _____ .
12. An **optometer** is an instrument for measuring the refractive error of an _____ .
13. A **palpus** is an organ attached to the head of creatures such as insects or lobsters that they use to _____ things.
14. **Osmics** is the science dealing with the sense of _____ .
15. **Rhinology** is the science dealing with diseases of the _____ .

EXERCISE 8-J
- **Fill in the Blank (no cue)**
- **Skills: word parts, context**

*Once again, use a **meaning** from List 2 to fill in the blank in each statement. This time, however, you will have to find the word part yourself in the difficult or technical word. **Do not use a dictionary**. Do not focus on the size or difficulty of the words. Look only for the simple word part; it will lead you to the correct answer.*

Example: √Dermatoplasty means _____ grafting.

        Answer: *skin* [> DERM]

1. Audiovisual materials are meant to be heard and _____ .
2. A savory meal _____ good.
3. A consonant is a group of letters that form a speech _____ .
4. A horoscope is a diagram that allows the user to _____ the position of the heavens at the hour of his or her birth.
5. The auditory canal, unless blocked, allows us to _____ .
6. Microscopic particles are too small to be _____ .
7. Infrasonic waves are below the normal range of _____ frequency.
8. To envision a plan is to _____ it mentally.

9. When a doctor palpates you, he or she examines you by _____ .
10. Insipid means without _____ .
11. The olfactory nerves transmit _____ to the brain.
12. Anosmia is the loss of the sense of _____ .
13. The rhinoscope is an instrument used to examine the _____ .
14. Otitis is inflammation of the _____ .
15. A dermatophyte is a fungus that grows on _____ .

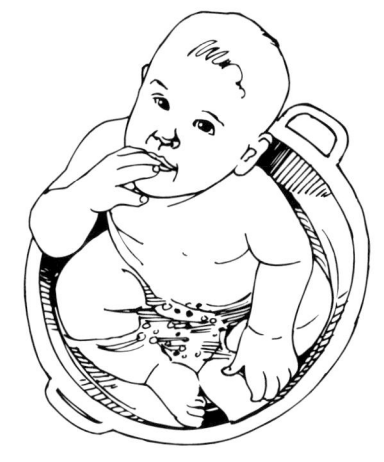

Here's to DERM, which means our skin;
It forms our body's suit.
And when arranged correctly,
DERM is also CUT.

EXERCISE 8-K
- **Matching Columns**
- **Skill: word parts**

Memory check. Do not look back at List 2 or use a dictionary.

1. ____ SCOP	(a) skin
2. ____ SON	(b) smell
3. ____ PALP	(c) taste
4. ____ OLFACT	(d) nose
5. ____ DERM	(e) hear
6. ____ RHIN	(f) sound
7. ____ OT	(g) eye
8. ____ AUD	(h) ear
9. ____ OP	(i) see
10. ____ SAV	(j) touch

EXERCISE 8-L
- **Fill in (two cues)**
- **Skills: word parts, dictionary, context**

*To finish each word, fill in the blank with one of the **word parts** from your version of List 2. **You must use a college-level dictionary** to make sure that what you write really is a word and that it fits in the sentence. The word in boldface will give you the meaning of the word part that you must write.*

Example: √ _ _ _ion is the ability to **see**.

          Answer: *VIS* [> see]

1. Something capable of giving out a rich, deep **sound** is _ _ _orous.
2. That which is _ _ _ _able is capable of being **touched** or felt.
3. _ _ _ _abrasion removes scars by scraping the **skin**.
4. _ _itis is an inflammation of the **ear**.
5. When we _ _ _ualize, we **see** a picture in our mind.
6. _ _ _ _metry is the profession of testing the **eyes** for defects in order to prescribe corrective glasses.
7. _ _ _orless food has no **taste**; it is totally bland.
8. People who have _ _ _ions **see** things that others do not.
9. Dis_ _ _ance is harsh or inharmonious **sound**.
10. A peri_ _ _ _ _ allows submariners to **see** what is above the surface of the water.
11. An _ _ _itory hallucination seems to be **heard**.
12. _ _ _ _orrhea is a mucous discharge from the **nose**.
13. _ _ _ _ _ _ion is the act of **smelling**.
14. An _ _ olith is a blockage in the inner **ear**.
15. The absence or loss of the sense of **smell** is called an_ _ _ia.

EXERCISE 8-M
- **Fill in (one cue)**
- **Skills: word parts, dictionary, context**

*Continue filling in **word parts** from your version of List 2 as you have been, **using a college-level dictionary** to check accuracy. This time, however, there will be no word in boldface. You will have to search the sentence for a clue.*

Example: √An _ _tician makes or sells glasses to improve the customer's eyes.

   Answer: *op-* [> eyes]

1. Something that is in_ _ _ible cannot be heard.
2. The epi_ _ _ _is is the outer layer of skin.
3. A windshield _ _ _or allows a driver to see without interference from sun glare.
4. A choir singing in uni_ _ _ makes a unified sound.
5. A _ _ _eo tape is meant to be seen.
6. An _ _ _io tape is meant to be heard.
7. The science of the ear and its diseases is called _ _ology.
8. _ _ _ic means of or pertaining to sound.
9. A micro_ _ _ _ _ allows the user to see very small materials clearly.
10. _ _ _atic animals have a keenly developed sense of smell.
11. _ _tics is the branch of science that deals with the eye and the way that it uses light.
12. _ _ _ _ _ory organs contribute to our sense of smell.
13. An oscillo_ _ _ _ _ is an instrument that allows the user to see changes in electrical power on a screen.
14. Infra_ _ _ic sounds are below the normal range of hearing.
15. Inflammation of the nose is called _ _ _ _itis.

234 CHAPTER 8 THE SENSES

EXERCISE 8-N
- **Paragraph Examples**
- **Skills: word parts, dictionary, context**

Answer these four questions after each paragraph:

(a) *What word part inside the boldfaced word helps you to understand that word? What does that word part mean?*

_____

(b) *Using only the context of the word and the word part that it contains, what do you think the boldfaced word means? (See Chapter 1, Section 2.)*

_____

(c) *Choose one context clue that helped you. (See Chapter 1, Section 2.)*
    1. word signals   4. examples or description
    2. punctuation signals   5. contrast or opposites
    3. synonyms (substitution) 6. prior knowledge; common sense
       If 6, explain: _____

_____

(d) *How does the dictionary define the boldfaced word as it is used in the paragraph?*

_____

1. During evolution, the midbrain has changed more in function than in size or structure. In fish and amphibians it is the principal area for association of sensory input with suitable motor output. In these lower vertebrates, a major part of the midbrain is the **optic** tectum, which receives signals from the optic nerves, carrying visual information from the eyes. In mammals, the analysis of vision has moved out of the midbrain and into part of the forebrain.
                [Arms, et. al., *A Journey into Life*, 3rd Ed., 597]

  (a) _____
  (b) _____
  (c) _____
  (d) _____

2. Breaths come in pairs, except at two times in our lives—the beginning and the end. At birth, we inhale for the first time; at death, we exhale for the last. In between, through all the lather of one's life, each breath passes air over our **olfactory** sites. Each day we breathe about 23,040 times and move around 438 cubic

feet of air. It takes us about five seconds to breathe—two seconds to inhale and three seconds to exhale—and, in that time, molecules of odor flood through our systems. Inhaling and exhaling, we smell odors.

        [Diane Ackerman, *A Natural History of the Senses*, 6–7]

(a) _____
(b) _____
(c) _____
(d) _____

3. If you or someone you know needs a hearing aid, buy from a reputable dispenser. If you don't get a hearing test **(audiogram)** from a medical facility, a dispenser will give you one. This person then takes an impression of your ear, chooses the most appropriate aid and adjusts the device to fit well. These are complex tasks, and skills of dispensers vary. FDA plans to issue new requirements for people who sell hearing aids. Until the regulations are available, ask your physician to recommend a reputable dispenser.

        ["Hearing Aids," *The Mayo Clinic Health Letter*, May 1994, 6]

(a) _____
(b) _____
(c) _____
(d) _____

4. If a bundle of parallel fibers is used to construct an optical transmission line, images can be transferred from one point to another. This technique is used in a sizable industry known as fiber optics. Physicians often use fiber optics cables to aid in the diagnosis and repair of certain medical problems, without the intrusive effects of major surgery. Damaged knees or other joints in athletes can sometimes be repaired using a process called **arthroscopic** surgery. In this technique, a small incision is made into the joint. Repair is accomplished by inserting a small fiber optics cable through the cut to provide illumination and then by trimming cartilage or damaged tissue with a small knife at the end of a second cable.

        [Serway & Faughn, *College Physics*, 3rd Ed., 770–71]

(a) _____
(b) _____
(c) _____
(d) _____

I don't want to insult the rhinoceros,
But the size of his nose is prepoceros.

5. According to various theories, there are several basic odors: flowery, minty, musky, camphoraceous, ethereal, pungent, and putrid. Other odors can then be broken down into combinations of basic odors. According to one theory, we smell substances whose molecules fit the shapes of receptor sites (Amoore, 1970). This theory receives some support from the fact that we can develop an **anosmia**, or "smell blindness," for a particular odor—suggesting that one kind of receptor has been damaged or degenerated.
   [Spencer A. Rathus, *Psychology*, 4th Ed., 129]

   (a) _____
   (b) _____
   (c) _____
   (d) _____

SECTION 3: CHAPTER REVIEW (LISTS 1 AND 2 COMBINED)

Word Parts Covered in This Chapter:

WORD PART	MEANING	COMMON EXAMPLE	TEXTBOOK EXAMPLE
ACOUST	sound; hearing	*acoustical tile*	*acoustician*
AUD	hear	*audiotape*	*audiometer*
AUR	ear; hearing	*aural*	*auricular*
CUT	skin	*cuticle*	*subcutaneous*
DERM	skin	*dermatologist*	*epidermis*
GUST	taste	*disgusting*	*gustation*
NAS	nose	*nasal*	*nasopharynx*
OCUL	eye	*binoculars*	*oculomotor*
ODOR	smell	*odorous*	*odoriferous*
OLFACT	smell	*olfactory*	*olfactometer*
OP	eye	*optician*	*optical scan*
OPSY	see	*biopsy*	*necropsy*
OPTO	eye	*optometrist*	*optometer*
OR	mouth	*oral*	*oratorical*
OSM	smell	*osmatic*	*osmidrosis*
OT	ear	*otic*	*parotic*
PALP	touch	*palpable*	*palpate*
PHON	sound	*phonics*	*phonometer*
RHIN	nose	*rhinoceros*	*rhinitis*
SAP	taste	*insipid*	*sapidity*
SAV	taste	*savor*	*savorless*
SCOPE	see	*horoscope*	*oscilloscope*
SENS	senses	*sensual*	*sensorimotor*
SON	sound	*sonic*	*soniferous*
SPEC	see; look	*inspect*	*spectrograph*
SPIC	see; look	*conspicuous*	*despicable*
TACT	touch; feel	*contact*	*tactile*
TANG	touch; feel	*tangible*	*tangential*
VID	see	*videotape*	*vide*
VIS	see	*visible*	*revisionary*

238 CHAPTER 8 THE SENSES

PRE-EXERCISE ACTIVITY 3
- **List Making**
- **Skill: word parts**

*In the blanks that follow, rewrite the combined word parts list. This time, however, reverse the order by writing the **meanings** in the first column. Then gather all the word parts in the list which have that meaning and write them on one line in the second column. This will let you make necessary connections and help you in the process of long-term memorization. The first one has already been done to show you how.*

	MEANING	WORD PARTS	
1.	ear	aur, ot	*Note:* This list will be more useful if you write it in alphabetical order.
2.			
3.			
4.			
5.			
6.			
7.			
8.			
9.			
10.			
11.			
12.			
13.			
14.			

Copyright © 1996 Harcourt Brace & Company. All rights reserved.

EXERCISE 8-O
- **Matching Columns**
- **Skill: word parts**

Memory check. Do not look back at the combined list or use a dictionary.

1. ____	AUR	(a)	hear
2. ____	RHIN	(b)	skin
3. ____	GUST	(c)	see
4. ____	OLFACT	(d)	touch
5. ____	CUT	(e)	nose
6. ____	PHON	(f)	smell
7. ____	OCUL	(g)	eye
8. ____	SCOPE	(h)	ear
9. ____	TANG	(i)	sound
10. ____	AUD	(j)	taste

EXERCISE 8-P
- **Cross Out**
- **Skills: dictionary, word parts, context**

One word in each set does not contain the word part and meaning that is given, even though it has a set of similar letters. **Use a college-level dictionary** *to find the one that does* **not** *fit.*

	WORD PART	MEANING	CROSS OUT THE ONE WORD THAT DOES NOT FIT.
Example:	√VIS	see	invisible, television, viscid

Answer: The dictionary shows that *invisible* and *television* have the word *see* or *view* in their definitions. *Viscid* (sticky) does not; cross it out.

WORD PART	MEANING	CROSS OUT THE ONE WORD THAT DOES NOT FIT.
1. SAV	taste	savory, savagery, savorless
2. OP	eye	oppugn, optical, myopia

3. PHON	sound	euphony, phony, phonograph
4. AUD	hear	audience, audition, audacious
5. NAS	nose	nasal, nastic, nasopharynx
6. AUR	ear	auriferous, auricular, auricle
7. GUST	taste	gustatory, degust, gusty
8. TACT	touch	contact, tactile, tactical
9. OSM	smell	osmatic, anosmia, osmosis
10. VID	see	videotape, invidious, videocassette

EXERCISE 8-Q
- **Extended Answer**
- **Skills: word parts, dictionary, context**

Answer the following questions by using a college-level dictionary.

Example: √How is the meaning *nose* involved in the word **rhinoceros?**

Answer: A rhinoceros has an upright horn on its snout (nose).

1. How is the meaning *taste* involved in the word **gustatory?**

2. How is the meaning *smell* involved in the word **olfactometer?**

3. How is the meaning *sound* involved in the word **sonar?**

4. How is the meaning *skin* involved in the word **pachyderm?**

5. How is the meaning *touch* involved in the word **contact?**

6. How is the meaning *see* involved in the word **spectator?**

7. How is the meaning *hear* involved in the word **audiophile?**

8. How is the meaning *feel* involved in the word **insensitivity?**

9. How is the meaning *nose* involved in the word **nasology**?

10. How is the meaning *sound* involved in the word **cacophony**?

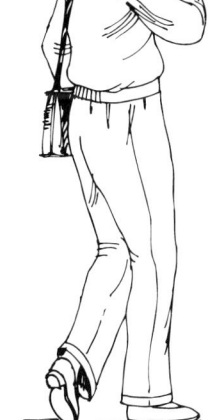

EXERCISE 8-R
- Fill in the Blank
- Skills: word parts, context

Answer each question by filling in the blank. Use the combined list.

Example: √A synonym for *skin* is _____.
          Answer: *hide*

1. A synonym for *to hear* is to _____.
2. A synonym for *to see* is to _____.
3. A synonym for *to smell* is to _____.
4. A synonym for *to taste* is to _____.
5. A synonym for *to touch* is to _____.

ODOR says it clearly,
OSM not as well;
OLFACT sneaks up behind you,
But, believe me, they all smell.

EXERCISE 8-S
- Fill in the Blanks
- Skill: word parts

Memory check. Do not look back at the combined list or use a dictionary.

1. Name two word parts that mean *see*: _____ and _____.
2. Name two word parts that mean *skin*: _____ and _____.

3. Name two word parts that
   mean *sound*: _____ and _____ .
4. Name two word parts that
   mean *smell*: _____ and _____ .
5. Name two word parts that
   mean *touch*: _____ and _____ .
6. Name two word parts that
   mean *taste*: _____ and _____ .
7. Name two word parts that
   mean *nose*: _____ and _____ .
8. Name two word parts that
   mean *ear*: _____ and _____ .
9. Name two word parts that
   mean *eye*: _____ and _____ .
10. Name two word parts that
    mean *hear*: _____ and _____ .

EXERCISE 8-T
- **Paragraph Examples**
- **Skills: word parts, dictionary, context**

Answer these four questions after each paragraph:

(a) *What word part inside the boldfaced word helps you to understand that word? What does that word part mean?*

_____

(b) *Using only the context of the word and the word part that it contains, what do you think the boldfaced word means? (See Chapter 1, Section 2.)*

_____

(c) *Choose one context clue that helped you. (See Chapter 1, Section 2.)*
   1. *word signals*   4. *examples or description*
   2. *punctuation signals*   5. *contrast or opposites*
   3. *synonyms (substitution)*   6. *prior knowledge; common sense*
      If 6, explain: _____

(d) *How does the dictionary define the boldfaced word as it is used in the paragraph?*

_____

1. Physiological fatigue, which is normal, often occurs during exercise. The more rapidly the exercise is performed, the sooner muscular fatigue ensues. In other words, the more concentrated the output of muscular energy, the more quickly fatigue comes on. Also, fatigue in one set of muscles affects other sets of muscles. This explains, for example, why eye fatigue—excessive use of the **ocular** muscles—or tired feet can induce lethargy in the whole body. Finally, fatigue is a protective mechanism during exercise. When the feeling of fatigue becomes a sensation of pain, this must always be regarded as a warning that physiological limits have been reached.
   [J. J. Schifferes, *Essentials of Healthier Living*, 29]

   (a) _____
   (b) _____
   (c) _____
   (d) _____

2. Touch is the first of your senses to develop and usually the last to diminish. Newborn babies process most information through their skin. And even a frail 90-year-old with failing sight clearly understands the grasp of a caring hand. One of the most dramatic realizations regarding the power of human **contact** came earlier in this century. Pediatricians noticed that babies in orphanages and hospitals, who were not held and cuddled, failed to grow and often died. In the 1930s, Bellevue Hospital in New York City started a "mothering" policy to make sure babies were talked to, held, and cuddled. As a result, the infant mortality rate fell from 30 to 35 percent to less than 10 percent.
   ["Touch," *The Mayo Clinic Health Letter*, June 1994, 7]

   (a) _____
   (b) _____
   (c) _____
   (d) _____

3. The external ear is composed of a funnel-shaped auricle that collects sound waves and helps localize the source of sound, and a passageway called the external auditory meatus, that directs the sound waves from the auricle to the eardrum. The **auricle**

has an elastic cartilage framework covered with skin. The meatus is lined with skin and has fine hairs surrounding its entrance. Oil-secreting and wax-secreting glands empty into it.
     [Alexander P. Spence, *Biology of Human Aging*, 117]

   (a) _____
   (b) _____
   (c) _____
   (d) _____

4. Wilhelm Wundt, like Aristotle, claimed that the mind was a natural event and could be studied scientifically, just like light, heat, and the flow of blood. Wundt used the method of **introspection**, recommended by Socrates, to try to discover the basic elements of experience. When presented with various sights and sounds, he and his colleagues tried to look inward as objectively as possible to describe their sensations and feelings.
     [Spencer A. Rathus, *Psychology*, 4th Ed., 9]

   (a) _____
   (b) _____
   (c) _____
   (d) _____

5. In many ways, touch is difficult to research. Every other sense has a key organ to study; for touch that organ is the skin, and it stretches over the whole body. Every sense has at least one key research center, except touch. Touch is a sensory system, the influence of which is hard to isolate or eliminate. Scientists can study people who are blind to learn more about vision, and people who are deaf or **anosmic** to learn more about hearing and smell, but this is virtually impossible to do with touch.
     [Diane Ackerman, *A Natural History of the Senses*, 77]

   (a) _____
   (b) _____
   (c) _____
   (d) _____

6. When musical sounds (also called tones) of different frequency are played together, we also perceive a third tone that results from the difference in their frequencies. If the combination of tones is pleasant, we say that they are in harmony, or consonant (from Latin roots meaning "together" and "sound"). Unpleasant combinations of tones are labeled dissonant ("the opposite of"

and "sound"). The expression that something "strikes a **dissonant** chord" means that we find it disagreeable.

[Spencer A. Rathus, *Psychology,* 4th Ed., 124]

(a) _____
(b) _____
(c) _____
(d) _____

7. The words are nice. They have melody. But I do not understand what I am reading, and I feel silly. I cannot read aloud anymore. Even though I am discouraged, Joseph Brodsky, poet and winner of the 1987 Nobel Prize in Literature, tells me that reading aloud is indeed the best way to find Walt Whitman. "Poetry *is* meant to be read aloud," he explains. "It's much more engaging than reading silently. You hear not only content, you hear the entire **euphony** of the words. Nothing beats the spoken word even if you are speaking to yourself."

[Joel L. Swerdlow, "America's Poet: Walt Whitman," *National Geographic,* December 1994, 121]

(a) _____
(b) _____
(c) _____
(d) _____

8. Language is steeped in metaphors of touch. We call our emotions feelings, and we care most deeply when something "touches" us. Problems can be thorny, ticklish, sticky, or need to be handled with kid gloves. Touchy people, especially if they're coarse, get on our nerves. . . . What seems real we call **"tangible,"** as if it were a fruit whose rind we could feel.

[Diane Ackerman, *A Natural History of the Senses,* 70–71]

(a) _____
(b) _____
(c) _____
(d) _____

9. Video signals displayed on your television screen use two forms of **optical** deception, one of which is used in motion pictures, the other in photography. The optical deception used in motion pictures involves the fact that a series of still pictures scanned rapidly by the eye is perceived as continuous motion in the scene that was photographed. A theater movie projector

flashes 24 different still pictures before your eyes each second. Each picture is only slightly different from the preceding one, and the persistence of eye vision blends them together as continuous action. In the case of television signals, 30 different pictures appear on the television screen each second.

[Serway & Faughn, *College Physics*, 3rd Ed., 736–37]

(a) _____
(b) _____
(c) _____
(d) _____

10. A revolution in surgery stemming mainly from innovative technology has changed what you may expect from your next operation. The key development: endoscopic surgery. Endoscopic surgery relies on the endoscope, a pencil-thin, hollow tube with its own lighting system and miniature video camera. It allows a surgeon to see inside your body without "cutting you open." Your surgeon inserts the **endoscope** through a tiny incision less than an inch long. Then while viewing the procedure on a video screen, your surgeon operates with miniature instruments inserted through one or more other small incisions.

["Endoscopic Surgery," *The Mayo Clinic Health Letter*, September 1994, 6]

(a) _____
(b) _____
(c) _____
(d) _____

CHAPTER 9 ACTION

SECTION 1

List 1
Here are some word parts that are used to signify action.

WORD PART	MEANING
CAP	take; hold
CED	move; go
CEP	take; hold
CESS	move; go
CID	kill
CIP	take; hold
CIS	cut
CUR	run; flow
CURS	run; flow
FER	carry; bear
FLECT	bend
FLEX	bend
FRACT	break
FRAG	break
MUT	change
SEQU	follow
-VERGE	turn; bend
VERS	turn; bend
VERT	turn; bend

Copyright © 1996 Harcourt Brace & Company. All rights reserved.

PRE-EXERCISE ACTIVITY 1
- **List Making**
- **Skill: word parts**

*In the blanks that follow, rewrite List 1. This time, however, reverse the order by writing the **meanings** in the first column. Then gather all the word parts in the list which have that meaning and write them on one line in the second column. This will let you make necessary connections and help you in the process of long-term memorization. The first one has already been done to show you how.*

	MEANING	WORD PARTS
1.	bend	flect, flex, -verge, verse, vert
2.	_____	_____
3.	_____	_____
4.	_____	_____
5.	_____	_____
6.	_____	_____
7.	_____	_____
8.	_____	_____
9.	_____	_____
10.	_____	_____
11.	_____	_____
12.	_____	_____
13.	_____	_____
14.	_____	_____
15.	_____	_____

Note: This list will be more useful if you write it in alphabetical order.

EXERCISE 9-A
- **Multiple Choice**
- **Skill: word parts**

A meaning is in boldface for each of the following phrases. From the four choices given, pick the one answer which contains a word part with that meaning. Use both versions of List 1 to help you. **Do not use a dictionary.** *Do not focus on the size or difficulty of the words. Look only for the simple word part; it will lead you to the correct answer.*

Example: √To **bend** or turn aside
    (A) degrade   (C) deflect
    (B) deplore   (D) deduce

    Answer: (C) The reason for this answer is that the FLECT part of *deflect* means "bend."

1. To **move** from a position and acknowledge that an opponent is correct
   (A) converge   (C) confer
   (B) concede   (D) contract

2. To **turn** back to a former way of doing things
   (A) refine   (C) revert
   (B) reflect   (D) repulse

3. To **carry** on a discussion or deliberation
   (A) converge   (C) confer
   (B) concede   (D) contract

4. To attract and **hold** attention or interest
   (A) motivate   (C) captivate
   (B) predicate   (D) perpetrate

5. To **bend or turn** toward each other and intersect
   (A) converge   (C) confer
   (B) concede   (D) contract

6. The act of **killing** one's own brother
   (A) fraternization   (C) fratery
   (B) fratricide   (D) fraternity

Copyright © 1996 Harcourt Brace & Company. All rights reserved.

7. To **carry** from one person or place to another
   - (A) transcribe
   - (B) transfigure
   - (C) transcend
   - (D) transfer

8. A result that **follows** an action
   - (A) constellation
   - (B) consequence
   - (C) conscript
   - (D) contortion

9. Done on the **run** in a hasty way
   - (A) cursory
   - (B) cutaneous
   - (C) cumulative
   - (D) custodial

10. A **breaking** of the rules
    - (A) involution
    - (B) inference
    - (C) infraction
    - (D) intercession

EXERCISE 9-B
- Fill in the Blank (one cue)
- Skill: word parts

*Use a **meaning** from List 1 to fill in the blank in each statement. The word part whose meaning you are defining will be found inside the boldfaced word. **Do not use a dictionary.** Do not focus on the size or difficulty of the words. Look only for the simple word part; it will lead you to the correct answer.*

Example: √**Fratricide** involves _____ing one's own brother.

                Answer: *killing* [> CID]

1. Explanations that are _____ down to the fewest possible words are **concise**.
2. A **captive** is someone who is _____ or imprisoned.
3. To **reverse** is to _____ around and go the other way.
4. **Unflexed** muscles are not _____ at that moment.
5. When floodwaters **recede**, they _____ back.

6. A **genuflection** is a _____ of the knee to show respect.
7. Being **receptive** to an idea means _____ it in and agreeing with it.
8. To **avert** your gaze is to _____ it away.
9. _____ another human being is classified as **homicide**.
10. **Cursive** writing allows you to _____ right along because of the joined letters.
11. A person who makes a **concession** _____ aside and concedes a point.
12. In a **conference**, participants _____ on a discussion with each other.
13. **Sequential** events _____ each other.
14. To **fractionate** is to _____ something into its component parts.
15. **Commutation** is the act of _____ something through substitution.

EXERCISE 9-C
- **Fill in the Blank (no cue)**
- **Skills: word parts, context**

Once again, use a **meaning** *from List 1 to fill in the blank in each statement. This time, however, you will have to find the word part yourself in the difficult or technical word.* **Do not use a dictionary.** *Do not focus on the size or difficulty of the words. Look only for the simple word part; it will lead you to the correct answer.*

Example: √Mutation is the act or process of _____ .

       Answer: *changing* [> MUT]

1. When you precede someone, you _____ before that person.
2. A mind that _____ through difficult problems is incisive.

3. Commutation is the act of _____ or substituting one thing for another.
4. Something fragile is easily _____.
5. A concession is a _____ toward an agreement.
6. Refraction _____ up light waves, causing them to change direction.
7. The systematic _____ of an entire race or group is called genocide.
8. A recipient _____ what is offered.
9. To deflect is to _____ or turn aside.
10. To prefer something is to _____ it forward to a place of priority.
11. Electrical current _____ through a wire.
12. A funeral procession _____ from the place of service to the cemetery.
13. Flection is the act of _____ing.
14. When the principal design side of a coin is _____ toward you, you are looking at the obverse side.
15. An abnormal condition that _____ from a previous disease is a sequela.

CED and CESS mean move or go,
While CUR and CURS mean run or flow.
CID and CIS mean kill and cut;
One is legal, one is nut.

EXERCISE 9-D
- **Matching Columns**
- **Skill: word parts**

Memory check. Do not look back at List 1 or use a dictionary.

1. ____ FLEX   (a) take
2. ____ FRACT   (b) move
3. ____ CAP   (c) kill

4. ____ CESS   (d) break
5. ____ CUR   (e) turn
6. ____ SEQU   (f) carry
7. ____ VERGE   (g) follow
8. ____ CID   (h) change
9. ____ FER   (i) run; flow
10. ____ MUT   (j) bend

EXERCISE 9-E
- **Fill in (two cues)**
- **Skills: word parts, dictionary, context**

*To finish each word, fill in the blank with one of the **word parts** from your version of List 1. **You must use a college-level dictionary** to make sure that what you write really is a word and that it fits in the sentence. The word in boldface will give you the meaning of the word part that you must write.*

Example: √A _ _ _ tive is *held* as a prisoner.

　　　　　Answer: *CAP* [> held]

1. Something which can be **bent** without harm is _ _ _ ible.
2. A _ _ _ atile mind is able to **turn** easily to other thoughts.
3. A _ _ _ _ ured pipe has **broken**.
4. _ _ _ tivity is the state of being **held** against one's will.
5. To de _ _ _ something is to **carry** it until a later time, to put it off.
6. A definition that is clear-**cut** and definite is pre _ _ _ e.
7. The act of **bending** is known as _ _ _ ion.
8. To di _ _ _ attention is to **turn** it away to something else.
9. A disease that is just beginning to **take hold** in the body is in _ _ _ ient.
10. Sui _ _ e is the act of killing oneself.
11. A lamp that is shattered and **broken** is _ _ _ mented.
12. When you in _ _ _ someone's anger, you **run** right into it.

13. When a governor com___es a prisoner's sentence, he or she **changes** it.
14. A movie ___el **follows** an original popular hit.
15. Lines that di_____ **turn** away in different directions.

EXERCISE 9-F
- Fill in (one cue)
- Skills: word parts, dictionary, context

Continue filling in **word parts** *from your version of List 1 as you have been doing,* **using a college-level dictionary** *to check accuracy. This time, however, there will be no word in boldface. You will have to search each sentence for a clue.*

Example: √Lines that con_____ turn toward each other and meet.

Answer: *VERGE* [> turn]

1. Something that has been turned in another direction or position is in____ed.
2. Your per___tion is the understanding or awareness that you hold in your mind.
3. Con____ences are the results that follow our actions.
4. A surgeon who makes an in___ion cuts into a patient.
5. In a re___ion, the economy moves downward.
6. An in___ible piece of material will not bend.
7. Laws of nature that cannot be changed are said to be im___able.
8. A ____ory glance is a running glance, a quick once-over.
9. To con____ something is to turn it to another use.
10. A re___rent thought runs through our mind repeatedly.
11. A pesti___e is a chemical preparation designed to kill plant, fungal, or animal pests.
12. A broken bone is referred to as a _____ure.

13. A _ _ _tive is held in confinement.
14. Coni_ _ _s are cone-bearing trees.
15. Regi_ _ _e is the killing of a king.

EXERCISE 9-G
- **Paragraph Examples**
- **Skills: word parts, dictionary, context**

Answer these four questions after each paragraph:

(a) *What word part inside the boldfaced word helps you to understand that word? What does that word part mean?*

(b) *Using only the context of the word and the word part that it contains, what do you think the boldfaced word means? (See Chapter 1, Section 2.)*

(c) *Choose one context clue that helped you. (See Chapter 1, Section 2.)*
   1. *word signals*
   2. *punctuation signals*
   3. *synonyms (substitution)*
   4. *examples or description*
   5. *contrast or opposites*
   6. *prior knowledge; common sense*
      If 6, explain: _____

(d) *How does the dictionary define the boldfaced word as it is used in the paragraph?*

1. Whenever electric charges move, a **current** is said to exist. To define current more precisely, suppose the charges are moving perpendicular to a surface of area A. This area could be the cross-sectional area of a wire, for example. The current is the rate at which charge flows through this surface. The charges flowing through a surface can be positive, negative, or both.
   [Serway & Faughn, *College Physics*, 3rd Ed., 569–70]

   (a) _____
   (b) _____
   (c) _____
   (d) _____

2. Too many companies are content to prepare their organizations only for the likely snags. It's easier on the brain, after all. But to survive, top managers must stretch their imaginations and work up wide-ranging creative paranoia. Says Tamara Erickson, an Arthur D. Little managing director: "You should ask yourself if your strategy is **flexible** enough to deal with the wildest-case scenario. You should contemplate the absurd and include it in your planning."

[Kenneth Labich, "Why Companies Fail," *Fortune*, 14 Nov. 1994, 54]

(a) _____
(b) _____
(c) _____
(d) _____

3. Fragmentation refers to the fourth stage of a social movement, when the movement gradually begins to fall apart. Organizational structures no longer seem necessary because the changes they sought to bring about have been institutionalized or the changes they sought to block have been prevented. Disputes over doctrine may drive dissident members out, as when the United Auto Workers (UAW) and the Teamsters left the AFL-CIO. Also, demographic changes may transform a once strong social movement into a far less powerful force. Economic changes have been largely responsible for the **fragmentation** of the American labor movement.

[Henry L. Tischler, *Introduction to Sociology*, 4th Ed., 408]

(a) _____
(b) _____
(c) _____
(d) _____

4. Food enters the human gut by manipulations of the mouth. Besides taking in food, the mouth begins to dismantle it, using lips, tongue, teeth, and jaw muscles. **Incisors**, chisel-like teeth in the front of the mouth, cut bite-sized pieces of food from a larger portion. The tongue, a slippery, mobile platform, manipulates food during chewing, pushing it back to the molars, the millstones that mash food into small particles. All the while, saliva is released into the mouth to moisten the food, stick it together into a bolus (ball), and lubricate the food so that

it does not scratch the delicate mucous membranes of the digestive tract.

[Karen Arms, et al., *A Journey into Life,* 3rd Ed., 480]

(a) _____
(b) _____
(c) _____
(d) _____

5. The computer industry launches big ideas the way some people throw beach balls. The biggest and airiest of them all these days is called convergence. The theory goes something like this: the technologies of television, telephone, and computers are all moving along converging trajectories. When they intersect, bang! The world will change. People will make calls from their television sets. Or watch television with their phones. They'll pull out their pocket doodad in the middle of a traffic jam and accomplish what an advanced desktop computer does today. . . . For now, though, the only **convergence** going on is a passel of business mergers among digital wannabes.

[Laurent Belsie, "Computers for the Rest of Us," *The Christian Science Monitor,* 15 Nov. 1994, 13]

(a) _____
(b) _____
(c) _____
(d) _____

SECTION 2

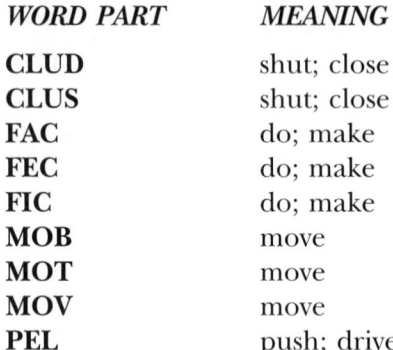

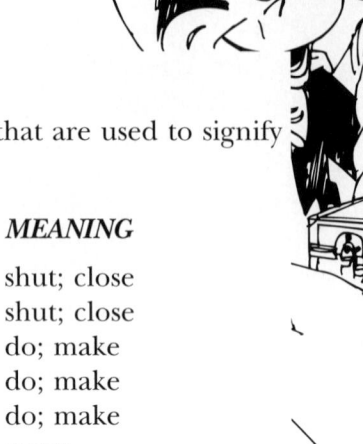

List 2
Here are more word parts that are used to signify action.

WORD PART	MEANING
CLUD	shut; close
CLUS	shut; close
FAC	do; make
FEC	do; make
FIC	do; make
MOB	move
MOT	move
MOV	move
PEL	push; drive
PORT	carry
PUL	push; drive
RUPT	break or burst
-TAIN	hold
TEN	hold
TRACT	pull
VEN	come
VENT	come
VOLUT	turn; roll
VOLV	turn; roll

PRE-EXERCISE ACTIVITY 2
- **List Making**
- **Skill: word parts**

*In the blanks that follow, rewrite List 2. This time, however, reverse the order by writing the **meanings** in the first column. Then gather all the word parts in the list which have that meaning and write them on one line in the second column. This will let you make necessary connections and help you in the process of long-term memorization. The first one has already been done to show you how.*

	MEANING	WORD PARTS	
1.	break or burst	rupt	*Note:* This list will be more useful if you write it in alphabetical order.
2.	_____	_____	
3.	_____	_____	
4.	_____	_____	
5.	_____	_____	
6.	_____	_____	
7.	_____	_____	
8.	_____	_____	
9.	_____	_____	
10.	_____	_____	
11.	_____	_____	
12.	_____	_____	
13.	_____	_____	
14.	_____	_____	

EXERCISE 9-H
- **Multiple Choice**
- **Skill: word parts**

A meaning is in boldface for each of the following phrases. From the four choices given, pick the one answer which contains a word part with that meaning. Use both versions of List 2 to help you. **Do not use a dictionary.** *Do not focus on the size or difficulty of the words. Look only for the simple word part; it will lead you to the correct answer.*

Example:　√To **drive** away
　　(A) relent　　　　　(C) regale
　　(B) resume　　　　 (D) repel

　　　Answer: (D) The reason for this answer is that the PEL part of *repel* means "drive."

1. To **shut** off from social contact
   (A) seclude　　　　(C) sequence
   (B) serrate　　　　 (D) secure

2. To **pull** back into a reduced state or to shrink
   (A) converge　　　(C) confer
   (B) concede　　　 (D) contract

3. To **hold** on to
   (A) regorge　　　　(C) retain
   (B) redirect　　　　(D) realign

4. The ability to **move**
   (A) motility　　　　(C) futility
   (B) disability　　　(D) tranquillity

5. One of the **turns** of a spiral shell
   (A) statute　　　　(C) parachute
   (B) institute　　　 (D) volute

6. A strong, **driving** force
   (A) impasse　　　 (C) implant
   (B) impulse　　　　(D) impound

7. To **come** together
   - (A) convey
   - (B) contort
   - (C) convene
   - (D) conjure

8. **Made** complete and without flaw
   - (A) perfused
   - (B) permeated
   - (C) personified
   - (D) perfected

9. To **carry** or bear the weight of something
   - (A) supplant
   - (B) support
   - (C) suppurate
   - (D) suppress

10. Not able to be **pulled** away from one's decision
    - (A) intractable
    - (B) invigorated
    - (C) introverted
    - (D) insolvent

EXERCISE 9-I
- Fill in the Blank (one cue)
- Skill: word parts

*Use a **meaning** from List 2 to fill in the blank in each statement. The word part whose meaning you are defining will be found inside the boldfaced word. **Do not use a dictionary**. Do not focus on the size or difficulty of the words. Look only for the simple word part; it will lead you to the correct answer.*

Example: √**Reporting** involves _____ing news to other people.

   Answer: *carrying* [> PORT]

1. Actions that _____ observers away in disgust are **repulsive**.
2. To **retain** something is to _____ it, to keep possession of it.
3. Someone who is **beatific** has been _____ blissfully happy.

4. **Seclusion** involves _____ someone away from distractions.
5. To _____ or burst inward suddenly is to **irrupt**.
6. To **convene** a meeting is to invite people to _____ together.
7. The **tractor** feed of a dot-matrix printer is a mechanism that _____ the paper into place by using pins that catch in the perforations along the edges of the paper.
8. The _____ of a wheel is called a **revolution**.
9. A **fictional** story is _____ up.
10. To **prevent** something is to stop it before it _____ about.
11. **Comportment** refers to the way that people _____ themselves—their behavior.
12. An **impulse** _____ us into action.
13. **Tenets** are beliefs that people _____ as true.
14. **Motile** cells are capable of _____ spontaneously.
15. A **volvulus** is an intestinal _____ing or twisting that causes an obstruction.

EXERCISE 9-J
- **Fill in the Blank (no cue)**
- **Skills: word parts, context**

*Once again, use a **meaning** from List 2 to fill in the blank in each statement. This time, however, you will have to find the word part yourself in the difficult or technical word.* **Do not use a dictionary.** *Do not focus on the size or difficulty of the words. Look only for the simple word part; it will lead you to the correct answer.*

Example: √A ruptured pipe has a _____ in it.

Answer: *break* [> RUPT]

1. To retain is to continue to _____ or have something.
2. A revolving door _____ in a circular course.

3. A recluse _____ himself or herself away from society.
4. A tenacious person _____ on even in the face of obstacles.
5. To _____ in on someone's conversation is to interrupt.
6. When an army mobilizes, it is ready to _____.
7. When you portage a canoe, you _____ it.
8. An inventor _____ upon something new through imagination and work.
9. A broken limb may be set in traction to _____ it back in place.
10. An immovable object cannot be _____.
11. When you compel someone, you _____ him or her into a course of action.
12. Anything that facilitates _____ something else easier.
13. To preclude is to _____ something out so it can't happen.
14. A defective piece of machinery fails to _____ what it was built for.
15. To convene a meeting is to invite people to _____ together.

PEL means push and TRACT means pull,
And though I cannot prove it.
MOB and MOT are stronger still
Since either one can move it.

EXERCISE 9-K
- **Matching Columns**
- **Skill: word parts**

Memory check. Do not look back at List 2 or use a dictionary.

1. _____ FAC   (a) break
2. _____ TRACT   (b) carry
3. _____ PORT   (c) come
4. _____ VOLV   (d) make

5. ____ RUPT   (e) hold
6. ____ CLUD   (f) move
7. ____ MOT   (g) pull
8. ____ PEL   (i) push
9. ____ -TAIN   (j) close
10. ____ VEN   (k) turn

EXERCISE 9-L
- Fill in (two cues)
- Skills: word parts, dictionary, context

*To finish each word, fill in the blank with one of the **word parts** from your version of List 2. **You must use a college-level dictionary** to make sure that what you write really is a word and that it fits in the sentence. The word in boldface will give you the meaning of the word part that you must write.*

Example: √When a wheel **turns**, it re_ _ _ _es.

        Answer: *VOLV* [> turns]

1. To pre_ _ _ _e a possibility is to **shut** out any hope of it happening.
2. Something that has been **made** contaminated by disease is in_ _ _ted.
3. Inter_ _ _ _ion is the act of **coming** between disagreeing people.
4. To be in_ _ _ _ed is to have **turned** your time and attention to something.
5. Com_ _ _ _sion is an uncontrollable **drive** to do something.
6. The religious observance of Ad_ _ _t commemorates the **coming** of Christ.
7. A _ _ _simile is a copy **made** exactly like the original.
8. A com_ _ _ion is an agitated **movement** or disturbance.
9. To re_ _ _ _ is to **carry** news to someone.
10. To **drive** something away is to re_ _ _ it.

11. Im____s consist of goods **carried** into a country.
12. A con_____ed argument twists and **turns** all over the place.
13. To in___t someone is to **make** that person diseased or contaminated.
14. A cor_____ politician has **broken** the rules of conduct.
15. A ___ile organism has the power to **move** on its own.

EXERCISE 9-M
- Fill in (one cue)
- Skills: word parts, dictionary, context

*Continue filling in **word parts** as you have been doing from your version of List 2, **using a college-level dictionary** to check on accuracy. This time, however, there will be no word in boldface. You will have to search the sentence for a clue.*

Example: √A re____sive sight drives our gaze away.

  Answer: *PUL* [> drives]

1. To ex_____ goods is to carry them for sale out of a country.
2. When you are unable to con_____ a laugh, you cannot hold it in.
3. A de_____or attempts to pull down someone's reputation.
4. When a living form changes and turns into another form, it is said to e____e.
5. To pre_____e something is to shut it down so it doesn't happen.
6. A cor____ government has broken down in its character and integrity.
7. The ability to hold on even in the face of opposition is called ____acity.
8. The power to move people to accomplish something is called ___ivation.
9. A manu____turer makes products on a large scale.
10. Pro___sion is the force that drives something forward or onward.

11. Ex___ion involves shutting someone out from an activity.
12. An at_____ion pulls us toward someone or something.
13. The ability to move freely is called ___ility.
14. A sopori___ is a preparation that makes people sleepy.
15. The fitting together of upper and lower teeth when the jaws are closed is called oc____ion.

EXERCISE 9-N
- **Paragraph Examples**
- **Skills: word parts, dictionary, context**

Answer these four questions after each paragraph:

(a) *What word part inside the boldfaced word helps you to understand that word? What does that word part mean?*

(b) *Using only the context of the word and the word part that it contains, what do you think the boldfaced word means? (See Chapter 1, Section 2.)*

(c) *Choose one context clue that helped you. (See Chapter 1, Section 2.)*
  1. *word signals*
  2. *punctuation signals*
  3. *synonyms (substitution)*
  4. *examples or description*
  5. *contrast or opposites*
  6. *prior knowledge; common sense*
     If 6, explain: _____

(d) *How does the dictionary define the boldfaced word as it is used in the paragraph?*

1. Linnaeus's system of classification had two kingdoms, the plants (Plantae) and animals (Animalia). This seemed reasonable in his day, since the familiar land plants and animals were clearly different. Plants did not move around; they did not eat, but seemed to need only water in order to grow. Animals were **motile**; that is, they could move from place to place. Animals had

to eat plants, or each other. Today, however, it is apparent that many forms of life do not fit neatly into either the plant or the animal camp.

[Karen Arms, et al., *A Journey into Life*, 3rd Ed., 362]

(a) _____
(b) _____
(c) _____
(d) _____

2. In 1961, the ruling in the case of Mapp v. Ohio incorporated Fourth Amendment protections against "unreasonable searches and seizures." This ruling limits the power of police to gather evidence without a proper search warrant. In particular, illegally obtained evidence cannot be used in a trial as a basis for convicting a defendant. The case involved a search of the house of Dollree Mapp. Police were looking for evidence relating to the bombing of the house of Don King, who later became a famed boxing promoter. What the police found, instead, was pornographic material which they seized and used in successfully prosecuting Mapp. The Supreme Court ruling **excluding** the use of this illegally obtained evidence against Mapp has become known as the exclusionary rule.

[W. Lance Bennett, *Inside the System*, 164]

(a) _____
(b) _____
(c) _____
(d) _____

3. In 1785, Charles Augustin Coulomb (1736–1806) established the fundamental law of electric force between two stationary charged particles. Experiments show that an electric force has the following properties:
   (1) It is inversely proportional to the square of the separation, r, between the two particles and is along the line joining them.
   (2) It is proportional to the product of the magnitudes of the charges $|q_1|$ and $|q_2|$ on the two particles.
   (3) It is attractive if the charges are of opposite sign and **repulsive** if the charges have the same sign.

[Serway & Faughn, *College Physics*, 3rd Ed., 506]

(a) _____
(b) _____

268 CHAPTER 9 ACTION

     (c) _____
     (d) _____

4. Today, at least 50 genetic tests for hereditary diseases are available; by the turn of the century, DNA tests are almost certain to be a standard part of medical exams. From a single sample of a patient's blood, doctors will be able to spot genetic mutations that signal the approach not only of rare hereditary diseases but also the common killers, including breast cancer, heart disease, and diabetes—and defeat them. For all its promise, the ability to glimpse the future will not come without costs. Knowing a patient's genetic predispositions will be central to **preventive** medicine, a keystone of health care reform.

                      [Shannon Brownlee, et al., "Genes and Cancer,"
                                U.S. News & World Report, 22 Aug. 1994, 94]

     (a) _____
     (b) _____
     (c) _____
     (d) _____

5. Lakes can be divided into categories based on how much plant life they support. Eutrophic ("good food") lakes are rich in nutrients and organisms and are usually shallow. Such lakes **contain** little oxygen because decomposer organisms rapidly use it up, metabolizing the organic matter produced by the lake's many other residents. In the normal course of events, a lake ages as it is steadily filled in with minerals and organic matter, becoming more eutrophic as it ages. Natural eutrophication takes thousands of years, but the process may be speeded up to take only a few years if the lake becomes polluted. When nutrients in sewage or minerals such as chemical fertilizers wash into a lake, they speed plant growth and hence eutrophication.

                             [Arms, et al., *A Journey into Life,* 3rd Ed., 760]

A CAPtion **holds** notations,
seCLUSion **shuts** apart;
TENsion **holds** frustrations,
And eMOTion **moves** the heart.

     (a) _____
     (b) _____
     (c) _____
     (d) _____

SECTION 3: CHAPTER REVIEW (LISTS 1 AND 2 COMBINED)

Word Parts Covered in This Chapter:

WORD PART	MEANING	COMMON EXAMPLE	TEXTBOOK EXAMPLE
CAP	take; hold	*capture*	*encapsulated*
CED	move; go	*recede*	*precedent*
CEP	take; hold	*accept*	*receptor*
CESS	move; go	*recess*	*intercessory*
CID	kill	*homicide*	*regicide*
CIP	take; hold	*recipient*	*incipient*
CIS	cut	*incision*	*precision*
CLUD	shut; close	*include*	*preclude*
CLUS	shut; close	*seclusion*	*recluse*
CUR	run; flow	*current*	*incur*
CURS	run; flow	*cursory*	*incursive*
FAC	do; make	*factory*	*factitious*
FEC	do; make	*effect*	*defective*
FER	carry; bear	*offer*	*proffer*
FIC	do; make	*fiction*	*honorific*
FLECT	bend	*reflect*	*flection*
FLEX	bend	*flexible*	*reflexive*
FRACT	break	*fracture*	*fractionate*
FRAG	break	*fragile*	*fragmentation*
MOB	move	*mobile*	*mobility*
MOT	move	*remote*	*motile*
MOV	move	*movement*	*removable*
MUT	change	*mutant*	*immutable*
PEL	push; drive	*compel*	*repellent*
PUL	push; drive	*impulse*	*repulsion*
PORT	carry	*support*	*deportment*
RUPT	break or burst	*interrupt*	*irruption*
SEQU	follow	*sequel*	*sequela*
-TAIN	hold	*maintain*	*containment*
TEN	hold	*tenant*	*tenable*
TRACT	pull	*tractor*	*retractable*
VEN	come	*intervene*	*convene*
VENT	come	*intervention*	*convention*
-VERGE	turn; bend	*converge*	*diverge*
VERS	turn; bend	*reverse*	*versatility*
VERT	turn; bend	*convert*	*vertiginous*
VOLUT	turn	*revolution*	*involute*
VOLV	turn	*revolve*	*volvulus*

Copyright © 1996 Harcourt Brace & Company. All rights reserved.

PRE-EXERCISE ACTIVITY 3
- **List Making**
- **Skill: word parts**

*In the blanks that follow, rewrite the combined word parts list. This time, however, reverse the order by writing the **meanings** in the first column. Then gather all the word parts in the list which have that meaning and write them on one line in the second column. This will let you make necessary connections and help you in the process of long-term memorization. The first one has already been done to show you how.*

	MEANING	WORD PARTS	
1.	bear	fer	*Note:* This list will be more useful if you write it in alphabetical order.
2.			
3.			
4.			
5.			
6.			
7.			
8.			
9.			
10.			
11.			
12.			
13.			
14.			
15.			
16.			
17.			
18.			
19.			
20.			

Continued

21. _____	_____
22. _____	_____
23. _____	_____

EXERCISE 9-O
- **Matching Columns**
- **Skill: word parts**

Memory check. Do not look back at the combined list or use a dictionary.

1. _____ CLUD   (a) move; go
2. _____ MUT   (b) kill; cut
3. _____ VOLUT   (c) follow
4. _____ FIC   (d) hold
5. _____ CID   (e) shut; close
6. _____ PEL   (f) turn
7. _____ CESS   (g) do; make
8. _____ TEN   (h) break
9. _____ RUPT   (i) push; drive
10. _____ SEQU   (j) change

EXERCISE 9-P
- **Cross Out**
- **Skills: dictionary, word parts, context**

*One word in each set does not contain the word part and meaning that is given even though it has a set of similar letters. Use a **college-level dictionary** to find the one that does **not** fit.*

	Example:	WORD PART	MEANING	CROSS OUT THE ONE WORD THAT DOES NOT FIT.
		√PEL	push; drive	repel, peloid, compel

Answer: The dictionary shows that *repel* and *compel* have the meaning *push* or *drive* in their definitions. *Peloid* (mud) does not; cross it out.

	WORD PART	MEANING	CROSS OUT THE ONE WORD THAT DOES NOT FIT.
1.	FAC	do; make	facial, facilitate, factitious
2.	PORT	carry	import, portfolio, proportion
3.	CUR	run	recurrent, curtail, incurred
4.	CED	move; go	precede, recede, cedilla
5.	TEN	hold	tenacious, tenable, tendinitis
6.	VERT	turn; bend	covert, divert, extrovert
7.	CIS	cut; kill	precise, cistern, incision
8.	MOT	move	motility, demoted, motley
9.	PUL	push; drive	pulverize, impulse, propulsion
10.	VENT	come	convention, venture, ventriloquist

EXERCISE 9-Q

- **Extended Answer**
- **Skills: word parts, dictionary, context**

Answer the following questions by using a college-level dictionary.

Example: √How is the meaning *break* involved in the word **fracture**?

Answer: A fracture is the breaking of a bone, cartilage, or the like.

1. How is the meaning *carry* involved in the word **inference**?

2. How is the meaning *made* involved in the word **fictitious**?

3. How is the meaning *kill* involved in the word **sororicide?**

4. How is the meaning *run* involved in the word **recurrence?**

5. How is the meaning *turn* involved in the word **devolve?**

6. How is the meaning *follow* involved in the word **sequence?**

7. How is the meaning *move* involved in the word **immobilize?**

8. How is the meaning *shut* involved in the word **seclusion?**

9. How is the meaning *turn* involved in the word **conversion?**

10. How is the meaning *carry* involved in the word **comportment?**

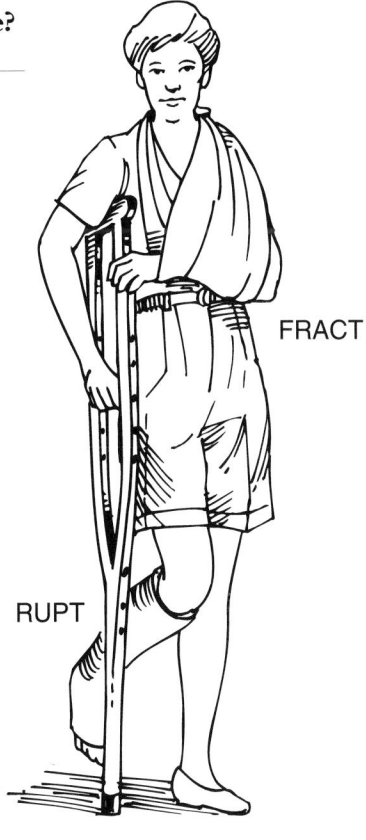

FRACT

RUPT

A fracture is a nasty break,
A rupture is torn tissue;
Unless precautions you do take,
We're really going to miss you.

EXERCISE 9-R
- **Fill in the Blank**
- **Skills: word parts, context**

Answer each question by filling in the blank. Use the combined list.

Example: √A synonym for *hold* is _____ .   Answer: *grasp*

1. A synonym for *come* is _____ .
2. A synonym for *do* is _____ .

Copyright © 1996 Harcourt Brace & Company. All rights reserved.

3. A synonym for *shut* is _____ .
4. A synonym for *pull* is _____ .
5. A synonym for *carry* is _____ .
6. A synonym for *move* is _____ .
7. A synonym for *kill* is _____ .
8. A synonym for *make* is _____ .
9. A synonym for *break* is _____ .
10. A synonym for *follow* is _____ .

EXERCISE 9-S
- **Fill in the Blanks**
- **Skill: word parts**

Memory check. Do not look back at the combined list or use a dictionary.

1. Name two word parts that mean *push*: _____ and _____ .
2. Name two word parts that mean *close*: _____ and _____ .
3. Name two word parts that mean *hold*: _____ and _____ .
4. Name two word parts that mean *make*: _____ and _____ .
5. Name two word parts that mean *come*: _____ and _____ .
6. Name two word parts that mean *bend*: _____ and _____ .
7. Name two word parts that mean *break*: _____ and _____ .
8. Name two word parts that mean *move*: _____ and _____ .
9. Name two word parts that mean *carry*: _____ and _____ .

EXERCISE 9-T
- **Paragraph Examples**
- **Skills: word parts, dictionary, context**

Answer these four questions after each paragraph:

(a) *What word part inside the boldfaced word helps you to understand that word? What does that word part mean?*

(b) *Using only the context of the word and the word part that it contains, what do you think the boldfaced word means? (See Chapter 1, Section 2.)*

(c) *Choose one context clue that helped you. (See Chapter 1, Section 2.)*

   1. *word signals*   4. *examples or description*
   2. *punctuation signals* 5. *contrast or opposites*
   3. *synonyms (substitution)* 6. *prior knowledge; common sense*
       If 6, explain: _____

(d) *How does the dictionary define the boldfaced word as it is used in the paragraph?*

1. Another sign of corporate cluelessness is a tendency on the part of management to **diversify** into fields far from the organization's central core, frequently through unwise mergers or acquisitions. The underlying psychology is often clear enough. Says Lawrence Graev, a prominent New York lawyer and dealmaker: "The guys running big companies know they have a limited time to make an impact, and they can be tempted to look for a panacea. Merger and acquisition can be a panacea."
   [Kenneth Labich, "Why Companies Fail," *Fortune*, 14 Nov. 1994, 53–54]

   (a) _____
   (b) _____
   (c) _____
   (d) _____

2. If you see a coin on the bottom of a swimming pool and want to dive for it, where do you aim? Not right at the coin, because **refraction** makes it hard for you to locate it. Instead, when you dive for the coin, aim in front of it. Refraction can also be

illustrated by holding a pencil in a glass of water so that the upper half of the pencil is above the water surface. When you view the pencil with your eye level to the water's surface, it will appear to be broken.

[Heimler & Price, *Focus on Physical Science*, 356]

(a) _____
(b) _____
(c) _____
(d) _____

3. The primary desire in all experiments is reduction of confusing variables: we bring all the buzzing and blooming confusion of the external world into our laboratories and, holding all else constant in our artificial simplicity, try to vary just one potential factor at a time. But many subjects defy the use of such an experimental method—particularly most social phenomena—because **importation** into the laboratory destroys the subject of the investigation, and then we must yearn for simplifying guides in nature.

[Stephen J. Gould, "Curveball," *New Yorker*, 28 Nov. 1994, 139]

(a) _____
(b) _____
(c) _____
(d) _____

4. In the second stage of the mate-selection process, the couple compares their values. They discuss their attitudes towards work, marriage, religion, culture, and society. The more similar their views are, the more likely it is that the attraction will deepen, since such **concurrence** enhances each party's self-image. Similar values and interests also lead to shared activities through which the couple may further confirm their suitability.

[Kathleen Berger, *The Developing Person Through the Life Span*, 2nd ed., 164]

(a) _____
(b) _____
(c) _____
(d) _____

5. There are four types of springs—springs that push, pull, bend, and twist. Compression springs, usually in the shape of a coil, push outward, thus compressing whatever it is that they exert their pressure on. Expansion springs pull toward the center of

the spring, thus expanding the length of the item being pulled. **Flexion** springs are usually flat strips of metal that bend at the center, thus creating a force at the ends. Torsion springs, which variously take the shape of a rod, a coil, or a flat strip of metal, create pressure by twisting.

[Walter Franklin, *Homeowner's Guide*, 117]

(a) _____
(b) _____
(c) _____
(d) _____

6. Many of the approximately 1,000 species of gymnosperm are **conifers**. Common temperate-zone conebearers are the pines, firs, spruces, cedars, and hemlocks. The giant California redwoods and the gnarled, ancient bristlecone pines also belong to this group.

[Greulach & Chiapetta, *Biology*, 417]

(a) _____
(b) _____
(c) _____
(d) _____

7. A revolution in surgery stemming mainly from innovative technology has changed what you may expect from your next operation. The key development: endoscopic surgery. Endoscopic surgery relies on the endoscope, a pencil-thin, hollow tube with its own lighting system and miniature video camera. It allows a surgeon to see inside your body without "cutting you open." Your surgeon inserts the endoscope through a tiny **incision** less than an inch long. Then while viewing the procedure on a video screen, your surgeon operates with miniature instruments inserted through one or more other small incisions.

["Endoscopic Surgery," *The Mayo Clinic Health Letter*, September 1994, 6]

(a) _____
(b) _____
(c) _____
(d) _____

8. Even though social scientists recognize that there is great variation in normal and deviant behavior and that no science can determine what acts are inherently deviant, there are certain acts

that are almost universally accepted as being deviant. For example, parent-child incest is severly disapproved of in nearly every society. **Genocide**, the willful killing of specific groups of people—as occurred in the Nazi extermination camps during World War II—also is considered to be wrong even if it is sanctioned by the government or an entire society.
    [Henry L. Tischler, *Introduction to Sociology*, 4th Ed., 120]

(a) _____
(b) _____
(c) _____
(d) _____

9, 10. No one knows exactly why female polar bears den in concentrated groups when they have so much potential denning habitat to choose from. Scientists believe that the need for **seclusion** may encourage bears to use a small number of areas that are free of disturbance. Once a female successfully rears cubs in a denning area, she will return to the same general area for each **subsequent** litter, as will her female offspring.
    [Wayne Lynch, "Den Mothers and Their Cubs," *International Wildlife*, November–December 1994, 15]

(a) _____
(b) _____
(c) _____
(d) _____

(a) _____
(b) _____
(c) _____
(d) _____

CHAPTER 10 QUALITIES

SECTION 1

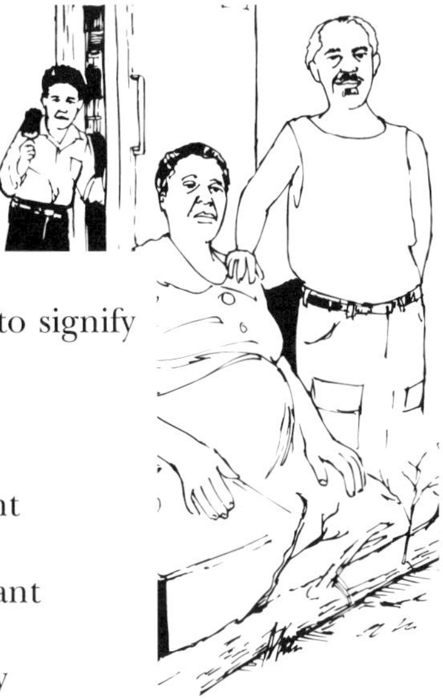

List 1
Here are some word parts that are used to signify qualities.

WORD PART	MEANING
BENE	good; pleasant
BIO	alive or life
CACO	bad; unpleasant
CAL	hot; warm
CELER	fast or speedy
CRYO	cold
DEBIL	weak
DUR	hard; lasting
FORC	strong
FORT	strong
JUVEN	young
LEN	soft; gentle; weak
MORT	dead or death
PLEN	full
PLET	full
SEN	old

PRE-EXERCISE ACTIVITY 1
- **List Making**
- **Skill: word parts**

*In the blanks that follow, rewrite List 1. This time, however, reverse the order by writing the **meanings** in the first column. Then gather all the word parts in the list which have that meaning and write them on one line in the second column. This will let you make necessary connections and help you in the process of long-term memorization. The first one has already been done to show you how.*

	MEANING	WORD PARTS	
1.	alive; life	bio	*Note:* This list will be more useful if you write it in alphabetical order.
2.	_____	_____	
3.	_____	_____	
4.	_____	_____	
5.	_____	_____	
6.	_____	_____	
7.	_____	_____	
8.	_____	_____	
9.	_____	_____	
10.	_____	_____	
11.	_____	_____	
12.	_____	_____	
13.	_____	_____	
14.	_____	_____	
15.	_____	_____	
16.	_____	_____	
17.	_____	_____	
18.	_____	_____	
19.	_____	_____	

Copyright © 1996 Harcourt Brace & Company. All rights reserved.

EXERCISE 10-A
- Multiple Choice
- Skill: word parts

A meaning is in boldface for each of the following phrases. From the four choices given, pick the one answer which contains a word part with that meaning. Use both versions of List 1 to help you. **Do not use a dictionary.** *Do not focus on the size or difficulty of the words. Look only for the simple word part; it will lead you to the correct answer.*

Example: √**Gentleness** or mildness
    (A) vitality   (C) vacuity
    (B) lenity   (D) salubrity

    Answer: (B) The reason for this answer is that the LEN part of *lenity* means "gentle."

1. **Strength** of mind
   (A) fortitude   (C) gratitude
   (B) latitude   (D) plenitude

2. The study of **living** matter
   (A) geology   (C) teleology
   (B) philology   (D) biology

3. A person who supervises the preparation of the **dead** for burial
   (A) obstetrician   (C) mortician
   (B) dietician   (D) clinician

4. Bringing about or doing **good**
   (A) magnificent   (C) beneficent
   (B) permanent   (D) maleficent

5. To **strengthen** against attack
   (A) mortify   (C) fortify
   (B) verify   (D) putrefy

6. An instrument for measuring very **cold** temperatures
   (A) thermometer   (C) hygrometer
   (B) cryometer   (D) sclerometer

7. The process of growing **old**
   - (A) juvenescence
   - (B) fluorescence
   - (C) senescence
   - (D) convalescence

8. The study of the activities of **living** organisms
   - (A) thermodynamics
   - (B) biodynamics
   - (C) isodynamics
   - (D) geodynamics

9. A **full** assembly, as a joint legislative assembly
   - (A) plectrum
   - (B) phenol
   - (C) presage
   - (D) plenum

10. Growing warm or increasing in **heat**
    - (A) marcescent
    - (B) calescent
    - (C) effervescent
    - (D) senescent

EXERCISE 10-B
- Fill in the Blank (one cue)
- Skill: word parts

*Use a **meaning** from List 1 to fill in the blank in each statement. The word part whose meaning you are defining will be found inside the boldfaced word. **Do not use a dictionary.** Do not focus on the size or difficulty of the words. Look only for the simple word part; it will lead you to the correct answer.*

Example: √A **cryometer** measures extremely _____ temperatures.

   Answer: *cold* [> CRYO]

1. A greeting that expresses _____ wishes is **benedictory**.
2. An argument that is _____ is **forceful**.
3. A **juvenile** is a _____ person.
4. To **decelerate** is to ease up on the _____ .
5. **Biodynamics** deals with the activity of _____ organisms.
6. To **accelerate** is to increase the _____ .
7. Something that is **durable** is _____ and lasting.

8. **Calories** are used to measure the _____ output of an organism.
9. **Lenient** punishment is _____ and merciful.
10. Something **complete** is _____ly done.
11. A **debility** is an abnormal _____ness.
12. A **mortiferous** disease is _____ly.
13. **Cryogenics** is the branch of physics that deals with very _____ temperatures.
14. **Plenipotent** means invested with or possessing _____ power.
15. **Cacography** is _____ handwriting.

EXERCISE 10-C
- Fill in the Blank (no cue)
- Skills: word parts, context

*Once again, use a **meaning** from List 1 to fill in the blank in each statement. This time, however, you will have to find the word part yourself in the difficult or technical word. **Do not use a dictionary.** Do not focus on the size or difficulty of the words. Look only for the simple word part; it will lead you to the correct answer.*

Example: √Literary or artistic work by _____ people is called juvenilia.

                Answer: *young* [> JUVEN]

1. A debilitating disease makes the victim _____.
2. Repletion is the condition of being _____.
3. A person's _____ point is his or her forte.
4. Originally, a senate was a governing body of _____ people.
5. Something perdurable is long-_____.
6. Immortal means not subject to _____.
7. Caloricity is the ability that animals have to produce _____.

CHAPTER 10 QUALITIES

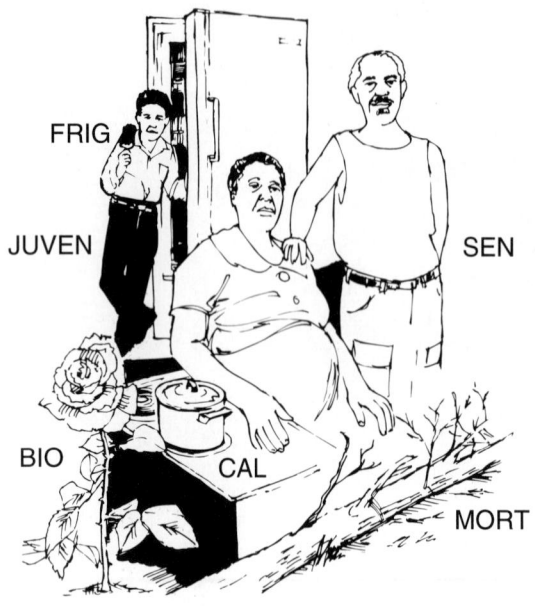

FRIG
JUVEN
SEN
BIO
CAL
MORT

JUVEN, SEN—young and old;
CAL and FRIG—hot and cold.
BIO means a livng thing;
MORT refers to death's cruel sting.

8. An accelerant is designed to make a process _____ .
9. A fortification is _____ enough to withstand attack.
10. A durable cover is _____ and protective.
11. Doing _____ things to others is known as benefaction.
12. Bioastronautics studies the effect of space travel on _____ things.
13. A lenis consonant has a relatively _____ sound effect.
14. In ecology, the cryochore is the region of perpetual _____ .
15. Cacodyl is a chemical that combines with other elements to form a _____ odor.

EXERCISE 10-D
- **Matching Columns**
- **Skill: word parts**

Memory check. Do not look back at List 1 or use a dictionary.

1. ___ CRYO   (a) good
2. ___ BIO   (b) fast
3. ___ PLET   (c) cold
4. ___ BENE   (d) soft
5. ___ CAL   (e) weak
6. ___ LEN   (f) bad
7. ___ JUVEN   (g) alive
8. ___ CELER   (h) hot
9. ___ CACO   (i) young
10. ___ DEBIL   (j) full

Copyright © 1996 Harcourt Brace & Company. All rights reserved.

EXERCISE 10-E
- **Fill in (two cues)**
- **Skills: word parts, dictionary, context**

To finish each word, fill in the blank with one of the **word parts** *from your version of List 1.* **You must use a college-level dictionary** *to make sure that what you write really is a word and that it fits in the sentence. The word in boldface will give you the meaning of the word part that you must write.*

Example: √A _ _ _ _ stat is an automatic apparatus that maintains a very **cold** constant temperature.

Answer: *CRYO* [> cold]

1. A **young** offender is called a _ _ _ _ ile delinquent.
2. _ _ _ _ ity is a **weakened** state.
3. When you re _ _ _ ish a glass, you **fill** it again.
4. To rein _ _ _ _ e is to make something **strong**.
5. The condition of being subject to **death** is called _ _ _ ality.
6. When you ac _ _ _ _ ate, you go **faster**.
7. _ _ _ _ volence is the disposition to do **good**.
8. **Strength** of mind and spirit is called _ _ _ itude.
9. When your money is de _ _ _ ed, your bank account is no longer **full**.
10. **Bad** handwriting is called _ _ _ graphy.
11. A _ _ _ cide is a substance capable of destroying **living** organisms.
12. Foods that produce **heat** are called _ _ _ orific.
13. In economics, _ _ _ able goods are those items that are **lasting** and reusable.
14. The physical and mental infirmities brought on by **old** age are known as _ _ _ ility.
15. **Unpleasant** and harsh sounds are referred to as _ _ _ phony.

EXERCISE 10-F
- **Fill in (one cue)**
- **Skills: word parts, dictionary, context**

*Continue filling in **word parts** from your version of List 1 as you have been doing, **using a college-level dictionary** to check accuracy. This time, however, there will be no word in boldface. You will have to search the sentence for a clue.*

Example: √ _ _ _ _therapy treats a condition by the use of cold, such as the application of ice packs.

Answer: *CRYO* [> cold]

1. A _ _ _ _ _itated patient is in a weakened condition.
2. Laws that are relatively soft, gentle, and permissive are _ _ _ient.
3. Something that is good for you is _ _ _ _ficial.
4. Ef_ _ _ _ is the amount of strength or hard work put into a project.
5. To en_ _ _ _e a law is to take strong measures to be sure it is observed.
6. _ _ _oric means relating to heat.
7. When something is _ _ _ _tiful, it is in full supply.
8. _ _ _rhythm is an inherent rhythm that appears to control various life processes.
9. Youthful traits or mannerisms are called _ _ _ _ _ilities.
10. En_ _ _ance is long-lasting energy.
11. Creatures that are subject to death are called _ _ _ _al.
12. _ _ _ _ _ity is speed or swiftness of motion.
13. A _ _ _efacient is a heating or warming agent.
14. A _ _ _ _stat is a device for automatically maintaining extremely cold temperatures.
15. The _ _ _sphere is that portion of the earth that can support living creatures.

EXERCISE 10-G
- **Paragraph Examples**
- **Skills: word parts, dictionary, context**

Answer these four questions after each paragraph:

(a) What word part inside the boldfaced word helps you to understand that word? What does that word part mean?

(b) Using only the context of the word and the word part that it contains, what do you think the boldfaced word means? (See Chapter 1, Section 2.)

(c) Choose one context clue that helped you. (See Chapter 1, Section 2.)
   1. word signals
   2. punctuation signals
   3. synonyms (substitution)
   4. examples or description
   5. contrast or opposites
   6. prior knowledge; common sense
      If 6, explain: _____

(d) How does the dictionary define the boldfaced word as it is used in the paragraph?

1. Flowering, setting of seeds and fruit, and germination of seeds are events in a plant's life that occur predictably in response to environmental or genetic factors. **Senescence,** the process of aging that makes all or part of a plant more susceptible to death, is also an integral part of its life history. A wheat plant turns yellow, dries up, and dies after it has set seed; a plum tree drops its fruits during a short period in early summer and loses all its leaves during the fall.
   [Karen Arms, et al., *A Journey into Life*, 3rd Ed., 721]
   (a) _____
   (b) _____
   (c) _____
   (d) _____

2. Since we throw out a television set far less frequently than we do the daily newspaper, we tend not to think about it as part of a solid waste problem. But the low profile of durable goods—everything from refrigerators, TV sets, and computers to calculators, thermostats, and fluourescent bulbs—belies their potential

impact on the environment. The manufacture of such complex products consumes considerable energy—to mine and refine materials, power the asembly plant, and transport goods from plant to store. And it gobbles up valuable natural resources, for although millions of Americans have become accustomed to filling recycling bins with newspapers, bottles, and cans, there's no recycling bin for durable goods. Some are impossible to repair; others are tossed because they're simply not worth repairing. Because few **durable** goods are recycled, the metals, plastic, and such used in making them generally go up in smoke or back into the ground, and are lost to future use.

["Out of Sight, Out of Mind?" *Consumer Reports,* February 1994, 99]

(a) _____
(b) _____
(c) _____
(d) _____

3. Cryosurgery is an experimental treatment for prostate cancer. A surgeon inserts metal probes into the prostate. Liquid nitrogen then circulates through the probes to freeze the gland. No long-term studies show how well **cryosurgery** destroys cancer or what complications are possible.
["Second Opinion," *The Mayo Clinic Health Letter,* October 1994, 8]

(a) _____
(b) _____
(c) _____
(d) _____

4. Physical anthropology (or, alternatively, biological anthropology) is the branch of anthropology that focuses on humans as **biological** organisms, and one of its many interests is human evolution. Through the analysis of fossils and the observation of living primates, the physical anthropologist tries to trace the ancestry of the human species in order to understand how, when, and why we became the kind of animal we are today.

[William A. Haviland, *Cultural Anthropology,* 7th Ed., 8]

(a) _____
(b) _____
(c) _____
(d) _____

5. Touch is the first of your senses to develop and usually the last to diminish. Newborn babies process most information through their skin. And even a frail 90-year-old with failing sight clearly understands the grasp of a caring hand. One of the most dramatic realizations regarding the power of human contact came earlier in this century. Pediatricians noticed that babies in orphanages and hospitals, who were not held and cuddled, failed to grow and often died. In the 1930s, Bellevue Hospital in New York City started a "mothering" policy to make sure babies were talked to, held, and cuddled. As a result, the infant **mortality** rate fell from 30 to 35 percent to less than 10 percent.
 ["Touch," *The Mayo Clinic Health Letter*, June 1994, 7]

(a) _____
(b) _____
(c) _____
(d) _____

SECTION 2

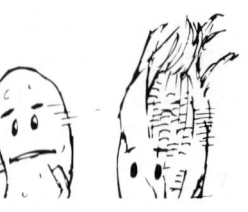

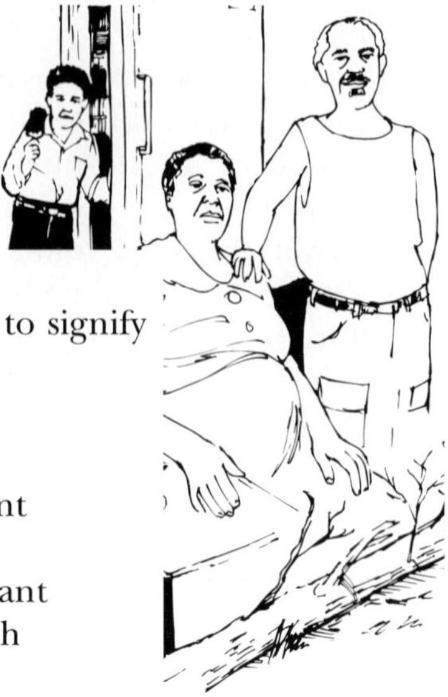

List 2

Here are more word parts that are used to signify qualities.

WORD PART	MEANING
EU	good; pleasant
FRIG	cold
MAL	bad; unpleasant
NECRO	dead or death
PATH	sick; disease
PSEUDO	false
SAN	healthy
SCLER	hard
TACH	fast
TACIT	quiet
TARD	slow
THERM	heat; hot; warm
VAC	empty
VER	true
VIT	alive or life
VIV	alive or life

PRE-EXERCISE ACTIVITY 2
- **List Making**
- **Skill: word parts**

*In the blanks that follow, rewrite List 2. This time, however, reverse the order by writing the **meanings** in the first column. Then gather all the word parts in the list which have that meaning and write them on one line in the second column. This will let you make necessary connections and help you in the process of long-term memorization. The first one has already been done to show you how.*

	MEANING	WORD PARTS	
1.	alive or life	vit, viv	*Note:* This list will be more useful if you write it in alphabetical order.
2.			
3.			
4.			
5.			
6.			
7.			
8.			
9.			
10.			
11.			
12.			
13.			
14.			
15.			
16.			
17.			
18.			
19.			

EXERCISE 10-H
- **Multiple Choice**
- **Skill: word parts**

A meaning is in boldface for each of the following phrases. From the four choices given, pick the one answer which contains a word part with that meaning. Use both versions of List 2 to help you. **Do not use a dictionary.** *Do not focus on the size or difficulty of the words. Look only for the simple word part; it will lead you to the correct answer.*

Example: √Causing or producing **cold**
    (A) calorific   (C) tenebrific
    (B) frigorific   (D) pacific

    Answer: (B) The reason for this answer is that the FRIG part of *frigorific* means "cold."

1. An instrument for measuring how **hot** something is
   - (A) thermometer
   - (B) cryometer
   - (C) hygrometer
   - (D) sclerometer

2. **Emptiness** or vacant space
   - (A) annuity
   - (B) perpetuity
   - (C) superfluity
   - (D) vacuity

3. An instrument for measuring the **hardness** of a substance, especially a mineral
   - (A) thermometer
   - (B) cryometer
   - (C) hygrometer
   - (D) sclerometer

4. **Pleasant** and agreeable sound
   - (A) cacophony
   - (B) euphony
   - (C) polyphony
   - (D) telephony

5. The medical science that studies the origin and nature of **disease**
   - (A) pathology
   - (B) biology
   - (C) cosmology
   - (D) philology

6. To confidently declare something as **true**
   - (A) assume
   - (B) abrade
   - (C) aver
   - (D) avenge

7. Wishing **bad** things on others
   - (A) confident
   - (B) benevolent
   - (C) diffident
   - (D) malevolent

8. A list of people who have **died** within a certain time
   - (A) biology
   - (B) necrology
   - (C) histology
   - (D) phrenology

9. A **false** name, often used to hide the identity of a writer
   - (A) heteronym
   - (B) pseudonym
   - (C) homonym
   - (D) synonym

10. A musical direction meaning **slow**
    - (A) tardo
    - (B) lento
    - (C) tacet
    - (D) molto

EXERCISE 10-I
- **Fill in the Blank (one cue)**
- **Skill: word parts**

Use a **meaning** from List 2 to fill in the blank in each statement. The word part whose meaning you are defining will be found inside the boldfaced word. **Do not use a dictionary.** Do not focus on the size or difficulty of the words. Look only for the simple word part; it will lead you to the correct answer.

Example: √**Necromancy** attempts to know the future by consulting the _____ .

   Answer: *dead* [> NECRO]

1. A **malefactor** is someone who does _____ things.
2. To **verify** is to prove that something is _____ .
3. A space entirely _____ of matter is called a **vacuum.**
4. Something **vivid** is full of _____ or animation.
5. **Unsanitary** conditions are not _____ .

294 CHAPTER 10 QUALITIES

6. A _____ adjustment or alteration is called a **maladaptation.**
7. Fire-**retardant** materials _____ the progress of a fire.
8. A **vita** is a brief account of one's _____, including career and education.
9. The science concerned with the conversion of mechanical energy into _____ is **thermodynamics.**
10. A **pathogen** is a _____-producing bacterium.
11. A **pseudomorph** is a _____ form, especially when one mineral imitates the appearance of another.
12. **Eugenic** means having _____ inherited characteristics.
13. Something **frigorific** causes _____.
14. A **tachometer** is an instrument that tells how _____ something is.
15. **Endothermic** reactions are the result of _____.

EXERCISE 10-J
- Fill in the Blank (no cue)
- Skills: word parts, context

Once again, use a **meaning** from List 2 to fill in the blank in each statement. This time, however, you will have to find the word part yourself in the difficult or technical word. **Do not use a dictionary.** Do not focus on the size or difficulty of the words. Look only for the simple word part; it will lead you to the correct answer.

Example: √Unsanitary conditions are un_____ conditions.

   Answer: *healthy* [> SAN]

1. A **maladroit** person handles situations _____ ly.
2. A **frigid** climate is very _____.
3. To **sanitize** is to make something _____ by eliminating dirt and germs.
4. A **taciturn** person is _____.

5. Vital signs indicate that a person is _____.
6. A vacuous look is an _____ look.
7. Veracious statements are _____.
8. A _____d condition of the nervous system is called neuropathy.
9. An abnormal fear of _____ is called necrophobia.
10. Eupepsia is _____ digestion.
11. Sclerenchyma is tough, _____ tissue that protects and supports plants.
12. Vivace is a musical direction meaning to play in a _____ly way.
13. Tardigrade animals are _____ in walking or moving.
14. Thermogenesis is the production of _____.
15. Pseudepigraphy means adding _____ names of authors to written works.

EXERCISE 10-K
- **Matching Columns**
- **Skill: word parts**

Memory check. Do not look back at List 2 or use a dictionary.

1. ____	FRIG	(a)	hard
2. ____	MAL	(b)	empty
3. ____	VAC	(c)	dead
4. ____	TACH	(d)	cold
5. ____	VIT	(e)	bad
6. ____	SCLER	(f)	slow
7. ____	EU	(g)	quiet
8. ____	NECRO	(h)	alive
9. ____	TACIT	(i)	pleasant
10. ____	TARD	(j)	fast

Celerity

EXERCISE 10-L
- Fill in (two cues)
- Skills: word parts, dictionary, context

*To finish each word, fill in the blank with one of the **word parts** from your version of List 2. **You must use a college-level dictionary** to make sure that what you write really is a word and that it fits in the sentence. The word in boldface will give you the meaning of the word part that you must write.*

Example: √A _ _ _ _ _ nym is a **false** name.

Answer: *PSEUDO* [> false]

1. To _ _ _ ify is to prove something **true**.
2. _ _ _ acity is **liveliness**.
3. A psycho _ _ _ has a **sick** mind.
4. An in _ _ _ e person does not have a **healthy,** balanced mind.
5. The power to **live** or grow is called _ _ _ ality.
6. _ _ _ _ id means very **cold** in temperature.
7. A speech that says **good** things about a person is known as a _ _ logy.
8. _ _ _ feasance is **bad** or unlawful conduct, especially by a public official.
9. To re _ _ _ _ a process is to **slow** it down.
10. A _ _ _ ant apartment is **empty.**
11. A **false** science, like astrology, is a _ _ _ _ _ _ science.
12. _ _ _ _ _ onuclear reactions require extremely **hot** temperatures.
13. The **death** of tissue caused by infection or burns is called _ _ _ _ _ sis.
14. An excessively **fast** heartbeat is called _ _ _ _ ycardia.
15. _ _ _ _ _ oderma is a disease in which connective body tissues become **hard.**

EXERCISE 10-M
- Fill in (one cue)
- Skills: word parts, dictionary, context

*Continue filling in **word parts** from your version of List 2 as you have been doing, **using a college-level dictionary** to check accuracy. This time, however, there will be no word in boldface. You will have to search the sentence for a clue.*

Example: √ _ _ _al signs are life signs.

   Answer: *VIT* [> life]

1. A _ _ _itarian is a specialist in public health.
2. Someone who commits bad deeds is a _ _ _efactor.
3. _ _phoria is an exaggerated pleasant feeling.
4. When a building is e_ _ _uated during a fire, it is emptied of all people.
5. A false pregnancy is called a _ _ _ _ _ _pregnancy.
6. _ _ _ _ology is the study of disease and its causes.
7. Someone who is _ _ _acious is lively.
8. _ _ _ification is the act of declaring something to be true.
9. A _ _ _ign person has bad intentions toward others.
10. _ _ _ _igrade means slow in pace or movement.
11. The hardening of a tissue or part is called _ _ _ _ _osis.
12. The abnormal fear of death or of corpses is called _ _ _ _ _phobia.
13. The _ _ _ _ometer is an instrument used to measure how fast an object is moving.
14. _ _ _ _ _urnity is the quality of being quiet or reserved in conversation.
15. _ _ _ _ _oplastic materials become soft in the presence of heat.

EXERCISE 10-N
- Paragraph Examples
- Skills: word parts, dictionary, context

Answer these four questions after each paragraph:

(a) *What word part inside the boldfaced word helps you to understand that word? What does that word part mean?*

(b) *Using only the context of the word and the word part that it contains, what do you think the boldfaced word means? (See Chapter 1, Section 2.)*

(c) *Choose one context clue that helped you. (See Chapter 1, Section 2.)*
   1. *word signals*
   2. *punctuation signals*
   3. *synonyms (substitution)*
   4. *examples or description*
   5. *contrast or opposites*
   6. *prior knowledge; common sense*
      If 6, explain: _____

(d) *How does the dictionary define the boldfaced word as it is used in the paragraph?*

1. Euthanasia, in Greek, means "the good death"—the active intervention of a doctor, usually at the patient's request, to bring that patient's life to an end. Even when asked for, euthanasia is illegal everywhere. In the United States it counts as assistance in a suicide; in Britain it is classed as attempted murder. In Holland, where since 1973 the practice has been winked at, the statutory penalty for **euthanasia** is up to twelve years in prison.
   [Henry L. Tischler, *Introduction to Sociology*, 4th Ed., 235]
   (a) _____
   (b) _____
   (c) _____
   (d) _____

2. A process in which an ideal gas expands (or is compressed) at a constant temperature is of such importance that we shall consider it separately from the processes described earlier. An expansion or compression of a substance at constant temperature is referred to as an isothermal process. The **isothermal** expansion

of a gas can be achieved by placing the gas in thermal contact with a heat reservoir at the same temperature.
           [Serway & Faughn, *College Physics*, 3rd Ed., 377]

   (a) _____
   (b) _____
   (c) _____
   (d) _____

3. In warm seasons and hot climes, few animals can long survive the full force of the sun's withering power. All species have an optimum internal temperature at which they function best. Too much sun, and the inner furnace oversteps its bounds. In overheated vertebrates, the body dehydrates, loss of fluid impedes blood flow, the brain **malfunctions**, and death strikes. For a desert creature, shade cast by a cactus across parched earth may mean survival.
           [Roger DiSilvestro, "Sweet Shadows," *International Wildlife*, November–December 1994, 51]

   (a) _____
   (b) _____
   (c) _____
   (d) _____

4. **Vital** signs are among the common observations made by physicians and nurses working with patients. They include measuring body temperature and blood pressure, and observing rates and types of pulse and breathing movements. There is a close relationship between these signs and the characteristics of life, since vital signs are the results of metabolic activities. In fact, death is recognized by the absence of such signs.
       [John W. Hole, Jr., *Human Anatomy and Physiology*, 4th Ed., 10]

   (a) _____
   (b) _____
   (c) _____
   (d) _____

5. About 3200 B.C., the local kingdoms of Egypt had grown powerful enough to check each other's ambitions, and constant war became a feature of life in the Nile Valley. During this period, the rulers of Hierakonpolis, which had become one of the royal centers, began again to use the old cemetery, continuing the ancient tradition of worship of the dead. The cemetery was built

300 CHAPTER 10 QUALITIES

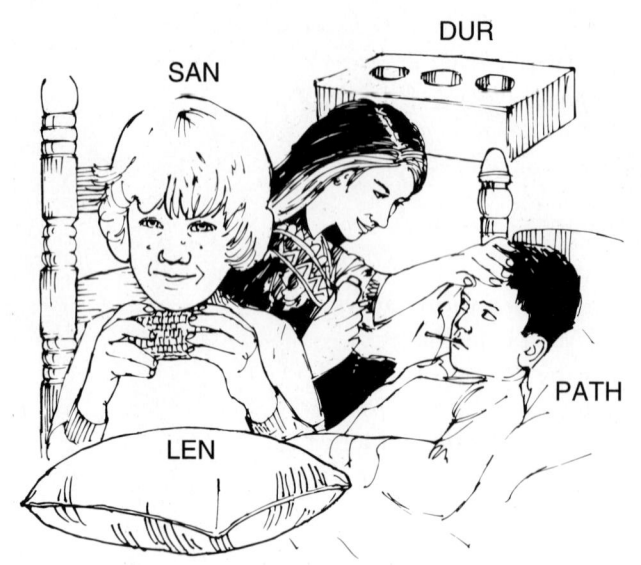

SCLER and DUR are tough and hard,
While LEN is soft and gentle.
SAN is wellness—health on guard—
But PATH is detrimental.

in the form of a **necropolis,** a city of the dead, to symbolize the society of the living. It was laid out along a dry stream (a *wadi*), which represented the Nile.

[Chodorow, et al., *The Mainstream of Civilization*, 6th Ed., 16]

(a) _____

(b) _____

(c) _____

(d) _____

SECTION 3: CHAPTER REVIEW (LISTS 1 AND 2 COMBINED)

Word Parts Covered in This Chapter:

WORD PART	MEANING	COMMON EXAMPLE	TEXTBOOK EXAMPLE
BENE	good; pleasant	*benefit*	*beneficence*
BIO	alive or life	*biography*	*bioluminescence*
CACO	bad; unpleasant	*cacophony*	*cacogenics*
CAL	hot; warm	*calorie*	*caloricity*
CELER	fast or speedy	*accelerate*	*celerity*
CRYO	cold	*cryogenics*	*cryoplankton*
DEBIL	weak	*debility*	*debilitate*
DUR	hard; lasting	*durable*	*duress*
EU	good; pleasant	*euphoria*	*eupepsia*
FORC	strong	*force*	*forcible*
FORT	strong	*effort*	*fortissimo*
FRIG	cold	*frigid*	*frigorific*
JUVEN	young	*juvenile*	*juvenescence*
LEN	soft; gentle; weak	*lenient*	*lenitive*
MAL	bad; unpleasant	*malicious*	*malignancy*
MORT	dead or death	*mortal*	*mortification*
NECRO	dead or death	*necrophilia*	*necrosis*
PATH	sick; disease	*pathologist*	*pathogenesis*
PLEN	full	*plenty*	*plenitude*
PLET	full	*complete*	*plethora*
PSEUDO	false	*pseudonym*	*pseudomorph*
SAN	healthy	*sanitation*	*sanative*
SCLER	hard	*sclerosis*	*scleroderma*
SEN	old	*senior citizen*	*senescence*
TACH	fast	*tachometer*	*tachycardia*
TACIT	quiet	*tacit*	*taciturnity*
TARD	slow	*tardy*	*tardigrade*
THERM	heat; hot; warm	*thermometer*	*thermotaxis*
VAC	empty	*vacant*	*vacuity*
VER	true	*verify*	*veracity*
VIT	alive or life	*vital*	*vitalism*
VIV	alive or life	*revive*	*viviparous*

Copyright © 1996 Harcourt Brace & Company. All rights reserved.

302   CHAPTER 10 QUALITIES

PRE-EXERCISE ACTIVITY 3
- List Making
- Skill: word parts

*In the blanks that follow, rewrite the combined word parts list. This time, however, reverse the order by writing the **meanings** in the first column. Then gather all the word parts in the list which have that meaning and write them on one line in the second column. This will let you make necessary connections and help you in the process of long-term memorization. The first one has already been done to show you how.*

	MEANING	WORD PARTS	
1.	alive	bio, vit, viv	*Note:* This list will be more useful if you write it in alphabetical order.
2.	_____	_____	
3.	_____	_____	
4.	_____	_____	
5.	_____	_____	
6.	_____	_____	
7.	_____	_____	
8.	_____	_____	
9.	_____	_____	
10.	_____	_____	
11.	_____	_____	
12.	_____	_____	
13.	_____	_____	
14.	_____	_____	
15.	_____	_____	
16.	_____	_____	
17.	_____	_____	
18.	_____	_____	
19.	_____	_____	
20.	_____	_____	*Continued*

21.	_____	_____
22.	_____	_____
23.	_____	_____
24.	_____	_____
25.	_____	_____
26.	_____	_____
27.	_____	_____

EXERCISE 10-O
- **Matching Columns**
- **Skill: word parts**

Memory check. Do not look back at the combined list or use a dictionary.

1. ____ BIO	(a) bad
2. ____ VER	(b) sick
3. ____ MAL	(c) old
4. ____ CELER	(d) empty
5. ____ VAC	(e) true
6. ____ SEN	(f) cold
7. ____ EU	(g) warm
8. ____ PATH	(h) good
9. ____ CRYO	(i) alive
10. ____ CAL	(j) fast

EXERCISE 10-P
- **Cross Out**
- **Skills: dictionary, word parts, context**

*One word in each set does not contain the word part and meaning that is given, even though it has a set of similar letters. Use a college-level dictionary to find the one that does **not** fit.*

	WORD		**CROSS OUT THE ONE WORD**
Example:	**PART**	**MEANING**	**THAT DOES NOT FIT.**
	√VER	true	veracity, verdant, verification

Answer: The dictionary shows that *veracity* and *verification* have the word *true* in their definitions. *Verdant* (green) does not; cross it out.

WORD PART	**MEANING**	**CROSS OUT THE ONE WORD THAT DOES NOT FIT.**
1. SAN	healthy	unsanitary, sanity, sanguine
2. CAL	hot; warm	calcareous, calorimeter, calescence
3. PLET	full	plethora, couplet, completion
4. CELER	fast	celery, celerity, accelerate
5. VIV	alive	revive, vivacious, viverrine
6. DUR	hard; lasting	duration, endure, durian
7. FORC	strong	forceps, forcible, reinforce
8. VAC	empty	vacillate, evacuate, vacuous
9. LEN	soft; gentle	lenity, leniency, lenticular
10. PATH	sick	pathology, psychopathic, pathfinder

EXERCISE 10-Q
- **Extended Answer**
- **Skills: word parts, dictionary, context**

Answer the following questions by using a college-level dictionary.

Example: √How is the meaning *old* involved in the word **senectitude**?

Answer: Senectitude means old age.

1. How is the meaning *slow* involved in the word **tardy?**

2. How is the meaning *living* involved in the word **biodegradable?**

3. How is the meaning *alive* involved in the word **survival?**

4. How is the meaning *good* involved in the word **benefactor?**

5. How is the meaning *false* involved in the word **pseudo-intellectual?**

6. How is the meaning *full* involved in the word **plenitude?**

7. How is the meaning *death* involved in the word **mortuary?**

8. How is the meaning *fast* involved in the word **tachistoscope?**

9. How is the meaning *cold* involved in the word **cryobiology?**

10. How is the meaning *bad* involved in the word **cacogenics?**

EXERCISE 10-R
- **Fill in the Blank**
- **Skills: word parts, context**

Answer each question by filling in the blank. Use the combined list.

Example: √The opposite of CRYO is _____.   Answer: THERM (etc.)

√A synonym for *dead* is _____.   Answer: *deceased*

1. The opposite of JUVEN is _____.   [Write another word part.]

Cryogenics is the art of
making dead folks freeze
In hopes that when they
wake up, they'll be cured
of their disease.
But every time I'm tempted,
one thing brings me to my
knees:
When the thermostat is
turned too low, I always
cough and sneeze.

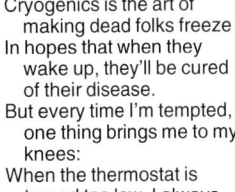

2. The opposite of MAL is _____. *[Write another word part.]*
3. The opposite of BIO is _____. *[Write another word part.]*
4. The opposite of DEBIL is _____. *[Write another word part.]*
5. The opposite of VAC is _____. *[Write another word part.]*
6. A synonym for *noisy* is _____. *[Write a regular word.]*
7. A synonym for *alive* is _____. *[Write a regular word.]*
8. A synonym for *sick* is _____. *[Write a regular word.]*
9. A synonym for *fast* is _____. *[Write a regular word.]*
10. A synonym for *cold* is _____. *[Write a regular word.]*

EXERCISE 10-S
- **Fill in the Blank**
- **Skill: word parts**

Memory check. Do not look back at the combined list or use a dictionary.

1. Name two word parts that mean *cold*: _____ and _____.
2. Name two word parts that mean *hot*: _____ and _____.
3. Name two word parts that mean *alive*: _____ and _____.
4. Name two word parts that mean *hard*: _____ and _____.
5. Name two word parts that mean *good*: _____ and _____.
6. Name two word parts that mean *fast*: _____ and _____.
7. Name two word parts that mean *strong*: _____ and _____.
8. Name two word parts that mean *dead*: _____ and _____.

Copyright © 1996 Harcourt Brace & Company. All rights reserved.

9. Name two word parts that
   mean *bad*: _____ and _____ .
10. Name two word parts that
    mean *full*: _____ and _____ .
11. Name two word parts that
    mean *weak*: _____ and _____ .

EXERCISE 10-T
- **Paragraph Examples**
- **Skills: word parts, dictionary, context**

Answer these four questions after each paragraph:

(a) What word part inside the boldfaced word helps you to understand that word? What does that word part mean?
   _____

(b) Using only the context of the word and the word part that it contains, what do you think the boldfaced word means? *(See Chapter 1, Section 2.)*
   _____

(c) Choose one context clue that helped you. *(See Chapter 1, Section 2.)*

   1. word signals   4. examples or description
   2. punctuation signals   5. contrast or opposites
   3. synonyms (substitution)   6. prior knowledge; common sense
      If 6, explain: _____

(d) How does the dictionary define the boldfaced word as it is used in the paragraph?
   _____

1. Most mammals are **viviparous** ("alive-bearing")—the young develop in the mother's uterus, nourished and supplied with oxygen by her blood, which flows through vessels close to those of the embryo. Viviparity permits the mammalian mother to remain mobile while incubating embryos that must be warm to survive. All female mammals nourish their young with milk produced in mammary glands.
   [Karen Arms, et al., *A Journey into Life*, 3rd Ed., 462]

(a) _____
(b) _____
(c) _____
(d) _____

2. On some beaches, sand is being removed faster than it is being **replenished.** When this happens, beaches become narrower and less attractive for swimming. Where erosion is severe, building close to the beach can be undermined and destroyed by waves as the shoreline moves inland on a disappearing beach. The sand moved from the beach may be redeposited in inconvenient places, such as across the mouth of a harbor where it must be dredged out periodically.

[Plummer & McGeary, *Physical Geology*, 206]

(a) _____
(b) _____
(c) _____
(d) _____

3. Scientists are rediscovering useful microbes that once were prevalent in farmland. Biological control, as the approach is known, has been harnessed for more than 100 years in the fight against insect infestations. But the field is still in its infancy when dealing with plant diseases. . . . Success rates at dealing with plant diseases have been lower using biocontrol methods. Yet biocontrols for plant **maladies** are beginning to edge their way into the marketplace.

[Peter N. Spotts, "Micro Bugs," *The Christian Science Monitor*, 15 Nov. 1994, 2]

(a) _____
(b) _____
(c) _____
(d) _____

4. Behaviorists are concerned that mental processes are private, not public, events that cannot be verified by observation or use of laboratory instruments. Sometimes mental processes are accepted as being present on the basis of self-report of the person experiencing them. Other times, however, mental processes can be indirectly **verified** by laboratory instruments, as in the case of dreams.

[Spencer A. Rathus, *Psychology*, 4th Ed., 2]

(a) _____
(b) _____
(c) _____
(d) _____

5. It is incorrect to call reptiles "cold-blooded." Most maintain a body temperature considerably higher than their surroundings, but they are **ectothermic,** taking most of their heat from the environment. Many reptiles must lie in the sun before they warm up enough to be active. Birds and mammals, on the other hand, are endothermic, generating most of their heat by their metabolism. Thus, they can be active at any time, which gives them an enormous advantage over reptiles.
　　　　　[Karen Arms, et al., *A Journey into Life,* 3rd Ed., 459]
(a) _____
(b) _____
(c) _____
(d) _____

6. On a calm, clear day in February 1977, Jack Corliss and two fellow explorers wedged themselves into the tiny, cramped cabin of the research submarine *Alvin,* said good-bye to the two support ships at the surface, and began a long descent into darkness. About 90 minutes later *Alvin* was gliding along the seafloor a mile and a half below the surface of the Pacific, and Corliss, a burly Oregon State University marine geologist, was peering out the porthole, searching for a phenomenon that had been suspected but never seen: submarine hot springs. Searchlights blazing, *Alvin* cruised through black water above the Galapagos Rift, an undersea volcanic ridge along the equator 200 miles west of Ecuador. It was in just such a place, Corliss and the others surmised, that these so-called **hydrothermal** vents would be found—if they existed.
　　　　　[Peter Radetsky, "How Did Life Start?" *Discover,*
　　　　　Special Issue, 1993, 34]
(a) _____
(b) _____
(c) _____
(d) _____

7. Many disease germs have had to evolve tricks to let them spread among potential victims. We've evolved countertricks, to which

the bugs have responded by evolving counter-countertricks. We and our **pathogens** are now locked in an escalating evolutionary contest, with the death of one contestant the price of defeat, and with natural selection playing the role of umpire.

[Jared Diamond, "The Arrow of Disease," *Discover*, Special Issue, 1993, 54]

(a) _____
(b) _____
(c) _____
(d) _____

8. The underlying disorder in multiple **sclerosis** is visible in the nervous system as small patches of abnormal tissue. The patches, originally perceived as a hardening of the nervous tissue, were the basis for the term "sclerosis," which comes from the Greek word meaning hard. These patches, ranging in size from a millimeter to several centimeters, have proved to be areas where the insulating material of the central nervous system, myelin, has been severely damaged or destroyed by attacking immune and inflammatory cells. The nerve cells themselves are not damaged, but without their myelin, which is formed by adjoining cells of another type, normal function is impossible.
[*Harvard Medical School Health Letter*, Volume 13, Number 1, p. 1]

(a) _____
(b) _____
(c) _____
(d) _____

9. For conservationists, what fuels the efforts to save the rainforests is the fear that **biodiversity**—a newly popular term that describes all aspects of biological diversity, including all the world's species as well as their genes, interactions, behaviors, and even the ecosystem they comprise—is taking a fast and furious nosedive. Hard data on the number of species lost each year are impossible to come by. But even conservative estimates show the situation to be bleak.

[Carol Kaesuk Yoon, "Drugs from Bugs," *Garbage*, Summer 1994, 24]

(a) _____
(b) _____
(c) _____
(d) _____

10. In psychology, stress is the demand made on an organism to adapt, to cope, or to adjust. Some stress is healthful and necessary to keep us alert and occupied. Stress researcher Hans Selye (1980) referred to healthful stress as **eustress.** But stress that is too intense or prolonged can overtax our adjustive capacity, dampen our moods, and have harmful physical effects.
[Spencer A. Rathus, *Psychology*, 4th Ed., 431]

(a) _____
(b) _____
(c) _____
(d) _____

CHAPTER 11 BODY PARTS

SECTION 1

List 1
Here are some word parts that are used to signify body parts.

WORD PART	MEANING
AUR	ear
BRACH	arm
BRONCH	windpipe
CARD	heart
CEPHAL	head; skull
CEREBR	brain
CORP	body
CUT	skin
DACTYL	finger; toe
DENT	tooth
DONT	tooth
NEPHR	kidney
OCUL	eye
PED	foot
PIL	hair
POD	foot
RHIN	nose
SANGUI	blood
TRICHO	hair

PRE-EXERCISE ACTIVITY 1
- **List Making**
- **Skill: word parts**

*In the blanks that follow, rewrite List 1. This time, however, reverse the order by writing the **meanings** in the first column. Then gather all the word parts in the list which have that meaning and write them on one line in the second column. This will let you make necessary connections and help you in the process of long-term memorization. The first one has already been done to show you how.*

	MEANING	WORD PARTS	
1.	arm	brach	*Note:* This list will be more useful if you write it in alphabetical order.
2.	_____	_____	
3.	_____	_____	
4.	_____	_____	
5.	_____	_____	
6.	_____	_____	
7.	_____	_____	
8.	_____	_____	
9.	_____	_____	
10.	_____	_____	
11.	_____	_____	
12.	_____	_____	
13.	_____	_____	
14.	_____	_____	
15.	_____	_____	
16.	_____	_____	
17.	_____	_____	
18.	_____	_____	

Copyright © 1996 Harcourt Brace & Company. All rights reserved.

EXERCISE 11-A
- **Multiple Choice**
- **Skill: word parts**

A meaning is in boldface for each of the following phrases. From the four choices given, pick the one answer which contains a word part with that meaning. Use both versions of List 1 to help you. **Do not use a dictionary.** *Do not focus on the size or difficulty of the words. Look only for the simple word part; it will lead you to the correct answer.*

Example: √Pertaining to the **ear**
    (A) pedal   (C) nasal
    (B) aural   (D) brachial

    Answer: (B) The reason for this answer is that the AUR part of *aural* means "ear."

1. Medical examination of the **windpipe**
   - (A) bronchoscopy
   - (B) hepatoscopy
   - (C) otoscopy
   - (D) rhinoscopy

2. The condition of having an oversized **head**
   - (A) megalomania
   - (B) megalocardia
   - (C) megalocephaly
   - (D) megalopsia

3. Medical examination of the **nose**
   - (A) bronchoscopy
   - (B) hepatoscopy
   - (C) otoscopy
   - (D) rhinoscopy

4. Pain in the **kidney**
   - (A) brachialgia
   - (B) nephralgia
   - (C) odontalgia
   - (D) cardialgia

5. A **heart**-shaped curve
   - (A) trapezoid
   - (B) ellipsoid
   - (C) cardioid
   - (D) cuboid

6. Pain in the **arm**
   - (A) brachialgia
   - (B) nephralgia
   - (C) odontalgia
   - (D) cardialgia

7. To use the **brain** to think
   - (A) celebrate
   - (B) cerebrate
   - (C) calibrate
   - (D) colligate

8. Pain in the **tooth**
   - (A) brachialgia
   - (B) nephralgia
   - (C) odontalgia
   - (D) cardialgia

9. Any disease of the **hair**
   - (A) osmosis
   - (B) pediculosis
   - (C) halitosis
   - (D) trichosis

10. Pain in the **heart**
    - (A) brachialgia
    - (B) nephralgia
    - (C) odontalgia
    - (D) cardialgia

EXERCISE 11-B

- Fill in the Blank (one cue)
- Skill: word parts

Use a **meaning** from List 1 to fill in the blank in each statement. The word part whose meaning you are defining will be found inside the boldfaced word. **Do not use a dictionary.** Do not focus on the size or difficulty of the words. Look only for the simple word part; it will lead you to the correct answer.

Example: √**Subcutaneous** means under the _____ .

Answer: *skin* [> CUT]

1. A **biped** has two _____ .
2. The word **corporeal** refers to the physical _____ .
3. A **denticulate** leaf has _____ -like margins or projections.
4. Something **cerebroid** resembles the shape of the _____ .
5. In zoology, the term **brachiate** means having _____ .
6. The **bronchia** are the branches of the _____ .

7. The **oculomotor** muscles help move the _____ .
8. **Cardiac** arrest involves the _____ .
9. **Pilar** means of or pertaining to _____ .
10. A **dentifrice** is used to clean _____ .
11. **Rhinoplasty** is plastic surgery of the _____ .
12. **Trichology** is the science dealing with the _____ .
13. Parasites that live in the _____ are called **sanguicolous.**
14. Certain reptiles are **tridactylous;** they have three _____ .
15. A **cutaneous** infection involves the _____ .

EXERCISE 11-C
- **Fill in the Blank (no cue)**
- **Skills: word parts, context**

*Once again, use a **meaning** from List 1 to fill in the blank in each statement. This time, however, you will have to find the word part yourself in the difficult or technical word. **Do not use a dictionary.** Do not focus on the size or difficulty of the words. Look only for the simple word part; it will lead you to the correct answer.*

Example: √Inflammation of the _____ is called nephritis.

Answer: *kidney* [> NEPHR]

1. A monocular creature has only one _____ .
2. Rhinitis involves inflammation of the membranes of the _____ .
3. A cerebral hemorrhage takes place in the _____ .
4. Pain in the _____ is called brachialgia.
5. Professional care and treatment of the _____ is called pedicure.
6. A dentation is a _____ like projection.
7. Corpulence refers to a large _____ size.

8. A bronchoscope is an instrument for inspecting the _____.
9. The cerebrospinal portion of the nervous system involves the spinal cord and the _____.
10. A cephalopod has tentacles attached to its _____.
11. Something trichoid is _____ like.
12. Tachycardia refers to an excessively fast _____.
13. Some vessels are sanguiferous; they carry _____.
14. Something which is piliferous has or produces _____.
15. Most mammals are diphyodonts; they have two successive sets of _____.

EXERCISE 11-D
- **Matching Columns**
- **Skill: word parts**

Memory check. Do not look back at List 1 or use a dictionary.

1. ____	BRACH	(a)	blood
2. ____	CEPHAL	(b)	arm
3. ____	NEPHR	(c)	ear
4. ____	SANGUI	(d)	hair
5. ____	DACTYL	(e)	heart
6. ____	RHIN	(f)	skull
7. ____	PIL	(g)	finger
8. ____	OCUL	(h)	eye
9. ____	CARD	(i)	nose
10. ____	AUR	(j)	kidney

Cardiologists at play.

EXERCISE 11-E
- Fill in (two cues)
- Skills: word parts, dictionary, context

*To finish each word, fill in the blank with one of the **word parts** from your version of List 1. **You must use a college-level dictionary** to make sure that what you write really is a word and that it fits in the sentence. The word in boldface will give you the meaning of the word part that you must write.*

Example: √A _ _ _ _oceros has a large **nose** or snout.

Answer: *RHIN* [> nose]

1. The _ _ _ _omotor nerves control the muscles of the **eye**.
2. A _ _ _ _oid structure resembles **hair**.
3. A pedo_ _ _ _ist specializes in treating children's **teeth**.
4. _ _ _iform means resembling **hair**.
5. Brady_ _ _ _ia is a slow **heart**beat rate.
6. The technique of communicating by signs made with the **fingers** is called _ _ _ _ _ology.
7. _ _ _ _ism is a condition caused by chronic disease of the **kidney**.
8. _ _ _ _ _nary means characterized by or full of **blood**.
9. The tendency of animals to have important organs or parts in or near the **head** is called _ _ _ _ _ization.
10. The hardened **skin** at the base of a fingernail is called the _ _ _icle.
11. _ _ _ _ _orrhagia is bleeding from the **windpipe**.
12. A _ _ _estrian travels on **foot**.
13. The _ _ _ _ium is the upper part of the **arm**.
14. The _ _ icle is the projecting outer portion of the **ear**.
15. _ _ _ _oral punishment is directed to the **body**.

EXERCISE 11-F
- Fill in (one cue)
- Skills: word parts, dictionary, context

*Continue filling in **word parts** from your version of List 1 as you have been doing, **using a college-level dictionary** to check accuracy. This time, however, there will be no word in boldface. You will have to search the sentence for a clue.*

Example: √To _ _ _ _ _ate is to use the brain—in other words, to think.

Answer: *CEREBR* [> brain]

1. A dead body is known as a _ _ _ _se.
2. A _ _ _ _ _ _logist treats the hair.
3. Some insects are _ _ _ _ _ _vorous; they feed on blood.
4. For bin_ _ _ _ar vision, we need two eyes.
5. _ _ _ _ _iation is locomotion accomplished by swinging by the arms from one hold to another.
6. The science dealing with the nose and its diseases is called _ _ _ _ _ology.
7. A small tooth or toothlike part is called a _ _ _ _icle.
8. The branch of medical science that deals with the kidney is called _ _ _ _ _ology.
9. _ _ _ _ _ _al activities take place in the brain.
10. A de_ _ _ _atory is a cream used to remove unwanted hair.
11. The _ _ _ _ _ _us is one of two primary subdivisions of the windpipe.
12. Perio_ _ _ _al disease affects the gums and roots of teeth.
13. _ _ _ _ _iology is the study of the heart and its functions in health and in disease.
14. _ _ _ _ _ _neous color has the same color as blood.
15. A patient who has foot problems may need to see a _ _ _iatrist.

EXERCISE 11-G
- **Paragraph Examples**
- **Skills: word parts, dictionary, context**

Answer these four questions after each paragraph:

(a) *What word part inside the boldfaced word helps you to understand that word? What does that word part mean?*

(b) *Using only the context of the word and the word part that it contains, what do you think the boldfaced word means? (See Chapter 1, Section 2.)*

(c) *Choose one context clue that helped you. (See Chapter 1, Section 2.)*

    1. *word signals*   4. *examples or description*
    2. *punctuation signals*   5. *contrast or opposites*
    3. *synonyms (substitution)* 6. *prior knowledge; common sense*
        If 6, explain: _____

(d) *How does the dictionary define the boldfaced word as it is used in the paragraph?*

1. Your doctor may use ultrasound—high frequency sound waves that "see" inside your body—to look at your heart. Physicians call ultrasound imagery of the heart echocardiography (echo = reflected sound, cardio = heart, graphy = record). Echocardiography lets physicians quickly and easily find abnormalities or pinpoint damage. By studying your heart's movements, your physician can spot a defective valve or an enlarged chamber, a congenital defect or an abnormality in the sac that surrounds your heart (**pericardium**).
        ["Diagnostic Ultrasound," *The Mayo Clinic Health Letter*, April 1992, 4]

    (a) _____
    (b) _____
    (c) _____
    (d) _____

2. Unquestionably, rock concerts are loud; the decibel level of some concerts reportedly exceeds that attained by a jet plane on take-off. In addition, this **aural** assault is often intensified by an

out-of-tune guitar, by the faltering voice of the performer, or by the bad acoustics in the concert hall.

[Jennifer Young, "The Rock Fantasy," *The Essay Connection*, 228]

(a) _____
(b) _____
(c) _____
(d) _____

3. Animals with well-developed muscular systems can move and obtain food more efficiently if they are bilaterally symmetrical, with only one plane that divides the body into two mirror-image halves. Bilateral symmetry allows an animal to have a more streamlined shape and to concentrate the power of its muscles and appendages into producing motion in one direction. Along with the trend toward bilateral symmetry in animals goes the evolution of **cephalization**—the development of a head, with a concentration of sensory and nervous tissue that monitors the area the animal is entering.

[Karen Arms, et al., *A Journey into Life*, 3rd Ed., 434]

(a) _____
(b) _____
(c) _____
(d) _____

4. Cardiovascular disorders are the cause of nearly half the deaths in the United States. Cardiovascular diseases include heart disease and disorders of the circulatory system, the most common of which is stroke. Once cardiovascular disease has been diagnosed, there are a number of medical treatments, including surgery and medication. However, persons who have not encountered **cardiovascular** disease (as well as those who have) can profit from behavior modification that is intended to reduce the risk factors. These methods include the following:

   (1) Stopping smoking.
   (2) Weight control.
   (3) Reducing hypertension.
   (4) Lowering serum cholesterol.
   (5) Modifying Type A behavior.
   (6) Exercise.

[Spencer A. Rathus, *Psychology*, 4th Ed., 506]

(a) _____
(b) _____

(c) _____
(d) _____

5. There are four main types of stroke: two caused by clots, and two by hemorrhage. Cerebral thrombosis is the most common type of stroke. It occurs when a blood clot (thrombus) forms and blocks blood flow in an artery bringing blood to part of the brain. One identifying feature of **cerebral** thrombotic strokes is that they usually occur at night or first thing in the morning, when blood pressure is low.

[*The Johns Hopkins Medical Handbook*, 292]

(a) _____
(b) _____
(c) _____
(d) _____

SECTION 2

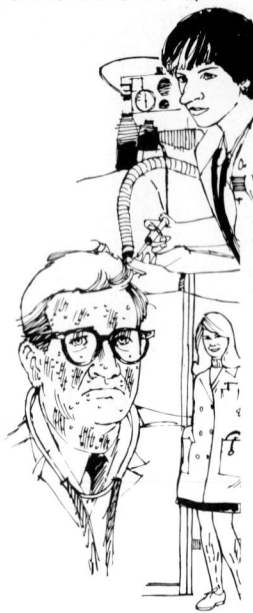

List 2

Here are more word parts that are used to signify body parts.

WORD PART	MEANING
ADEN	gland
CARN	flesh
CRANIO	skull
DERM	skin
DIGIT	finger; toe
ENTER	intestine
GASTR	stomach
GNATH	jaw
HEPAT	liver
MANU	hand
NAS	nose
OP	eye
OR	mouth
OSS	bone
OSTEO	bone
OT	ear
PHLEB	vein
PULMO	lung
SOMAT	body

PRE-EXERCISE ACTIVITY 2
- **List Making**
- **Skill: word parts**

*In the blanks that follow, rewrite List 2. This time, however, reverse the order by writing the **meanings** in the first column. Then gather all the word parts in the list which have that meaning and write them on one line in the second column. This will let you make necessary connections and help you in the process of long-term memorization. The first one has already been done to show you how.*

	MEANING	WORD PARTS	
1.	body	somat	*Note:* This list will be more useful if you write it in alphabetical order.
2.			
3.			
4.			
5.			
6.			
7.			
8.			
9.			
10.			
11.			
12.			
13.			
14.			
15.			
16.			
17.			
18.			
19.			

EXERCISE 11-H
- **Multiple Choice**
- **Skill: word parts**

A meaning is in boldface for each of the following phrases. From the four choices given, pick the one answer which contains a word part with that meaning. Use both versions of List 2 to help you. **Do not use a dictionary.** *Do not focus on the size or difficulty of the words. Look only for the simple word part; it will lead you to the correct answer.*

Example: √Pertaining to the **nose**
    (A) dermal   (C) nasal
    (B) carnal   (D) manual

Answer: (C) The reason for this answer is that the NAS part of *nasal* means "nose."

1. Pertaining to the **mouth**
   (A) aural   (C) visual
   (B) nasal   (D) oral

2. Pertaining to the **hand**
   (A) dermal   (C) nasal
   (B) carnal   (D) manual

3. Pertaining to the **body**
   (A) phlegmatic   (C) psychotic
   (B) somatic   (D) demotic

4. The study and treatment of the **skin**
   (A) enterology   (C) adenology
   (B) dermatology   (D) gastrology

5. Disease of the **liver**
   (A) bronchitis   (C) otitis
   (B) hepatitis   (D) phlebitis

6. Pertaining to the **lungs**
   (A) plenary   (C) predatory
   (B) pulmonary   (D) peccary

7. The study and treatment of the **stomach**
   - (A) enterology
   - (B) dermatology
   - (C) adenology
   - (D) gastrology

8. The study and treatment of the **glands**
   - (A) enterology
   - (B) dermatology
   - (C) adenology
   - (D) gastrology

9. The study and treatment of the **intestines**
   - (A) enterology
   - (B) dermatology
   - (C) adenology
   - (D) gastrology

10. Medical examination of the **ear**
    - (A) bronchoscopy
    - (B) proctoscopy
    - (C) otoscopy
    - (D) rhinoscopy

EXERCISE 11-I
- Fill in the Blank (one cue)
- Skill: word parts

*Use a **meaning** from List 2 to fill in the blank in each statement. The word part whose meaning you are defining will be found inside the boldfaced word.* **Do not use a dictionary.** *Do not focus on the size or difficulty of the words. Look only for the simple word part; it will lead you to the correct answer.*

Example: √The **optic** nerve carries impulses from the _____ to the brain.

Answer: *eye* [> OP]

1. **Oral** messages involve the _____ .
2. A **carnivore** is a _____-eating animal.
3. Originally, a **manuscript** was a _____-written document.
4. A **craniometer** measures the size of the _____ .
5. _____ that is dry, hard, and scaly is suffering from **xeroderma**.

6. **Pulmotor** devices inflate the _____ during emergency life-saving procedures.
7. A **nasalized** tone comes through the _____.
8. **Gastroenteritis** is inflammation of the _____ and intestines.
9. An **ossicle** is a small _____.
10. Various _____ types are referred to as **somatotypes**.
11. Pain in a _____ is called **adenalgia**.
12. The operation that removes part of the _____ is called a **hepatectomy**.
13. A **phlebotomy** involves cutting open a _____.
14. An **otolith** is a hard calciumlike build-up in the _____.
15. **Osteology** is the science dealing with _____.

EXERCISE 11-J
- Fill in the Blank (no cue)
- Skills: word parts, context

*Once again, use a **meaning** from List 2 to fill in the blank in each statement. This time, however, you will have to find the word part yourself in the difficult or technical word. **Do not use a dictionary**. Do not focus on the size or difficulty of the words. Look only for the simple word part; it will lead you to the correct answer.*

Example: √Osteoplasty is surgical reconstruction of a _____.

Answer: *bone* [> OSTEO]

1. The process of dermabrasion involves scraping off _____.
2. Originally, manufactured items were made by _____.
3. Oronasal means pertaining to the _____ and the nose.
4. Otology is the branch of medicine that focuses on the _____.

5. In botany, digitate refers to leaflets that are shaped like _____.
6. Phlebitis is inflammation of a _____.
7. Carnival means goodbye to _____ and originally referred to the start of Lenten fasting.
8. The cranium is the _____.
9. Somatology is the branch of anthropology that deals with the human _____ and its characteristics.
10. The entire _____ is called the enteron.
11. An adenoma is a benign tumor originating in a _____.
12. The largest Eurasian bird of prey is referred to as an ossifrage because it is capable of breaking _____ with its beak.
13. The gnathion is the lower end of the _____.
14. Pulmonates have _____ or organs like them.
15. Pain in the _____ is called gastralgia.

EXERCISE 11-K
- Matching Columns
- Skills: word parts, context

Memory check. Do not look back at List 2 or use a dictionary.

1.	____	CARN	(a)	vein
2.	____	PULMO	(b)	flesh
3.	____	GASTR	(c)	finger; toe
4.	____	GNATH	(d)	skull
5.	____	PHLEB	(e)	ear
6.	____	CRANIO	(f)	lung
7.	____	ENTERO	(g)	stomach
8.	____	DIGIT	(h)	intestines
9.	____	MANU	(i)	hand
10.	____	OT	(j)	jaw

Dental hygiene is a matter of tooth or consequences.

Oculists don't always see eye to eye.

Podiatrists get underfoot.

EXERCISE 11-L
- Fill in (two cues)
- Skills: word parts, dictionary, context

To finish each word, fill in the blank with one of the **word parts** *from your version of List 2.* **You must use a college-level dictionary** *to make sure that what you write really is a word and that it fits in the sentence. The word in boldface will give you the meaning of the word part that you must write.*

Example: √___tometry tests the **eyes** for defects.

Answer: *OP* [> eye]

1. ___algia is the name for pain in the **ear**.
2. ____assial teeth are adapted for tearing off **flesh**.
3. An operation to fix a loss of **bone** is called _____plasty.
4. The epi____is is the outer layer of **skin**.
5. A psycho____ic illness is a **bodily** disorder caused or influenced by the mind.
6. The science dealing with the function and diseases of **glands** is ____ology.
7. Most four-footed mammals are ____igrade, meaning that they walk on the **toes**.
8. An ____ostomy is an artificial opening made into the **intestines**.
9. The operation that opens the **skull** for brain surgery is called a _____tomy.
10. _____osclerosis is a hardening of the walls of **veins**.
11. Something ____ic resembles the **liver**.
12. A pro____ous individual has a **jaw** that thrusts out considerably.
13. An ___ifice is a **mouth**like opening or hole.
14. ____al labor requires the use of **hands**.
15. Inflammation of the **stomach** is called _____itis.

EXERCISE 11-M
- Fill in (one cue)
- Skills: word parts, dictionary, context

*Continue filling in **word parts** from your version of List 2 as you have been doing, **using a college-level dictionary** to check accuracy. This time, however, there will be no word in boldface. You will have to search each sentence for a clue.*

Example: √An _ _ _ _ oma is a tumor that starts in a gland.

     Answer: *ADEN* [> gland]

1. The _ _ _ _ _ ic juices are found in the stomach.
2. _ _ _ _ _ ic problems center in the jaw.
3. _ _ _ _ _ ogenic changes arise within the body.
4. _ _ ology is the medical specialty that focuses on diseases of the ear.
5. A _ _ _ _ _ nary disease affects the lungs.
6. _ _ _ _ mission, releasing a slave, literally meant opening one's hand and letting him or her go free.
7. An _ _ _ _ _ ostomy is the surgical formation of an opening into the intestine.
8. Something that is _ _ _ ified is hardened like or into bone.
9. There is a dark reddish brown color called _ _ _ _ _ ic because it is the same color as the liver.
10. The _ _ _ _ _ al index is a ratio used for measuring skulls.
11. _ _ _ _ _ ic means of or pertaining to the jaw.
12. _ _ _ _ oids, which are enlarged glands in the throat, can interfere with breathing.
13. In _ _ _ _ ate means invested with flesh or human form.
14. Pre _ _ al parts are located in front of the mouth.
15. A pachy _ _ _ _ , such as an elephant, has thick skin.

EXERCISE 11-N
- **Paragraph Examples**
- **Skills: word parts, dictionary, context**

Answer these four questions after each paragraph:

(a) *What word part inside the boldfaced word helps you to understand that word? What does that word part mean?*

(b) *Using only the context of the word and the word part that it contains, what do you think the boldfaced word means? (See Chapter 1, Section 2.)*

(c) *Choose one context clue that helped you. (See Chapter 1, Section 2.)*
   1. *word signals*
   2. *punctuation signals*
   3. *synonyms (substitution)*
   4. *examples or description*
   5. *contrast or opposites*
   6. *prior knowledge; common sense*
      If 6, explain: _____

(d) *How does the dictionary define the boldfaced word as it is used in the paragraph?*

1. Late in the Triassic Period, a dog-size carnivore dashed through the forest on its two hind legs, terrorizing mouse-size animals with its sharp teeth and claws. Some 228 million years later, a team led by University of Chicago paleontologist Paul Sereno unearthed this creature's skeleton from the Ischigualasto Badlands of Northwestern Argentina. Eoraptor ("dawn plunderer"), as it is called, has neither the specialized teeth and heavy bill of plant-eating dinosaurs nor the mobile jaw joint found in most carnivorous dinosaurs. The evidence says that it was a **carnivore**, though—it had the claws and sharp teeth needed to kill prey, even if it lacked the jaw joint to subdue its prey first.
   [Robert Naeye, "Dawn of the Dinosaurs," *Discover*, January 1994, 51]

   (a) _____
   (b) _____
   (c) _____
   (d) _____

2. The liver's main function is to control the level of many substances in the blood. Digested food molecules absorbed into the bloodstream from the intestine pass directly to the liver by way of the **hepatic** portal vein. Before these molecules pass to the rest of the body, the liver may change their concentrations and even their chemical structures. The liver detoxifies some otherwise poisonous substances.
   [Karen Arms, et al., *A Journey into Life,* 3rd Ed., 488]
   (a) _____
   (b) _____
   (c) _____
   (d) _____

3. During the first year of life, a child experiences much of its world through the mouth. If it fits, into the mouth it goes. This is the oral stage. Freud argued that oral activities such as sucking and biting bring the child sexual gratification as well as nourishment. Freud believed that children would encounter conflicts during each stage of psychosocial development. During the oral stage, conflict would center around the nature and extent of oral gratification. Insufficient or excessive gratification in any stage could lead to fixation in that stage and to the development of traits characteristic of that stage. **Oral** traits include dependency, gullibility, and optimism or pessimism.
   [Spencer A. Rathus, *Psychology,* 4th Ed., 438]
   (a) _____
   (b) _____
   (c) _____
   (d) _____

4. In the United States, more than 600,000 bone fractures a year are attributed to brittle bones. Part of the reason osteoporosis is so common is that people live much longer nowadays, and degeneration of bone is a serious problem in many older people. Osteoporosis is a condition in which bones have lost so much inorganic mineral matter that they become light, brittle, and easily broken. The most effective ways to prevent or treat **osteoporosis** appear to be exercise, which stimulates addition of material to bone, and increasing calcium in the diet, especially from organic sources such as dairy products.
   [Karen Arms, et al., *A Journey into Life,* 3rd Ed., 625]

334 CHAPTER 11 BODY PARTS

(a) _____
(b) _____
(c) _____
(d) _____

5. Among the many fibs of vision are **optical** illusions. A puddle forms on the highway in front of you. But, unlike a real puddle, it keeps moving farther away as you approach it. Because it is a hot summer day, with a layer of hot air sitting below a layer of cold air, a reflection (of the sky) is cast onto the road. The word "mirage" slowly forms in your mind. Its etymology means "to wonder at."
[Diane Ackerman, *A Natural History of the Senses,* 230]

(a) _____
(b) _____
(c) _____
(d) _____

The epidermis is our skin;
  it helps us keep in touch.
They change its name to
  corpulence when there is
  too much.
Cerebral is the word they use
  to talk about our brain.
It's hard to have too much of
  it unless the user's vain.

SECTION 3: CHAPTER REVIEW (LISTS 1 AND 2 COMBINED)

Word Parts Covered in This Chapter:

WORD PART	MEANING	COMMON EXAMPLE	TEXTBOOK EXAMPLE
ADEN	gland	*adenoids*	*adenectomy*
AUR	ear	*aural*	*auricle*
BRACH	arm	*brachial*	*brachialgia*
BRONCH	windpipe	*bronchitis*	*bronchoscope*
CARD	heart	*cardiac*	*bradycardia*
CARN	flesh	*carnal*	*carnivorous*
CEPHAL	head; skull	*cephalic*	*microcephalous*
CEREBR	brain	*cerebral*	*cerebrate*
CORP	body	*corpse*	*corporeity*
CRANIO	skull	*cranium*	*craniometry*
CUT	skin	*cuticle*	*subcutaneous*
DACTYL	finger; toe	*dactylic*	*pterodactyl*
DENT	tooth	*dentist*	*dentiform*
DERM	skin	*epidermis*	*dermatophyte*
DIGIT	finger; toe	*digital*	*digitigrade*
DONT	tooth	*orthodontist*	*odontalgia*
ENTER	intestine	*enteritis*	*enterectomy*
GASTR	stomach	*gastric*	*gastronomy*
GNATH	jaw	*gnathic*	*prognathous*
HEPAT	liver	*hepatitis*	*hepatization*
MANU	hand	*manual*	*manumission*
NAS	nose	*nasal*	*nasopharynx*
NEPHR	kidney	*nephritis*	*nephrolith*
OCUL	eye	*binoculars*	*oculomotor*
OP	eye	*optometrist*	*presbyopia*
OR	mouth	*oral*	*oracular*
OSS	bone	*ossify*	*ossification*
OSTEO	bone	*osteopath*	*osteoclasis*
OT	ear	*otic*	*otologist*
PED	foot	*pedal*	*pediform*
PHLEB	vein	*phlebitis*	*phlebotomy*
PIL	hair	*depilatory*	*piligerous*
POD	foot	*podiatrist*	*monopode*
PULMO	lung	*pulmonary*	*pulmonate*
RHIN	nose	*rhinoceros*	*rhinorrhea*
SANGUI	blood	*sanguine*	*sanguicolous*
SOMAT	body	*somatic*	*psychosomatic*
TRICHO	hair	*trichosis*	*trichologist*

Copyright © 1996 Harcourt Brace & Company. All rights reserved.

PRE-EXERCISE ACTIVITY 3
- List Making
- Skill: word parts

*In the blanks that follow, rewrite the combined word parts list. This time, however, reverse the order by writing the **meanings** in the first column. Then gather all the word parts in the list which have that meaning and write them on one line in the second column. This will let you make necessary connections and help you in the process of long-term memorization. The first one has already been done to show you how.*

	MEANING	WORD PARTS	
1.	arm	brach	*Note:* This list will be more useful if you write it in alphabetical order.
2.			
3.			
4.			
5.			
6.			
7.			
8.			
9.			
10.			
11.			
12.			
13.			
14.			
15.			
16.			
17.			
18.			
19.			
20.			

Continued

21. _____   _____
22. _____   _____
23. _____   _____
24. _____   _____
25. _____   _____
26. _____   _____
27. _____   _____
28. _____   _____
29. _____   _____

EXERCISE 11-O
- **Matching Columns**
- **Skill: word parts**

Memory check. Do not look back at the combined list or use a dictionary.

1. ____ POD   (a) nose
2. ____ GASTR   (b) bone
3. ____ DONT   (c) vein
4. ____ PHLEB   (d) hand
5. ____ RHIN   (e) body
6. ____ PULMO   (f) stomach
7. ____ OSS   (g) eye
8. ____ SOMAT   (h) tooth
9. ____ OCUL   (i) foot
10. ____ MANU   (j) lung

EXERCISE 11-P
- Cross Out
- Skills: dictionary, word parts, context

One word in each set does not contain the word part and meaning that is given, even though it has a set of similar letters. **Use a college-level dictionary** *to find the one that does* **not** *fit.*

Example:

	WORD PART	MEANING	CROSS OUT THE ONE WORD THAT DOES NOT FIT.
	√ADEN	gland	adenoid, adenalgia, cadence

Answer: The dictionary shows that *adenoid* and *adenalgia* have the word *gland* in their definitions. *Cadence* does not; cross it out.

WORD PART	MEANING	CROSS OUT THE ONE WORD THAT DOES NOT FIT.
1. CARD	heart	tachycardia, cardinal, cardiology
2. DENT	tooth	dented, dentifrice, dentation
3. OR	mouth	oropharynx, orogeny, oration
4. TRICHO	hair	trichocyst, trichoid, trichotomy
5. OT	ear	otitis, otiose, otologist
6. PIL	hair	pileous, depilatory, pilfer
7. OS	bone	osculate, osteophyte, ossify
8. PED	foot	pediform, pedal, pediatrician
9. CARN	flesh	carnivorous, carnallite, carnage
10. MANU	hand	manumit, manufacture, manure

EXERCISE 11-Q
- Extended Answer
- Skills: word parts, dictionary, context

Answer the following questions by using a college-level dictionary.

Example: √How is the meaning *lung* involved in the word **pulmonary**?

Answer: Pulmonary means of or pertaining to the lungs.

1. How is the meaning *body* involved in the word **somatic**?

2. How is the meaning *finger/toe* involved in the word **pentadactyl**?

3. How is the meaning *ear* involved in the word **otolaryngology**?

4. How is the meaning *stomach* involved in the word **gastronomy**?

5. How is the meaning *skin* involved in the word **epidermis**?

6. How is the meaning *flesh* involved in the word **carnivorous**?

7. How is the meaning *heart* involved in the word **megalocardia**?

8. How is the meaning *body* involved in the word **incorporation**?

9. How is the meaning *nose* involved in the word **rhinoceros**?

10. How is the meaning *foot* involved in the word **monopode**?

My rhinologist thinks she nose it all;
My gastrologist can't stomach pain.
My dermatologist is a thin-skinned man,
And my phlebologist is very vein.

EXERCISE 11-R
- **Fill in the Blank**
- **Skill: word parts**

Memory check. Do not look back at the combined list or use a dictionary.

1. Name two word parts that mean *skull*: _____ and _____ .

2. Name two word parts that
   mean *hair*: _____ and _____.
3. Name two word parts that
   mean *finger*: _____ and _____.
4. Name two word parts that
   mean *body*: _____ and _____.
5. Name two word parts that
   mean *tooth*: _____ and _____.
6. Name two word parts that
   mean *skin*: _____ and _____.
7. Name two word parts that
   mean *nose*: _____ and _____.
8. Name two word parts that
   mean *eye*: _____ and _____.
9. Name two word parts that
   mean *ear*: _____ and _____.

EXERCISE 11-S
- **Paragraph Examples**
- **Skills: word parts, dictionary, context**

Answer these four questions after each paragraph:

(a) What word part inside the boldfaced word helps you to understand that word? What does that word part mean?

(b) Using only the context of the word and the word part that it contains, what do you think the boldfaced word means? (See Chapter 1, Section 2.)

(c) Choose one context clue that helped you. (See Chapter 1, Section 2.)
   1. word signals
   2. punctuation signals
   3. synonyms (substitution)
   4. examples or description
   5. contrast or opposites
   6. prior knowledge; common sense

   If 6, explain: _____

(d) *How does the dictionary define the boldfaced word as it is used in the paragraph?*

_____

1. Throughout our young life, the bones build and strengthen. Young individuals typically enjoy a relatively calcium-rich diet, and this large surplus of calcium is stored almost exclusively in the bones. As this occurs, the bones become more dense and solid, a process known as ossification. By about age 35, **ossification** is complete, and the bones are as hard—and as strong—as they will ever be.
   [*The Johns Hopkins Medical Handbook*, 340]
   (a) _____
   (b) _____
   (c) _____
   (d) _____

2. Every action involving the body's muscles is initiated by electrical activity. The voltages produced by muscular action in the heart are particularly important to physicians. Voltage pulses cause the heart to beat, and the waves of electrical excitation associated with the heartbeat are conducted through the body via the body fluids. These voltage pulses are large enough to be detected by suitable monitoring equipment attached to the skin. Standard electric devices can be used to record these voltage pulses because the amplitude of a typical pulse associated with heart activity is of the order of 1 mV. These voltage pulses are recorded on an instrument called an electrocardiograph, and the pattern recorded by this instrument is called an **electrocardiogram** (EKG).
   [Spencer A. Rathus, *Psychology*, 4th Ed., 611]
   (a) _____
   (b) _____
   (c) _____
   (d) _____

3. **Phlebitis,** or inflammation of a vein, is a relatively common disorder, and although it may occur in association with an injury or infection or as an aftermath of surgery, it sometimes develops for no apparent reason. If such an inflammation is restricted to a superficial vein, the blood flow may be rechanneled through other vessels. If it occurs in a deep vein, however,

the consequences can be quite serious, particularly if the blood within the affected vessel clots and blocks the normal circulation.

[John W. Hole, Jr., *Human Anatomy and Physiology*, 4th Ed., 676]

(a) _____

(b) _____

(c) _____

(d) _____

4. Most diving animals show bradycardia (slowing of the heart rate) when they dive. For example, a seal's heart rate drops from 150 to 10 beats per minute. In penguins, the heart rate drops to one-fifth of the normal, resting rate. Bradycardia is seen in other animals, including humans when they submerge, and, interestingly, fish undergo bradycardia when they are removed from water. The advantage of **bradycardia** is probably that it saves the body energy and oxygen. In addition, blood vessels constrict and reduce the circulation to the kidneys, gut, and so forth. This conserves oxygen for use by the brain, which must not be deprived of oxygen.

[Karen Arms, et al., *A Journey into Life*, 3rd Ed., 521]

(a) _____

(b) _____

(c) _____

(d) _____

5. In somatoform disorders, people show or complain of physical problems such as paralysis, pain, or the persistent belief that they have a serious disease, yet no evidence of a physical abnormality can be found. In this section, we discuss two **somatoform** disorders: conversion disorder and hypochondriasis. Conversion disorder is characterized by a major change in, or loss of, physical functioning, although there are no medical findings to explain the loss of functioning. The behaviors are not intentionally produced; that is, the person is not faking. Persons with hypochondriasis insist that they are suffering from profound illness, even though no medical evidence can be found. They become preoccupied with minor physical sensations and maintain their belief despite medical reassurance. Hypochondriacs may run from doctor to doctor, seeking the one who will find the causes of the sensations. Fear may disrupt work or home life.

[Spencer A. Rathus, *Psychology*, 4th Ed., 548]

(a) _____
(b) _____
(c) _____
(d) _____

6. The epidermis is your skin's outer layer. Thickness averages about the width of the mark from a sharp pencil. Your back, soles, and palms have the thickest skin; your eyelids, the thinnest. Men generally have thicker skin than women. As you age, your skin becomes thinner. The outermost layer of the **epidermis** is the *stratum corneum*. It's made up of dead cells that are constantly shedding.
["Anatomy of Your Skin," *The Mayo Clinic Health Letter,* July 1991, 5]

(a) _____
(b) _____
(c) _____
(d) _____

7. Externally, the mosque often gave an impression of an overwhelming material power and magnificence, though the minarets flanking the dome served as a reminder that this was made possible by the will of God. But internally the mosque remained faithful to the desert origins of Islam and continued to represent a totally different view of life from that conveyed in the Christian church. The church was an organization of inner space planned to express the belief in divine immanence in nature. The altar where God became **incarnate** in the Eucharist was the center on which the eyes and attention of the congregation were irresistibly concentrated, each individual member feeling himself to be part of an organic collectivity engaged in the worship of a manifest divinity. But the mosque had no center. It remained merely a section of ground and air set aside for communion with a transcendent spirit.
[Henry Parkes, *The Divine Order,* 117]

(a) _____
(b) _____
(c) _____
(d) _____

8. The chief cause of death by inhaling fumes from spray cans is the fluorocarbon gases, such as Freon or fluorotrichloromethane. Inhaling large quantities of some of these gases can

cause **pulmonary** edema. The lungs fill up with fluid, preventing the victim from breathing. In view of the growing concern about fluorocarbons, some manufacturers of spray products have begun introducing pump-type cans as alternatives to aerosols.

[Greulach & Chiapetta, *Biology*, 514]

(a) _____
(b) _____
(c) _____
(d) _____

9. The embryonic stage lasts from implantation until about the eighth week of development. During this stage, the major body organ systems differentiate. Development follows two general trends—**cephalocaudal** and proximodistal. As you can note from the relatively large heads of embryos and fetuses during prenatal development, the growth of the head takes precedence over the growth of the lower parts of the body. If you also think of the body as containing a central axis that coincides with the spinal cord, the growth of the organ systems close to this axis (that is, *proximal*) takes precedence over the growth of the extremities (*distal* areas). Relatively early maturation of the brain and the major organ systems allows them to participate in the nourishment and further development of the unborn child.

[Spencer A. Rathus, *Psychology*, 4th Ed., 346]

(a) _____
(b) _____
(c) _____
(d) _____

10. Herbs are natural substances. But don't believe that "natural" means safe. Since 1960, sassafras has been banned as a flavoring agent because of its cancer-causing properties. And in the July 15, 1992, issue of *Annals of Internal Medicine*, doctors report seven cases of **hepatitis** (liver toxicity) resulting from use of the herb germander in tea or capsules. Reports of herbal poisoning are not unusual.

["Herbal Supplements," *The Mayo Clinic Health Letter*, December 1992, 7]

(a) _____
(b) _____
(c) _____
(d) _____

CHAPTER 12 NATURE

SECTION 1

List 1
Here are some word parts that are used to signify elements of nature.

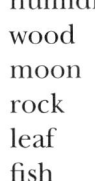

WORD PART	MEANING
ARBOR	tree
AREN	sand
ASTR	star; celestial body
DENDR	tree
HELIO	sun
HYDR	water; fluid
HYGR	humidity; moisture
LIGN	wood
LUN	moon
PETR	rock
PHYLL	leaf
PISC	fish
TERR	earth; ground
ZO	animal

PRE-EXERCISE ACTIVITY 1
- **List Making**
- **Skill: word parts**

*In the blanks that follow, rewrite List 1. This time, however, reverse the order by writing the **meanings** in the first column. Then gather all the word parts in the list which have that meaning and write them on one line in the second column. This will let you make necessary connections and help you in the process of long-term memorization. The first one has already been done to show you how.*

	MEANING	WORD PARTS
1.	animal	zo
2.		
3.		
4.		
5.		
6.		
7.		
8.		
9.		
10.		
11.		
12.		
13.		
14.		
15.		
16.		
17.		

Note: This list will be more useful if you write it in alphabetical order.

EXERCISE 12-A
- **Multiple Choice**
- **Skill: word parts**

A meaning is in boldface for each of the following phrases. From the four choices given, pick the one answer which contains a word part with that meaning. Use both versions of List 1 to help you. **Do not use a dictionary.** *Do not focus on the size or difficulty of the words. Look only for the simple word part; it will lead you to the correct answer.*

Example: √Pertaining to the **moon**
    (A) solar   (C) arboreal
    (B) terrestrial   (D) lunar

    Answer: (D) The reason for this answer is that the LUN part of *lunar* means "moon."

1. The scientific study of **heavenly bodies**
   (A) zoology   (C) petrology
   (B) astronomy   (D) dendrology

2. The scientific study of **animals**
   (A) zoology   (C) petrology
   (B) astronomy   (D) dendrology

3. Living in the **ground**
   (A) arenicolous   (C) saxicolous
   (B) terricolous   (D) sanguicolous

4. The scientific study of **trees**
   (A) zoology   (C) petrology
   (B) astronomy   (D) dendrology

5. Worship of the **sun**
   (A) idolatry   (C) heliolatry
   (B) zoolatry   (D) bibliolatry

6. The scientific study of **water**
   (A) hydrology   (C) cosmology
   (B) geology   (D) piscatology

7. The scientific study of **rocks**
   - (A) zoology
   - (B) astronomy
   - (C) petrology
   - (D) dendrology

8. Worship of **animals**
   - (A) idolatry
   - (B) zoolatry
   - (C) heliolatry
   - (D) bibliolatry

9. The study of **fishing**
   - (A) hydrology
   - (B) geology
   - (C) cosmology
   - (D) piscatology

10. Living in **sand**
    - (A) arenicolous
    - (B) terricolous
    - (C) saxicolous
    - (D) sanguicolous

EXERCISE 12-B
- **Fill in the Blank (one cue)**
- **Skill: word parts**

*Use a **meaning** from List 1 to fill in the blank in each statement. The word part whose meaning you are defining will be found inside the boldfaced word. **Do not use a dictionary.** Do not focus on the size or difficulty of the words. Look only for the simple word part; it will lead you to the correct answer.*

Example: √**Zoology** is the scientific study of _____ .

Answer: *animals [> ZO]*

1. **Petrified** wood has been turned to _____ .
2. **Zoophobia** is the fear of _____ .
3. An **arboretum** displays _____ .
4. **Sublunary** means situated beneath the _____ .
5. An **astrocyte** is a _____-shaped cell.
6. Something that resembles a _____ in form is **dendroid**.
7. **Terricolous** means living on or in the _____ .
8. **Arenite** is rock that is made up chiefly of _____ .

9. A **hydrophyte** is a plant that grows in _____.
10. **Zooplasty** involves grafting _____ tissue into the human body.
11. A **diphyllous** stalk has two _____.
12. The movement of an organism toward or away from the _____ is called **heliotaxis**.
13. **Pisciculture** is also referred to as _____ farming.
14. **Lignography** is the engraving of _____.
15. A **hygrograph** is an instrument that records variations in _____.

EXERCISE 12-C
- Fill in the Blank (no cue)
- Skills: word parts, context

*Once again, use a **meaning** from List 1 to fill in the blank in each statement. This time, however, you will have to find the word part yourself in the difficult or technical word.* **Do not use a dictionary.** *Do not focus on the size or difficulty of the words. Look only for the simple word part; it will lead you to the correct answer.*

Example: √An astrolabe was an instrument that measured the altitude of _____ and used the information to help navigate ships.

  Answer: *stars* [> ASTRO]

1. Roman sports centers had oval areas covered with _____, which were called arenas.
2. The act or process of being turned to _____ is called petrifaction.
3. Lunar means of or pertaining to the _____.
4. The scientific attempt to describe _____ accurately is called zoography.
5. An arborist specializes in caring for _____.

6. An astronomer studies _____ .
7. Something terrigenous is produced by the _____ .
8. Hydroponics involves raising vegetables with their roots immersed in _____ instead of in soil.
9. The arrangement of _____ on a stem is called phyllotaxy.
10. Piscine means like a _____ .
11. Hygrometric measurements establish the amount of _____ in the air and in gases.
12. A helioscope is a telescope modified for safe viewing of the _____ .
13. Something ligneous resembles _____ .
14. Astrophotography is concerned with taking pictures of _____ .
15. Dendrochronology relates the growth of _____ to the passage of time.

EXERCISE 12-D
- **Matching Columns**
- **Skill: word parts**

Memory check. Do not look back at List 1 or use a dictionary.

"I've had my phyll; just leaf me alone"

1. _____ LUN   (a) rock
2. _____ AREN   (b) wood
3. _____ ARBOR   (c) water
4. _____ HELIO   (d) moon
5. _____ PETR   (e) fish
6. _____ HYDR   (f) sand
7. _____ PHYLL   (g) earth
8. _____ PISC   (h) tree
9. _____ TERR   (i) leaf
10. _____ LIGN   (j) sun

Copyright © 1996 Harcourt Brace & Company. All rights reserved.

EXERCISE 12-E
- Fill in (two cues)
- Skills: word parts, dictionary, context

*To finish each word, fill in the blank with one of the **word parts** from your version of List 1. **You must use a college-level dictionary** to make sure that what you write really is a word and that it fits in the sentence. The word in boldface will give you the meaning of the word part that you must write.*

Example: √_ _ _ _ _oid means resembling a **leaf**.

        Answer: *PHYLL* [> leaf]

1. A view of the universe that considers the **sun** as the center is _ _ _ _ _centric.
2. _ _ _ _ometry deals with the measurement of the positions and motions of **celestial bodies**.
3. _ _ _ _atorial means pertaining to **fish** or fishing.
4. A _ _ _ _rite is a **treelike** figure produced in a mineral by another mineral.
5. A region of **ground** or tract of land is called _ _ _ _ain.
6. Insects that feed on **leaves** are _ _ _ _ _ophagous.
7. The abnormal fear of **animals** is called _ _ ophobia.
8. A _ _ _ _oglyph is a prehistoric carving upon a **rock**.
9. The period of time from one new **moon** to the next is called _ _ _ation.
10. _ _ _ _omancy tries to tell the future by watching patterns and motion in **water**.
11. _ _ _ _iform means having the appearance of **wood**.
12. A creature that is _ _ _ _icolous lives in **sand**.
13. A single plant that has unlike kinds of **leaves** on it is called hetero_ _ _ _ _ous.
14. A _ _ _ _oscope shows variations in atmospheric **moisture**.
15. _ _ _ _ _eal creatures live in **trees**.

EXERCISE 12-F
- **Fill in (one cue)**
- **Skills: word parts, dictionary, context**

*Continue filling in **word parts** as you have been, **using a college-level dictionary** to check accuracy. This time, however, there will be no word in boldface. You will have to search the sentence for a clue.*

Example: √ _ _ _ igenous means produced by the earth.

      Answer: *TERR* [> earth]

1. A _ _ ophilous person is someone who is animal-loving.
2. Something _ _ _ _ iform is treelike in form.
3. Mono_ _ _ _ ous means consisting of one leaf.
4. _ _ _ ophysics deals with the makeup of celestial bodies.
5. A substance that is sandy or gritty is _ _ _ _ ose.
6. _ _ _ iers are small dogs that were originally bred to burrow into the ground in pursuit of game.
7. An _ _ _ _ eous area has many trees.
8. An upright outlet pipe from a water main that allows firefighters to draw water is called a _ _ _ _ ant.
9. An insect or animal that eats wood is referred to as _ _ _ _ ivorous.
10. The tendency of a plant to move toward or away from sunlight is called _ _ _ _ tropism.
11. A substance that is _ _ _ _ ous is as hard as a rock.
12. The study of trees is called _ _ _ _ ology.
13. A plant living under conditions of plentiful moisture is called a _ _ _ _ ophyte.
14. An animal that feeds on fish is called _ _ _ _ ivorous.
15. That part of a tidal movement due to the pull of the moon is called _ _ _ itidal.

EXERCISE 12-G
- **Paragraph Examples**
- **Skills: word parts, dictionary, context**

Answer these four questions after each paragraph:

(a) *What word part inside the boldfaced word helps you to understand that word? What does that word part mean?*

(b) *Using only the context of the word and the word part that it contains, what do you think the boldfaced word means? (See Chapter 1, Section 2.)*

(c) *Choose one context clue that helped you. (See Chapter 1, Section 2.)*
  1. *word signals*
  2. *punctuation signals*
  3. *synonyms (substitution)*
  4. *examples or description*
  5. *contrast or opposites*
  6. *prior knowledge; common sense*
     If 6, explain: _____

(d) *How does the dictionary define the boldfaced word as it is used in the paragraph?*

1. Important hints about how the solar system formed are provided by the organization of the planets in the solar system, which is very orderly. The planets' orbits lie in nearly the same plane, their orbits are nearly circular and are rather regularly spaced, they all revolve in the same direction—from west to east—and most rotate and most of the satellites of planets revolve from west to east as well. The four innermost planets—Mercury, Venus, Earth, and Mars—are small, rocky, and earthlike; these are the terrestrial planets. The four outermost planets (except for Pluto)—Jupiter, Saturn, Uranus, and Neptune—are giant, composed largely of light elements (hydrogen and helium) and are Jupiter-like; they are the Jovian planets. Tiny remote Pluto is more like a **terrestrial** planet. Its orbit is the most eccentric, and it may have had an origin different from that of the outer planets.
[George O. Abell, *Realm of the Universe*, 137]

(a) _____
(b) _____

(c) _____
(d) _____

2. During the two decades from 1960 to 1980, the subject of general relativity experienced a rebirth. Despite its enormous influence on scientific thought in its early years, by the late 1950s, general relativity had become a sterile, formalistic subject, cut off from the mainstream of physics. It was thought to have very little observational contact, and was believed to be an extremely difficult subject to learn and comprehend. . . . The turning point for general relativity came in the early 1960s, when discoveries of unusual astronomical objects such as quasars demonstrated that the theory would have important applications in **astrophysical** situations. Theorists found new ways to understand the theory and its observable consequences. Finally, the technological revolution of the last quarter century, together with the development of the interplanetary space program, provided new high-precision tools to carry out experimental tests of general relativity.

[Serway & Faughn, *College Physics*, 3rd Ed., 905]

(a) _____
(b) _____
(c) _____
(d) _____

3. What draws visitors to the Great Smoky Mountains National Park is Great Smoky's magnificent half-million acre forest, the most diverse in all North America and likely the nation's last large reservoir of old growth broadleaf stands. . . . But there was something else that drew me here, a rumor that this forest was in danger of dying—not from an excess of visitors trampling the terrain inside the park but from an excess of plagues drifting into the treetops from the Great Outside. . . . Some of the pests are not easily or affordably battled or may require control measures that if used, would be harmful to other life-forms in a particular ecosystem. And managers such as Superintendent Randall Pope are further frustrated by the fact that **arboreal** species might be less vulnerable to insect and fungus infestations if they weren't already so weakened by that other parkland intruder, dirty air.

[John G. Mitchell, "Our National Parks," *National Geographic*, October 1994, 29]

(a) _____
(b) _____
(c) _____
(d) _____

4. In Johnstone Strait I was no longer peering down at whales in a tank, I was among them. They swirled the water beneath me and rose beside me. I was the visitor; they were at home. I lowered my **hydrophone,** an underwater microphone, placed the headset over my ears and pressed the "record" button. Echoing in the vastness of the deep, numbing water were the familiar calls of whale dialect.
 [Alexandra Morton, "Life Among the Whales," *Smithsonian,* November 1994, 48]

(a) _____
(b) _____
(c) _____
(d) _____

5. The remains of the ceremonially buried horses which had been pressed against the burial chamber's outer wall emerged with patches of chestnut hair intact and the holes of the executioner's ax in their skulls. In their stomachs remained a partly digested mix of grass, twigs, and pine needles. Mathias Seifert, a Swiss **dendrochronologist** who spent the summer on Ukok [Siberia], collected these stomach contents and took core samples of the wood in the chamber; from them he was able to determine that the burial had been in spring.
 [Natalya Polosmak, "A Mummy Unearthed from the Pastures of Heaven," *National Geographic,* October 1994, 97]

(a) _____
(b) _____
(c) _____
(d) _____

SECTION 2

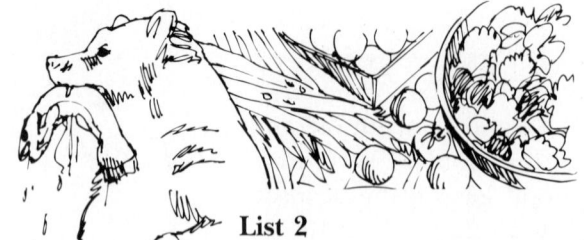

List 2
Here are more word parts that are used to signify elements of nature.

WORD PART	MEANING
ANEMO	wind
AQU	water
COSM	world; universe
ECO	environment
GEO	earth
HERB	green plant
ORO	mountain
PHYT	vegetation
SEISM	earthquake
SILV	tree; forest
SOL	sun
STELL	star
SYLV	tree; forest
XYL	wood

Copyright © 1996 Harcourt Brace & Company. All rights reserved.

PRE-EXERCISE ACTIVITY 2
- **List Making**
- **Skill: word parts**

*In the blanks that follow, rewrite List 2. This time, however, reverse the order by writing the **meanings** in the first column. Then gather all the word parts in the list which have that meaning and write them on one line in the second column. This will let you make necessary connections and help you in the process of long-term memorization. The first one has already been done to show you how.*

	MEANING	WORD PARTS	
1.	earth	geo	*Note:* This list will be more useful if you write it in alphabetical order.
2.	_____	_____	
3.	_____	_____	
4.	_____	_____	
5.	_____	_____	
6.	_____	_____	
7.	_____	_____	
8.	_____	_____	
9.	_____	_____	
10.	_____	_____	
11.	_____	_____	
12.	_____	_____	
13.	_____	_____	
14.	_____	_____	
15.	_____	_____	

EXERCISE 12-H
- **Multiple Choice**
- **Skill: word parts**

A meaning is in boldface for each of the following phrases. From the four choices given, pick the one answer which contains a word part with that meaning. Use both versions of List 2 to help you. **Do not use a dictionary.** *Do not focus on the size or difficulty of the words. Look only for the simple word part; it will lead you to the correct answer.*

Example: √A musical instrument built of **wooden** bars that are struck by small hammers:
   (A) sousaphone   (C) saxophone
   (B) xylophone   (D) megaphone

   Answer: (B) The reason for this answer is that the XYLO part of *xylophone* means "wood."

1. The scientific study of the history of the physical **earth**
   (A) geology   (C) phytology
   (B) orology   (D) herbology

2. The scientific study of the **environment**
   (A) anemology   (C) ecology
   (B) cosmology   (D) seismology

3. The scientific study of **earthquakes**
   (A) anemology   (C) ecology
   (B) cosmology   (D) seismology

4. The scientific study of **vegetation**
   (A) geology   (C) phytology
   (B) orology   (D) pharmacology

5. A method of plant cultivation that uses **water** instead of soil
   (A) pisciculture   (C) silviculture
   (B) aquiculture   (D) horticulture

6. The scientific study of **winds**
   (A) anemology   (C) ecology
   (B) cosmology   (D) seismology

7. The scientific study of **mountains**
   - (A) geology
   - (B) orology
   - (C) phytology
   - (D) herbology

8. The art of producing and caring for a **forest**
   - (A) pisciculture
   - (B) aquiculture
   - (C) silviculture
   - (D) horticulture

9. The scientific study of edible or medicinal **green plants**
   - (A) geology
   - (B) orology
   - (C) anemology
   - (D) herbology

10. The scientific study of the **universe**
    - (A) anemology
    - (B) cosmology
    - (C) ecology
    - (D) seismology

EXERCISE 12-I
- Fill in the Blank (one cue)
- Skill: word parts

*Use a **meaning** from List 2 to fill in the blank in each statement. The word part whose meaning you are defining will be found inside the boldfaced word. **Do not use a dictionary.** Do not focus on the size or difficulty of the words. Look only for the simple word part; it will lead you to the correct answer.*

Example: √**Orology** is the scientific study of _____ .

   Answer: *mountains* [> ORO]

1. **Aqueous** means of, like, or containing _____ .
2. **Seismic** disturbances are caused by _____ .
3. The **cosmos** is the _____ thought of as an orderly and harmonious system.
4. A **solar** flare is an outburst of gases from the surface of the _____ .
5. A **sylvan** landscape can be found only in a _____ .

6. Something **herbaceous** has the appearance of an ordinary _____.
7. Something **silvicolous** lives or grows among _____.
8. **Geodynamics** studies the forces within the _____.
9. **Anemometry** measures the speed of the _____.
10. An engraving on _____ is called a **xylograph**.
11. Animals that are **phytophagous** eat _____.
12. **Orographic** precipitation is caused by the movement of moist air over a _____.
13. **Xylotomy** is the art of preparing sections of _____ for microscopic viewing.
14. An **ecotone** is a transition area between two different _____.
15. To **stellify** is to transform into a _____.

EXERCISE 12-J
- **Fill in the Blank (no cue)**
- **Skills: word parts, context**

*Once again, use a **meaning** from List 2 to fill in the blank in each statement. This time, however, you will have to find the word part yourself in the difficult or technical word. **Do not use a dictionary.** Do not focus on the size or difficulty of the words. Look only for the simple word part; it will lead you to the correct answer.*

Example: √An aquarium is filled with _____.

   Answer: *water* [> AQU]

1. A formation that contains or conducts _____ is called an aquifer.
2. An ecosystem is formed by the interaction of organisms with their _____.
3. Stelliferous means having or abounding with _____.
4. An aquiferous source supplies _____.

5. A solarium is another name for a _____ room.
6. A herbivore eats _____.
7. Seismism is _____ activity.
8. The cultivation of _____ is known as silviculture.
9. A geophyte is a plant growing in _____.
10. Cosmogony is a theory or story about the origin and development of the _____.
11. The branch of physical geography dealing with _____ is called orography.
12. Xylem is a _____y tissue.
13. Geomorphology deals with the form of the _____.
14. Phytogenesis studies the origin and development of _____.
15. Anemotropism means turning in response to the _____.

EXERCISE 12-K
- **Matching Columns**
- **Skill: word parts**

Memory check. Do not look back at List 2 or use a dictionary.

1. ____	SILV	(a)	wind
2. ____	ANEMO	(b)	mountain
3. ____	SEISM	(c)	earth
4. ____	XYLO	(d)	environment
5. ____	ORO	(e)	vegetation
6. ____	AQU	(f)	tree
7. ____	ECO	(g)	sun
8. ____	GEO	(h)	earthquake
9. ____	PHYT	(i)	water
10. ____	SOL	(j)	wood

Carnivores eat animals and piscivores eat fish;
Herbivores put vegetables and plants upon their dish.
If it grows or runs or jumps or swims or flies upon the wing,
I cast my lot with omnivores—I'll eat most anything!

EXERCISE 12-L
- Fill in (two cues)
- Skills: word parts, dictionary, context

*To finish each word, fill in the blank with one of the **word parts** from your version of List 2. **You must use a college-level dictionary** to make sure that what you write really is a word and that it fits in the sentence. The word in boldface will give you the meaning of the word part that you must write.*

Example: √___desy studies the shape and size of the **earth**.

    Answer: *GEO* [> earth]

1. An ___educt is an artificial channel for conducting **water** from a distance, usually by means of gravity.
2. ___cide is the destruction of large areas of the natural **environment**.
3. Early ___centric theories taught that the **earth** was the center of the universe.
4. The scientific measuring of **earthquakes** is called _____ography.
5. _____ocidal chemicals kill **vegetation**.
6. Something that is **star**-shaped is _____iform.
7. ___ophagous insects destroy **wood**.
8. The process of **mountain** making is called ___geny.
9. The macro_____ is the **universe** at large.
10. A para___ is a light portable **sunshade**.
11. A sapro___e is any organism living in dead or decaying **vegetation**.
12. A _____atic disease is transmitted by **forest**-dwelling insects or animals.
13. A ___icide is a substance used to destroy **green plants**, especially weeds.
14. A _____ular gemstone is marked with **starlike** spots of color.
15. The dandelion is _____chorous; it is spread by the **wind**.

EXERCISE 12-M
- Fill in (one cue)
- Skills: word parts, dictionary, context

*Continue filling in **word parts** from your version of List 2 as you have been doing, **using a college-level dictionary** to check accuracy. This time, however, there will be no word in boldface. You will have to search the sentence for a clue.*

Example: √A _ _ _ _ _ic disturbance involves an earthquake.

       Answer: *SEISM* [> earthquake]

1. In a _ _ _ ar eclipse, part of the sun is obscured.
2. _ _ _ graphy is the science which studies mountains.
3. A _ _ _ syncline is a great downward bending of the earth's crust.
4. An _ _ _ system is a physical environment and all the elements that depend upon it for their very existence.
5. An _ _ _ _ _ meter is an instrument for measuring the force or velocity of the wind.
6. _ _ _ otomous insects bore or cut into wood.
7. A _ _ _ _ _ ometer measures the intensity and duration of earthquakes.
8. _ _ _ _ an means consisting of or abounding in woods or trees.
9. Animals or plants that live in water are _ _ _ atic.
10. A micro _ _ _ e is microscopically small vegetation.
11. _ _ _ _ ography is the science that describes and maps the main features of the universe.
12. _ _ _ _ ivorous animals eat green plants.
13. A _ _ _ _ _ iform figure has the shape of a star.
14. _ _ _ _ ics is the study of forests.
15. _ _ _ _ opathology studies diseases that attack vegetation.

EXERCISE 12-N
- **Paragraph Examples**
- **Skills: word parts, dictionary, context**

Answer these four questions after each paragraph:

(a) *What word part inside the boldfaced word helps you to understand that word? What does that word part mean?*

(b) *Using only the context of the word and the word part that it contains, what do you think the boldfaced word means? (See Chapter 1, Section 2.)*

(c) *Choose one context clue that helped you. (See Chapter 1, Section 2.)*
  1. *word signals*
  2. *punctuation signals*
  3. *synonyms (substitution)*
  4. *examples or description*
  5. *contrast or opposites*
  6. *prior knowledge; common sense*

  If 6, explain: _____

(d) *How does the dictionary define the boldfaced word as it is used in the paragraph?*

1. Animals are heterotrophs—organisms that cannot make their own food from inorganic substances, but must ingest organic molecules from the environment. Animals can be broadly divided into **herbivores,** which eat plants, carnivores, which eat animals, and omnivores, which eat both. Each mode of nutrition involves digestive systems suited to handling and digesting the type of food eaten.
   [Karen Arms, et al., *A Journey into Life*, 3rd Ed., 473]

   (a) _____
   (b) _____
   (c) _____
   (d) _____

2. According to the most modern idea, a real myth has nothing to do with religion. It is an explanation of something in nature; how, for instance, any and everything in the universe came into existence: humans, animals, this or that tree or flower, the sun, the moon, the stars, storms, eruptions, earthquakes, all that is and all that happens. Thunder and lightning are caused when

Zeus hurls his thunderbolt. A volcano erupts because a terrible creature is imprisoned in the mountain and every now and then struggles to get free. The Dipper, the **constellation** called also the Great Bear, does not set below the horizon because a goddess once was angry at it and decreed that it should never sink into the sea. Myths are early science, the result of people's first trying to explain what they saw around them.

[Edith Hamilton, *Mythology*, 7]

(a) _____
(b) _____
(c) _____
(d) _____

3. Early in the Devonian Era, nearly 400 million years ago, all the continents were grouped closely together and surrounded by sea. The climate ranged from periods of dry weather to periods of torrential rains, much as parts of the tropics do today. No flowering plants blossomed on land, for flowers had yet to evolve. No vertebrates—animals with backbones—walked the Earth, for those creatures that existed were entirely **aquatic.**

[Caroline Harding, "Fish Out of Water," *National Wildlife*, October–November 1994, 12]

(a) _____
(b) _____
(c) _____
(d) _____

4, 5. More than a century ago, it was discovered that sunspot activity is correlated with magnetic storms on earth. During geomagnetic storms, the earth's magnetic field is disturbed, and the compass needle shows fluctuations. Today we know that communication transmission interference and displays of the aurora are also correlated with **geomagnetic** storms and the sunspot cycle. Some investigators are of the opinion that even long-term changes in climate may be connected with **solar** activity. These effects are due to the ultraviolet and X-ray radiation from the sun, and also to the solar wind. The solar wind is the more or less continuous emission of charged atomic particles, mostly protons and electrons, from the sun.

[George O. Abell, *Realm of the Universe*, 283]

(a) _____
(b) _____

366 CHAPTER 12 NATURE

(c) _____
_____
(d) _____
_____
(a) _____
_____
(b) _____
_____
(c) _____
_____
(d) _____

Creatures living among
  trees
Are rightly called silvicolous.
Squirrels will flock there as
  they please,
But this is just ridiculous.

Copyright © 1996 Harcourt Brace & Company. All rights reserved.

SECTION 3: CHAPTER REVIEW (LISTS 1 AND 2 COMBINED)

Word Parts Covered in This Chapter:

WORD PART	MEANING	COMMON EXAMPLE	TEXTBOOK EXAMPLE
ANEMO	wind	*anemometer*	*anemochore*
AQU	water; fluid	*aquarium*	*aquiferous*
ARBOR	tree	*arboretum*	*arborization*
AREN	sand	*arena*	*arenaceous*
ASTR	star; celestial body	*astronomy*	*astronavigation*
COSM	world; universe	*cosmic*	*cosmology*
DENDR	tree	*rhododendron*	*dendriform*
ECO	environment	*ecology*	*ecotype*
GEO	earth	*geography*	*geomorphic*
HELIO	sun	*heliocentric*	*heliotaxis*
HERB	green plant	*herbs*	*herbivore*
HYDR	water; fluid	*hydrant*	*hydrophyte*
HYGR	humidity; moisture	*hygrometer*	*hygroscopic*
LIGN	wood	*ligneous*	*lignivorous*
LUN	moon	*lunar*	*lunular*
ORO	mountain	*orography*	*orogenesis*
PETR	rock	*petrified*	*petroglyph*
PHYLL	leaf	*chlorophyll*	*heterophyllous*
PHYT	vegetation	*phytogenic*	*phytocidal*
PISC	fish	*Pisces*	*piscatology*
SEISM	earthquake	*seismograph*	*seismicity*
SILV	tree; forest	*silvics*	*silviculture*
SOL	sun	*solar*	*solarimeter*
STELL	star	*stellar*	*stelliferous*
SYLV	tree; forest	*sylvan*	*sylvatic*
TERR	earth; ground	*terrain*	*terricolous*
XYL	wood	*xylophone*	*xylophagous*
ZO	animal	*zoo*	*zooplasty*

Copyright © 1996 Harcourt Brace & Company. All rights reserved.

PRE-EXERCISE ACTIVITY 3
- **List Making**
- **Skill: word parts**

*In the blanks that follow, rewrite the combined word parts list. This time, however, reverse the order by writing the **meanings** in the first column. Then gather all the word parts in the list which have that meaning and write them on one line in the second column. This will let you make necessary connections and help you in the process of long-term memorization. The first one has already been done to show you how.*

	MEANING	WORD PARTS	
1.	animal	zo	*Note:* This list will be more useful if you write it in alphabetical order.
2.	_____	_____	
3.	_____	_____	
4.	_____	_____	
5.	_____	_____	
6.	_____	_____	
7.	_____	_____	
8.	_____	_____	
9.	_____	_____	
10.	_____	_____	
11.	_____	_____	
12.	_____	_____	
13.	_____	_____	
14.	_____	_____	
15.	_____	_____	
16.	_____	_____	
17.	_____	_____	
18.	_____	_____	
19.	_____	_____	
20.	_____	_____	*Continued*

21. _____	_____
22. _____	_____
23. _____	_____
24. _____	_____
25. _____	_____
26. _____	_____

EXERCISE 12-O
- **Matching Columns**
- **Skill: word parts**

Memory check. Do not look back at the combined list or use a dictionary.

1. _____ AREN   (a) wood
2. _____ SOL   (b) sand
3. _____ TERR   (c) rock
4. _____ LIGN   (d) leaf
5. _____ ZO   (e) sun
6. _____ STELL   (f) star
7. _____ PHYLL   (g) mountain
8. _____ PETR   (h) wind
9. _____ ORO   (i) animal
10. _____ ANEMO   (j) earth; ground

EXERCISE 12-P
- **Cross Out**
- **Skills: dictionary, word parts, context**

One word in each set does not contain the word part and meaning that is given, even though it has a set of similar letters. **Use a college-level dictionary** *to find the one that does **not** fit.*

	WORD PART	MEANING	CROSS OUT THE ONE WORD THAT DOES NOT FIT.
Example:	√ZO	animal	zoanthropy, zoomorphic, zoisite

Answer: The dictionary shows that *zoanthropy* and *zoomorphic* have the meaning *animal* in their definitions. *Zoisite* (a mineral) does not; cross it out.

WORD PART	MEANING	CROSS OUT THE ONE WORD THAT DOES NOT FIT.
1. SILV	tree; woods	silviculture, silver, silvics
2. PISC	fish	piscivorous, episcopal, piscatorial
3. ASTR	star; universe	astrobiology, astromancy, astragalus
4. LIGN	wood	lignin, align, lignify
5. LUN	moon	lunisolar, lunate, lunge
6. ORO	mountain	oronasal, orogeny, orography
7. PETR	rock	petrel, petrology, petrified
8. SOL	sun	parasol, solarization, solitude
9. TERR	earth; ground	terrify, territorial, terrain
10. COSM	universe; world	macrocosm, cosmology, cosmetology

EXERCISE 12-Q
- **Extended Answer**
- **Skills: word parts, dictionary, context**

Answer the following questions by using a college-level dictionary.

Example: √How is the meaning *tree* involved in the word **arborescent?**

   Answer: Arborescent means having the form or characteristics of a tree.

1. How is the meaning *world* or *universe* involved in the word **microcosm?**

2. How is the meaning *animal* involved in the word **zoolatry?**

3. How is the meaning *wind* involved in the word **anemophilous?**

4. How is the meaning *wood* involved in the word **xylocarp?**

5. How is the meaning *leaf* involved in the word **chlorophyll?**

6. How is the meaning *water* involved in the word **aqueduct?**

7. How is the meaning *celestial bodies* involved in the word **astrophotography?**

8. How is the meaning *sand* involved in the word **arenaceous?**

9. How is the meaning *vegetation* involved in the word **phytoplankton?**

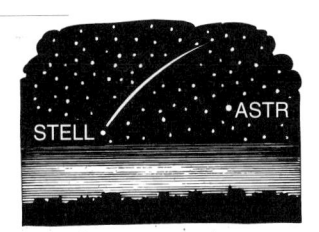

10. How is the meaning *ground* involved in the word **terricolous?**

Twinkle, twinkle, little stell;
What holds you up I cannot tell.
Twinkle, twinkle, little astr;
If you fall, it'll be a disastr.

EXERCISE 12-R
- **Fill in the Blank**
- **Skill: word parts**

Memory check. Do not look back at the combined list or use a dictionary.

1. Name two word parts that mean *wood*: _____ and _____ .
2. Name two word parts that mean *star*: _____ and _____ .
3. Name two word parts that mean *tree*: _____ and _____ .
4. Name two word parts that mean *earth*: _____ and _____ .
5. Name two word parts that mean *water*: _____ and _____ .
6. Name two word parts that mean *sun*: _____ and _____ .

EXERCISE 12-S
- **Paragraph Examples**
- **Skills: word parts, dictionary, context**

Answer these four questions after each paragraph:

(a) What word part inside the boldfaced word helps you to understand that word? What does that word part mean?
_____

(b) Using only the context of the word and the word part that it contains, what do you think the boldfaced word means? (See Chapter 1, Section 2.)
_____

(c) Choose one context clue that helped you. (See Chapter 1, Section 2.)

    1. word signals   4. examples or description
    2. punctuation signals   5. contrast or opposites
    3. synonyms (substitution)   6. prior knowledge; common sense
       If 6, explain: _____

(d) *How does the dictionary define the boldfaced word as it is used in the paragraph?*

1. The word "ecology," coined in 1869, is based on the Greek word *oikos,* meaning "house" or, more loosely, "habitat." The term ecosystem, from the same root, is the habitat or environment where organisms live and interact. The ecosystem includes abiotic (nonliving) factors such as sunlight, temperature, water, and soil and biotic factors (all the other organisms in the ecosystem). Each **ecosystem** contains several communities of organisms, collections of different species living together.
   [Arms, et al., *A Journey into Life,* 3rd Ed., 749]
   (a) _____
   (b) _____
   (c) _____
   (d) _____

2. In warm seasons and hot climes, few animals can long survive the full force of the sun's withering power. All species have an optimum internal temperature at which they function best. Too much sun, and the inner furnace oversteps its bounds. In overheated vertebrates, the body **dehydrates,** loss of fluid impedes blood flow, the brain malfunctions, and death strikes. For a desert creature, shade cast by a cactus across parched earth may mean survival.
   [Roger DiSilvestro, "Sweet Shadows," *International Wildlife,* November–December 1994, 51]
   (a) _____
   (b) _____
   (c) _____
   (d) _____

3. Over the years, researchers and government agencies have developed many definitions of wetlands. All share the recognition that wetlands are shallow-water systems, or areas where water is at or near the surface for some time. Most descriptions also note the presence of plants adapted to flooding, called **hydrophytes,** and hydric soils, which, when flooded, develop colors and odors that distinguish them from upland soils.
   [John A. Kusler, et al., "Wetlands," *Scientific American,* January 1994, 65]

(a) _____
(b) _____
(c) _____
(d) _____

4. We know from its 10 foot skeleton that the great elephantbird was built like a steamroller and plodded over the Madagascar landscape on massive legs and feet. But it had only shriveled wings. Yet those vestigial wing bones suggest that once upon a time, elephantbirds could indeed fly. They eventually lost that power through disuse as they adapted to a **terrestrial** lifestyle in a place free of predators.

[Les Line, "Have Wings, Can't Fly," *International Wildlife*, November–December 1994, 23]

(a) _____
(b) _____
(c) _____
(d) _____

5. Words do have areas of agreed-upon meaning or dictionary definitions. "Rat," for example, is the label agreed upon in English to identify a rodent that resembles a mouse but is larger and marked by a different sort of tooth structure. This identifying function of the word is its *denotation*. But what has happened to the word when a gangster refers to an accomplice as "a rat," or when he makes the word into a verb and says "he ratted on me," that is, "he gave information against me to the police"? The gangster does not mean that his accomplice is a rodent resembling a mouse but larger and having a different tooth-structure. For man, the language animal, not only invents words as labels (denotations), but tends to associate the word with the thing it labels. Most people think of rats as despicable, vicious, and filthy. So the word takes on that "feel." The gangster is not at all concerned with the **zoological** classification of *genus Rattus*. He has dropped the denotation in order to use the feeling of the words (connotation).

[John Ciardi, *How Does a Poem Mean?* 762]

(a) _____
(b) _____
(c) _____
(d) _____

6, 7. For hundreds of years, scientists and lay people regarded the Earth as the center of the Universe. This geocentric model was accepted by such notables as Aristotle (384 to 322 B.C.) and Claudius Ptolemy (about A.D. 140). Largely because of the authority of Aristotle, the **geocentric** model became the officially accepted theory of the Universe and maintained this position until the seventeenth century. The Polish astronomer Nicolaus Copernicus (1473–1543) suggested that the Earth and the other planets revolved in circular orbits around the Sun (the **heliocentric** model). This early knowledge formed the foundation for the work of Galileo Galilei (1564–1642). Galileo stands out as perhaps the dominant figure in leading the world of physics into the modern era.

[Serway & Faughn, *College Physics*, 3rd Ed., 27]

(a) _____
(b) _____
(c) _____
(d) _____

(a) _____
(b) _____
(c) _____
(d) _____

8. The young roots of a tall tree that absorb water and minerals may be many meters from the leaves. The roots and leaves are connected by the vascular tissues, xylem and phloem, which form a transport system linking the various parts of the plant and moving substances between them. In 1679, the Italian scientist Marcello Malpighi performed an experiment that showed the functions of xylem and phloem. He peeled off the bark in a complete ring around the trunk of the tree, a procedure known as girdling. This removes the phloem, which makes up the inner bark, but leaves the secondary xylem, or wood, intact. After this treatment, Malpighi found that a swelling appeared on the bark just above the stripped area. Fluid exuded from this swelling was sweet. The leaves showed no effects for days or months, but eventually they wilted and then died, and the entire tree was soon dead. From these observations, Malpighi concluded that phloem transports food and that **xylem** was transporting water to the leaves.

[Karen Arms, et al., *A Journey into Life*, 3rd Ed., 694]

(a) _____
(b) _____
(c) _____
(d) _____

9. One cannot fault the ancients for assuming that the luminous orbs in the sky, the stars and planets, are made of "heavenly" substances, and not of the earthly elements we find at home. In fact, the realization that celestial worlds are actually worlds and not ethereal substance is relatively recent in the history of science. Small wonder, then, that the ancients regarded the planets as having special significance. Thus the planets came to be associated with the gods of ancient mythologies; in some cases, they were themselves thought of as gods. Even in the comparatively sophisticated Greece of antiquity, the planets had the names of gods, and were even credited with having the same powers and influences as the gods whose names they bore. From such ideas grew the primitive religion of **astrology.**
[George O. Abell, *Realm of the Universe*, 19]

(a) _____
(b) _____
(c) _____
(d) _____

10. Invisible barriers in the physical sciences never fail to astonish us. The edge of the detectable Universe—the **cosmological** horizon—is one invisible barrier, and the relativistic speed limit, beyond which no object can accelerate, is another. The consternation they cause stems from the fact that the extremely large and the extraordinarily fast lie outside the realm of human experience. A third such barrier is the absolute zero of temperature, the state beyond which matter cannot be cooled, in which all molecular motion ceases.
[Serway & Faughn, *College Physics*, 3rd Ed., 408]

(a) _____
(b) _____
(c) _____
(d) _____

Appendix A HOW TO MEMORIZE

You're walking down the street trying to decide where to eat when a bright yellow school bus crammed with manic grade schoolers rumbles by. Suddenly, in your mind, you're in your third grade class again, fourth aisle, second seat, and Miss Ferndale is looming over you menacingly, a ruler clutched in her hand.

Or you're standing impatiently in front of the microwave one Friday night waiting for the popcorn to finish hotfooting its way across the bottom of the bag, and a scene from an old Clint Eastwood movie pops into your head unbidden, a movie you saw a few years ago in the mall quadruplex back home with old what's-his-name.

Or you're flopped in an overstuffed chair, just hanging out at a friend's place, when a song on the radio transports you back to your senior prom, and once again you're in your high school gym, the air stuffy, your new shoes too tight, other couples bumping into you as you try to do your "thang."

Or you're thumbing through the television listings and you notice that there's going to be yet another rerun of Ken Burns' *Civil War*, and out of nowhere, totally unasked for, the dates 1861–1865 flash onto your mental screen.

This is memory at work. Even without any conscious help from us, the brain cross-relates items through biochemical memory traces in cell assemblies that communicate constantly with each other. In service of memory, the brain hangs things on mental pegs and combines and connects and pigeonholes and correlates and categorizes and does all sorts of wondrous things that can be gathered together under the term *association*. Information is stored this way, and information is retrieved this way. Understanding some practical matters about memory input, storage, and output (to use computer terms) will make learning the word parts in this book a little bit easier. And make no mistake about it: when you try to increase your vocabulary, memory plays an absolutely necessary, even if not solitary, role.

MEMORY BOOSTERS

Both for placing items in your memory in the first place and for pulling them out later, here are some proven methods that you can use.

- In trying to associate a word part with its meaning, use good old-fashioned repetition. Take a word part like VIS and its meaning, *sight*. One of the things to do is to repeat that connection until you're sick of hearing it: "VIS means sight; VIS means sight; VIS means sight"—over and over. When you think that you'll *never* forget it, repeat it at least ten more times. Set it aside, but come back to it the next day and go through the repetitions again. Wait one day and go through the routine once more. Then give it 24 hours, and then . . . but you get the idea.
- Involve as many senses as possible in the memorizing process. Here are some ready examples; you will be able to think of others.

  SEE:
  √ Look intently at the word part and its meaning. Then turn away, stare at a blank wall, and try to see the letters as if they were spray-painted there.
  √ Use different colored highlighting pens for each list; associate the category for that list with a particular color. Alternatively, rewrite the lists using different colored pens, art pencils—even crayons! If you live near an office supply store, invest in different colored index cards—or cut out your own homemade flash cards from colored posterboard.
  √ Use your imagination to assign different sizes and shapes to word parts. For instance, in Chapter 5, just visualize micro and macro.

  HEAR:
  √ Recite the word parts and their meanings out loud—*very* loud.
  √ Use a tape recorder to record each list and play it back whenever you get a chance—at home, in the car, walking down the street.
  √ When possible, associate word parts with different sounds. Some word parts may sound happy to you; others may sound sad. Some word parts sound like a sneeze or a barking dog; others sound like yogurt splatting against a brick wall. Be weird; it works.

  FEEL:
  √ Write each word part and its meaning by hand on homemade flash cards.
  √ Draw the letters of each word part and its meaning in the air as if you were writing on a gigantic chalkboard for people at the back of the auditorium.

√ Pressing hard, trace the letters of each word part and its meaning on the palm of your hand with your finger. (No, it's not the same as writing the answers on your hand for a test.)
√ Associate word parts with different tactile feelings or textures. Some word parts may strike you as smooth to the touch; others are rough or jagged. Some are hot; others feel cold.

SMELL AND TASTE:
√ Assign each category or word part a different flavor and smell. (These senses are so intertwined that it often amounts to the same thing.) For instance, some word parts can be chocolate, some blueberry, some pepperoni pizza, some barbecued ribs. If you're really into food, it will be a verbal feast.

- As long as we've just considered sense association, let's mention a couple of other types of association at this point.
  √ Picture association tries to connect a word part and its meaning to some vivid mental picture. For instance, consider PHYT, which means *vegetation*. To remember it more easily, picture yourself fighting (phyting) giant weeds in your garden with a sword. To recall the meaning of TRICHO (*hair*), visualize an extremely long-haired magician unsuccessfully trying to perform a trick (trich). To bring back the meaning of AMBI (*both or two*), picture two cute little fawns—Bambi and his sister Ambi—running away from two hunters. Make your mental pictures vivid, active, exaggerated, even downright silly. Silly associations are likely to work more effectively. You can even turn your separate mental images into a connected short story.
  √ Word or letter association uses various methods. For instance, you might use rhyme to hook together word parts and meanings.

  One, two: MONO, DU;
  Three, four: TRI and QUAR(t).

  If you think that's wretched, try this on for size:

  MAXI, MINI: large and small;
  MICRO, ALTO: short and tall.

  Or here's another rollicking rap that uses numbers:

  AMBI, AMPHI, BI, DI, DU:
  All these word parts just mean two.

  Then there's the use of letters. If you're trying to remember the word parts that mean two (AMBI, AMPHI, BI, DI, DU), you could take their initial letters (A, A, B, D, D), rearrange them,

and come up with "2 BAD AD." A variation could be "2 BAADD for you." Or you could turn the first letter of each into a new word to construct a sentence: "An Aging Buffalo Doubly Dies." During a test, simply turn the letters back into the word parts that they represent. The only limit is your imagination and what works for you. If it takes too long to come up with a word or letter mnemonic (memory device), or if it's too hard to remember, then it's not worth the trouble. There's always repetition.

- Look for word parts that share a pattern. This book already establishes general patterns by devoting each chapter to a specific category. But you can enhance that by setting up your own specific patterns. Two patterns that you can use are similarity (synonyms) and difference (antonyms). Let's use Chapter 4 as an example. For a similarity pattern, you could link the following items on the basis of their shared meaning: *with* = CO, COL, COM, CON, COR, SYL, SYM, SYN, SYS. Then, for a difference pattern, you could contrast those word parts to the word parts that mean the opposite: *against* = ANTI, CONTRA, COUNTER. Here's another example from Chapter 4. The word parts ENDO, INTRA, and INTRO share a similar meaning—*inside*. You can set up a contrast pattern by grouping the word parts ECTO, EXTRA, and EXTRO, all of which mean *outside*. In fact, in the chapters where such groupings are possible, you will find exercises in Section 3, Chapter Review, which will require you to focus on synonyms and antonyms. And when you do the Pre-Exercises that begin each section, you will usually find yourself involved with patterns of similarity.
- Remember to make choices when you memorize. You can't remember everything, so decide what's going to be left behind. In this textbook, for instance, your first concern should be memorizing the word parts. Later, if there is time, you can go back and try to learn how to spell or pronounce some of the words that use the word parts.

TEST PREPARATION

- Review the material frequently. Thirty minutes each day for a week is better than cramming the night before a test. Don't forget to use your flash cards.

- Study with a classmate. Take turns drilling each other on word parts and their meanings. And don't forget to reverse the process by starting with a meaning and asking for a word part with that meaning.
- Redo all the chapter exercises even if they were covered in class or as homework.
- Construct your own test for each list. Set it aside; then take it a few days later.
- An hour or so before class begins, go to the room where the test will be given, sit in the chair where you will take the test, and do a final review there.
- As the test time approaches, use any relaxing technique that works for you: breathing exercises, pleasant mental images, motivational review, biofeedback, mantras, etc. If you don't know any relaxation techniques, go learn some now before the first test is scheduled.
- Just before you start the test, picture the place where you first memorized the word parts. Visualize yourself sitting there studying. Recreate the sights, the sounds, the smells, the feelings that you were experiencing then.
- As you retrieve memories of word parts and their meanings, use the sense, picture, word, and letter associations that were discussed in the last section.

STUDY HABITS

To maximize the job of memorizing, you must control your physical surroundings.

- Set up a specific place for study, and use it for nothing but study. If you can't set aside a small study room, at least set aside a desk, an old table, or a collapsible card table that is used only for study. Don't sit and talk on the phone there, don't read *The National Enquirer* there, and don't eat there. Just study there.
- Set up a specific study time. It's best if it's a standing priority set in advance. Let your friends or family know that you are not available during that time. Don't answer the phone during that time. Lock the door and pretend that you're not home.
- Allow no noise or distractions. That may mean waiting until your roommate or your kid brother is out. It may mean going to the quiet room of a library. It certainly means turning off the TV and the stereo and putting your personal headset way out of reach.

No matter how much you insist that you can't study without background noise, you must come to recognize that you can't successfully study and do something else at the same time. Without realizing it, your attention will shift from one to the other. That's just the way the brain operates.

- Make sure that the lighting is good (get a brighter bulb), keep the room temperature on the cool side, and sit on a chair which isn't so soft and comfortable that the next thing you know it's morning and time to get up. Give yourself regular breaks—but get up and away from your designated study place when you take a break every hour or so. If you find yourself nodding off periodically, stand up and pace the room as you study. If you still feel drowsy, face reality: go to bed and study another time.
- If you haven't had an eye exam for some time (or ever!), go get one. Even if you've had one within the last year, if you experience burning, itching, or watery eyes every time you read, or if blurry vision makes the print or the chalkboard hard to read, it's time for another checkup.

Once optimal physical conditions are in place, you must check on mental and emotional factors each time that you sit down to study.

- Make sure that you are motivated for this particular study session. If you don't see a reason to study some material, if you think it's a waste of time, it's not going to stick. You've got to work up some motivation, some positive emotion—and it's got to be based on *your* goals and reasons, not your parents' or mate's or instructor's goals or reasons. If you really believe that a course or a book is a steppingstone to something that you dearly want, something that you truly hunger for, then your motivation will carry you through dull or difficult material. It's a fact that information which has motivational or emotional significance for us stays longer in the memory.
- Call on all your powers of focus and concentration; work on developing self-discipline. If you do not fully pay attention to what you are studying, your brain cannot record information. You won't remember what you didn't notice. You've got to pull your attention back ruthlessly if your mind begins to wander. If your emotions or personal obligations entice you elsewhere during a study session, if you cannot intensely and exclusively focus on the matter at hand, you should close the book and go take care of

pressing business. Don't ever sit at that designated study desk or table if you don't mean it.

SUPPLIES

- Get some index cards—the ones that fit easily in a pocket—or make your own by cutting up sheets of paper. You'll use them to construct flash cards with a word part on one side and its meaning on the other. Since they are much more compact than the textbook, they will make studying easier.
- You'll want to devote a spiral notebook to vocabulary. Divide it into sections.
    √ Use one section to copy word part examples from textbooks, magazines, newspapers, etc. Write down the sentence in which you found the word and write down the meaning of the word.
    √ Use another notebook section to save interesting word part examples that you have found by looking up word parts in unabridged and specialty dictionaries—medical, legal, computer, etc. You'll find dictionaries of this nature in the library. Be sure to find one that fits your intended major.
    √ Use a different section of the notebook to record words that seem interesting or important even if they don't use recognizable word parts. Don't forget to include a dictionary definition and a sentence that uses the word.
    √ Use other sections of the notebook for vocabulary projects that your instructor gives you.
- Build a collection of different colored highlighters, pens, or pencils. You'll need them to color-code lists to make memorizing easier. This process was explained above.

EXERCISE

Following are ten word parts (and their meanings) that appear in various chapters of this book. Create a picture association for each one. Make each mental picture (or story) as concrete and as colorful as you can. If you like to draw, you may even want to make some sketches.

EXAMPLE: SPHER = round; globe-shaped

Picture myself in an Olympic spear- (*spher*) or javelin-throwing contest. The spear that I have been given has a round tip instead of a pointed tip. It looks like a globe map stuck on the end of a broom handle. Every time that I throw the spear at the target, it bounces off instead of sticking because it's round. From the corner of my eye, I can see Brent Musberger laughing as he comes forward, microphone in hand, to interview me for a national television audience.

1. MILLI = one thousand
   My story or picture:

2. CATA = down
   My story or picture:

3. SYN = with; together
   My story or picture:

4. BATHY = deep
   My story or picture:

5. ACU = pointed; sharp
   My story or picture:

6. NOCT = evening
   My story or picture:

7. GUST = taste
   My story or picture:

Copyright © 1996 Harcourt Brace & Company. All rights reserved.

8. **CURS** = to run
   My story or picture:

9. **CRYO** = cold
   My story or picture:

10. **CARD** = heart
    My story or picture:

Appendix B NEGATIVE WORD PARTS

Certain word parts have negative meanings, so when they are added to words, they tend to reverse the original meaning. Most negative word parts can be translated with the word *not*. For instance, the word *possible* gets translated as "not possible" when you add the letters IM- to form the word *impossible*. But sometimes the proper way to translate the negative word part is by using meanings such as *absent, missing, losing, leaving, lacking, removed, without, opposing, against,* and other "takeaway" or reversal words. Context will help you decide which meaning fits best; so will a dictionary.

As usual, remember the warning from Chapter 1: letter combinations sometimes come together only accidentally. For instance, an *atheist* is someone who does not believe in God, as opposed to a *theist*; the A- is a negative word part. But the A- in the word *achieve* has no negative meaning at all. Likewise, *counterclockwise* motion goes in the opposite direction of *clockwise* motion; COUNTER- is a negative word part in this word. But in the word *countertop*, there is no negative meaning in COUNTER-. As usual, let a dictionary be the final judge when you are not sure if a word is negative.

WORD PART	MEANING	EXAMPLES
A	not; without	achromatic: free from color asymmetric: not identical on both sides of a central line amoral: having no moral standards at all
AB	away from	abdicate: to leave a throne, high office, etc. abduct: to carry off or lead away by force aberrant: departing from the right, normal, or usual course
AN	not; without	anaerobic: living in the absence of air or free oxygen anarchy: a state of society without government or law anonymous: without any name acknowledged
ANTI	opposite of; against	antiallergenic: not aggravating an allergy antigay: opposed or hostile to homosexuals antisocial: hostile or unfriendly toward others

387

APPENDIX B NEGATIVE WORD PARTS

WORD PART	MEANING	EXAMPLES
APO	away; apart	apocope: loss or omission of the last letter or part of a word apostasy: a total departure from one's religion, cause, etc. apostrophe: a mark used to show a missing letter or letters
CONTRA	opposite; against	contraband: goods imported or exported illegally contraceptive: preventing conception or impregnation contradict: to assert the opposite of; to deny directly
COUNTER	opposite; against	counteract: to act in opposition to counterculture: culture of those who reject dominant values countermand: to revoke or cancel a command or order
DE	away; apart	defrost: to remove the frost or ice from demerit: a mark against a person for misconduct deranged: insane; thrown into disorder
DIS	away; apart	disagree: to fail to agree discontent: not content or satisfied disgrace: the loss of respect, honor, or esteem
EX-	no longer	ex-president: a former president ex-prisoner: a former prisoner ex-wife: a former wife
IL	not; without	illegal: forbidden by law or statute illiteracy: a lack of ability to read and write illogical: not logical
IM	not; without	imbalance: the state or condition of lacking balance immoral: not conforming to moral principles impeccable: without fault or flaw
IN	not; without	inarticulate: lacking the ability to express oneself inexpensive: not high in price; costing little invariable: not changing; static or constant
IR	not; without	irreducible: incapable of being reduced or diminished irrelevant: not relevant, applicable, or pertinent irrevocable: not to be revoked or recalled

WORD PART	MEANING	EXAMPLES
-LESS	without	childless: having no children feckless: not effective or competent; futile hopeless: without hope
MAL	not; badly	maladaptation: incomplete, inadequate, or faulty adaptation malcontent: not satisfied or content with current conditions malfunction: failure to function properly
MIS	not; wrongly	misconceive: to interpret wrongly misprint: a mistake in printing mistrust: lack of trust or confidence
NO-	not at all	no-account: worthless; good-for-nothing no-load: investment funds with no commission charges no-name: goods sold without a brand name; generic
NON	not	nonalcoholic: not being or containing alcohol nondurable: not resistant to wear, decay, etc. nonresident: not resident in a particular place
UN	not	unemployed: not employed; without a job unfair: not fair; beyond what is proper or fitting unpopular: not popular; disliked or ignored by the public
WITH	away; apart; opposed	withdraw: to draw back, away, or aside withhold: to hold back; restrain or check withstand: to stand or hold out against; resist or oppose

EXERCISE

Tell what the boldfaced word means in each of the following sentences. Use whatever will help—word parts, context, or dictionary. Be sure to circle the negative part of each meaning when you write it down.

Example: √She was left **inarticulate** by his bizarre statement. Her mouth was open, but no words came forth. She seemed to have forgotten how to speak.

Answer: *not* able to talk; speechless

1. Since fire and billowing smoke will quickly **deplete** the oxygen in a room starting at ceiling level, safety experts recommend that people drop to the floor and crawl out as quickly as possible before they become confused or lose consciousness.
   Meaning: _____

2. Because she did not witness the unfortunate incident that began the argument, she **misconstrued** what she saw and thought that I was to blame.
   Meaning: _____

3. The manager refused to make any concessions or modifications to the new work rules, even though all the employees thought that the rules were unreasonable. As a result of the manager's **uncompromising** position, half a dozen people handed in their resignations the next day.
   Meaning: _____

4. When the onboard computer failed to perform a relatively minor sequence just minutes before liftoff, worried NASA officials decided to **abort** the mission rather than take the chance of facing more serious computer problems when the spacecraft was in orbit.
   Meaning: _____

5. The sign on the electronic equipment was enough to scare off any would-be lawbreakers: "Unauthorized use of this device by personnel without top security clearance is **illicit** and violators will be punished to the full extent of the law."
   Meaning: _____

6. If you have been a couch potato for quite some time or are aware of an existing medical condition, be sure that you check with your doctor before beginning a vigorous exercise program. In some cases, vigorous exercise may be **contraindicated.**
   Meaning: _____

7. Since the threat of nuclear confrontation between the Soviet Union and the United States had existed since the 1950s, Americans and Russians breathed a sigh of relief when the **nonproliferation** treaty was signed and nuclear production and deployment began to wind down.

8. In the search for an **antidote** to teenage crime, some commentators urge the greater availability of jobs that pay more than

minimum wage, some point to the need to curb school dropouts, and others insist on a return to strong family values.

Meaning: _____

9. We did everything we could to **dissuade** him from smoking. We reminded him that his clothes and breath reeked of offensive smoke, we pointed out that he was burning up money by buying cartons of cigarettes, and we warned him about the dangers of lung cancer and heart disease.

Meaning: _____

10. In spite of the fact that they were in church and that the solemn ceremony was about to begin, their laughter was **irrepressible.** The sight of a stray dog with its front paws resting on the pulpit as if it were about to give a sermon was too much to take.

Meaning: _____

Sample Answers:
1. To *make less* by gradually using up
2. Took in a *wrong* sense; misunderstood
3. *Not* admitting of compromise or adjustment
4. To *stop* before the scheduled flight is under way
5. *Not* legally permitted or authorized
6. *Not* recommended; advised *against*
7. *Against* the spread of nuclear weapons
8. Something that works *against* unwanted effects
9. Advise *against*; persuade *not* to do something
10. *Not* able to be repressed or restrained; uncontrollable

Appendix C SUFFIXES

Suffixes are short word parts that are always added to the end of a word. Suffixes are not quite as useful as other word parts when it comes to figuring out what a word means. This is because the principal job of most suffixes is to tell how a word is being used, not what it means. In many cases, the suffix reveals only a vague or general meaning. For instance, the -IOUS in the word *spacious* is a suffix. These four ending letters tell us clearly enough that *spacious* is an adjective, but the only meaning that they carry is "characterized by or having." In other words, a spacious room has lots of space, an anxious person has anxiety, a furious person has fury, and so on. Such a generic meaning is better than nothing, but it is certainly not as valuable, for example, as the word part THERM in *thermometer*, which reveals instantly that it is heat that is being measured, or the CARD in *cardiac*, which tells precisely that the heart is involved.

Occasionally, a suffix will carry a more definite meaning. The -ETTE in *kitchenette* clearly tells us something about the size of the room, and the -ITIS in *colitis* unmistakably tells us that there is a medical problem involving the colon. But for the most part, suffixes are most consistently valuable when we look a word up in the dictionary, as Section 1 of Chapter 1 explains.

One final warning about suffixes. As with other word parts, the same letter combination can have widely different meanings and functions. Take the suffix -ATE. It can signal an adjective (*fortunate*), a noun (*magistrate*), or a verb (*originate*). To make matters worse, the word *graduate*, for example, could be a noun (a Harvard graduate), a verb (to graduate), or an adjective (graduate school). There is no way to tell from the spelling what the word is doing; we have to see it in actual use to tell. This drives home once again the repeated lesson of this book: to understand a word, always interweave the use of word parts, context, and dictionary use.

What follows is a sampling of suffixes:

MEANING	SUFFIX	EXAMPLES
able to; capable of being *(adjective)*	-ABLE	durable, laudable, solvable
	-ATIVE	correlative, regulative, remunerative
	-IBLE	horrible, sensible, visible
	-ILE	agile, docile, volatile

MEANING	SUFFIX	EXAMPLES
act; cause; do *(verb)*	**-ATE**	aggravate, calibrate, chlorinate
	-EN	fasten, strengthen, weaken
	-ESCE	coalesce, convalesce, phosphoresce
	-FY	dignify, simplify, vilify
	-IZE	apologize, patronize, sterilize
characteristic of; tending to *(adjective)*	**-AN**	African, agrarian, mammalian
	-ARY	honorary, legendary, voluntary
	-ATE	collegiate, desolate, separate
	-IAL	filial, imperial, nuptial
	-IC	angelic, cosmic, Hispanic
	-ILE	agile, juvenile, servile
	-ISH	Danish, childish, selfish
	-ISTIC	communistic, deistic, sadistic
	-IVE	creative, disruptive, massive
	-LIKE	childlike, lifelike, warlike
	-LY	cowardly, friendly, weekly
	-SOME	awesome, quarrelsome, tiresome
	-Y	gloomy, icy, rainy
characterized by; full of; having *(adjective)*	**-ACIOUS**	audacious, pugnacious, vivacious
	-ATE	desolate, passionate, proportionate
	-ED	bearded, bigoted, pileated
	-EOUS	aqueous, beauteous, vitreous
	-FUL	fateful, joyful, painful
	-IOUS	contentious, religious, suspicious
	-ITIOUS	ambitious, expeditious, fictitious
	-ORY	gustatory, advisory, justificatory
	-OUS	famous, glorious, joyous
	-ULOUS	meticulous, populous, ridiculous
condition; quality; state *(noun)*	**-ACITY**	pugnacity, tenacity, vivacity
	-ACY	delicacy, democracy, fallacy
	-AGE	bondage, carnage, marriage
	-ANCE	abundance, resistance, vigilance
	-ANCY	brilliancy, constancy, infancy
	-ATION	gratification, reformation, starvation
	-DOM	freedom, kingdom, wisdom
	-ENCE	dependence, excellence, prominence
	-ENCY	decency, emergency, urgency
	-ERY	slavery, snobbery, trickery
	-ESCENCE	adolescence, convalescence, effervescence

MEANING	SUFFIX	EXAMPLES
condition; quality; state *(continued)*	-HOOD	childhood, falsehood, likelihood
	-ICE	cowardice, malice, service
	-ILITY	ability, civility, sensibility
	-ION	ambition, fusion, union
	-ISM	heroism, patriotism, skepticism
	-ITY	maternity, nobility, parity
	-MENT	abridgement, astonishment, disappointment
	-NESS	fullness, greatness, kindness
	-OR	ardor, favor, terror
	-OSIS	metamorphosis, osmosis, psychosis
	-SHIP	citizenship, friendship, leadership
	-TUDE	amplitude, gratitude, solitude
	-TY	enmity, novelty, sanity
	-URE	composure, exposure, pressure
	-Y	infamy, jealousy, victory
disease; medical condition *(noun)*	-IA	anemia, malaria, pneumonia
	-IASIS	elephantiasis, hypochondriasis, psoriasis
	-ITIS	bronchitis, gastritis, phlebitis
	-OMA	carcinoma, glaucoma, sarcoma
	-OSIS	halitosis, neurosis, tuberculosis
in a specified way *(adverb)*	-ABLY	capably, comfortably, peaceably
	-IBLY	credibly, legibly, possibly
	-LY	carefully, gradually, quickly
location; place *(noun)*	-ARIUM	aquarium, herbarium, solarium
	-ARY	dictionary, granary, seminary
	-ERY	bakery, brewery, grocery
	-ORIUM	auditorium, emporium, sanatorium
	-ORY	dormitory, lavatory, observatory
person who is, has, or does *(noun)*	-ANT	accountant, litigant, servant
	-ARIAN	librarian, nonagenarian, vegetarian
	-ATE	advocate, delegate, magistrate
	-ATOR	aviator, educator, mediator
	-EE	devotee, employee, grantee
	-EER	auctioneer, engineer, profiteer
	-ENT	dependent, president, superintendent
	-ER	employer, farmer, teacher
	-ICIAN	beautician, patrician, theoretician
	-IER	brigadier, cashier, glazier

Copyright © 1996 Harcourt Brace & Company. All rights reserved.

MEANING	SUFFIX	EXAMPLES
person who is, has, or does *(continued)*	-IOR -IST -OR -STER	junior, senior, warrior novelist, machinist, theorist actor, grantor, inventor gangster, pollster, tipster
small; short *(noun)*	-ET -ETTE -LET -LING -ULE	eaglet, islet, minuet barrette, cigarette, kitchenette booklet, droplet, hamlet duckling, hatchling, inkling ampule, molecule, pustule
without; missing *(adjective)*	-LESS	childless, hopeless, thoughtless

EXERCISE

Go back through the examples very carefully. Write down all the words that you do not know. Then look up their meaning in a dictionary and write that down. Study your list until you know those words.

UNKNOWN WORD   DICTIONARY MEANING

INDEX OF WORD PARTS

The number in brackets indicates the chapter in which the word part appears; B = Appendix B, and C = Appendix C. A hyphen indicates a suffix.

a	not; without [B]	anti	against; opposed [4, B]	brev	small/short [5]
ab	away from [3, B]			bronch	windpipe [11]
-able	able to; capable of being [C]	antiq	ancient [7]		
		apo	away from; off; apart [3, B]	caco	bad; unpleasant [10]
-ably	in a specified way [C]	aqu	water [12]	cal	hot; warm [10]
-acious	characterized by; full of; having [C]	arbor	tree [12]	cap	take; hold [9]
		archaeo	ancient; primitive [7]	card	heart [11]
-acity	condition; quality; state [C]	aren	sand [12]	carn	flesh [11]
		-arian	person who is, has, or does [C]	cata	(going) down [3]
acoust	sound; hearing [8]			cata	lower; down from [4]
acro	pointed; tip end [6]	-arium	location; place [C]		
acu	pointed; sharp [6]	-ary	characteristic of; tending to [C]	ced	move; go [9]
-acy	condition; quality; state [C]			celer	fast or speedy [10]
		-ary	location; place [C]	cent	100 [2]
ad	to; toward [3]	astr	star; celestial body [12]	cep	take; hold [9]
aden	gland [11]			cephal	head; skull [11]
-age	condition; quality; state [C]	-ate	act; cause; do [C]	cerebr	brain [11]
		-ate	characteristic of; tending to [C]	cess	move; go [9]
alti	high [5]			chron	time [7]
alto	high [5]	-ate	characterized by; full of; having [C]	cid	kill [9]
ambi	both [2]			cinct	round or girdle-shaped [6]
amphi	both [2]	-ate	person who is, has, or does [C]		
ampl	large [5]			cip	take; hold [9]
-an	characteristic of; tending to [C]	-ation	condition; quality; state [C]	circul	round; circular [6]
				circum	around [4]
an	not; without [B]	-ative	able to; capable of being [C]	cis	kill [9]
ana	up(ward); going back [3]			clin	bent; sloped; leaning [6]
		-ator	person who is, has, or does [C]		
-ance	condition; quality; state [C]			clud	shut; close [9]
		aud	hear [8]	clus	shut; close [9]
-ancy	condition; quality; state [C]	aur	ear; hearing [8, 11]	co	at the same time; with [7]
anemo	wind [12]	bacill	rod-shaped [6]	co	with; together [4]
angul	angled; bent [6]	batho	deep [5]	col	with; together [4]
ann	year [7]	bathy	deep [5]	com	with; together [4]
-ant	person who is, has, or does [C]	bene	good; pleasant [10]	con	with; together [4]
		bi	two [2]	contra	against; opposite [4, B]
ante	earlier; in front of; before [4, 7]	bio	alive or life [10]		
		brach	arm [11]	cor	with; together [4]

397

corp	body [11]	endo	inside [4]	gnath	jaw [11]
cosm	world; universe [12]	enn	year [7]	gon	angled [6]
counter	against; opposite [4, B]	-ent	person who is, has, or does [C]	gust	taste [8]
cranio	skull [11]	enter	intestines [11]	gyr	spiral; rotating [6]
cryo	cold [10]	-eous	characterized by; full of; having [C]	hecto	100 [2]
cur	run; flow [9]			-hedral	faceted [6]
curs	run; flow [9]	epi	upon; outer; near [4]	-hedron	faceted [6]
curv	bent; curved [6]	-er	person who is, has, or does [C]	helio	sun [12]
cut	skin [8, 11]			hemi	half [2]
cycl	round; circular [6]	-ery	condition; quality; state [C]	hepat	liver [11]
				hepta	seven [2]
dactyl	finger; toe [11]	-ery	location; place [C]	herb	green plant [12]
de	away from; down; apart [3, B]	-esce	act; cause; do [C]	hetero	different; other [4]
		-escence	condition; quality; state [C]	hex	six [2]
debil	weak [10]			homo	same; alike [4]
dec	ten [2]	-et	small; short [C]	-hood	condition; quality; state [C]
deka	ten [2]	-ette	small/short [5, C]		
dendr	tree [12]	eu	good; pleasant [10]	horo	hour; time [7]
dent	tooth [11]	eury	wide [5]	hydr	water; fluid [12]
derm	skin [8, 11]	ex-	no longer [B]	hygr	humidity; moisture [12]
di	two [2]	ex	out of [3]		
dia	through; across [3]	exo	outside [4]	hyper	excessive; over; above [4]
digit	finger; toe [11]	extra	outside [4]		
dis	away; apart [B]	extro	outside [4]	hypo	insufficient; under [4]
-dom	condition; quality; state [C]	fac	do; make [9]		
dont	tooth [11]	fec	do; make [9]	-ia	disease; medical condition [C]
du	two [2]	fer	carry; bear [9]		
dur	hard; lasting [10]	fic	do; make [9]	-ial	characteristic of; tending to [C]
		flect	bend [9]		
e	out of; away from [3]	flect	bent [6]	-iasis	disease; medical condition [C]
ec	out of; away from [3]	flex	bent [6]		
eco	environment [12]	flex	bend [9]	-ible	able to; capable of being [C]
ecto	outside [4]	forc	strong [10]		
-ed	characterized by; full of; having [C]	fore	earlier; before [7]	-ibly	in a specified way [C]
		-form	shaped like [6]		
-ee	person who is, has, or does [C]	fort	strong [10]	-ic	characteristic of; tending to [C]
		fract	break [9]		
-eer	person who is, has, or does [C]	frag	break [9]	-ice	condition; quality; state [C]
		frig	cold [10]		
ef	out of; away from [3]	-ful	characterized by; full of; having [C]	-ician	person who is, has, or does [C]
em	into [3]				
-en	act; cause; do [C]	-fy	act; cause; do [C]	-ier	person who is, has, or does [C]
en	into [3]				
-ence	condition; quality; state [C]	gastr	stomach [11]	il	into [3]
		geo	earth [12]	il	not; without [B]
-ency	condition; quality; state [C]	ger	old; elderly [7]	-ile	able to; capable of being [C]
		geronto	old; elderly [7]		

INDEX OF WORD PARTS 399

-ile	characteristic of; tending to [C]	-less	without [B, C]	ob	to; toward [3]
-ility	condition; quality; state [C]	-let	small; short [C]	oc	to; toward [3]
		lign	wood [12]	octa	eight [2]
im	into [3]	-like	characteristic of; tending to [C]	octo	eight [2]
im	not; without [B]			ocul	eye [8, 11]
in	into [3]	-ling	small; short [C]	odor	smell [8]
in	not; without [B]	lun	moon [12]	of	to; toward [3]
infra	under [4]	-ly	characteristic of; tending to [C]	-oid	shaped like; resembling [6]
inter	between [4]			olfact	smell [8]
intra	inside [4]	-ly	in a specified way [C]	-oma	disease; medical condition [C]
intro	inside [4]	macro	large/long [5]		
-ion	condition; quality; state [C]	magni	large [5]	op	eye [8, 11]
		maj	large; great [5]	op	to; toward [3]
-ior	person who is, has, or does [C]	mal	bad; unpleasant; not [10, B]	opsy	see [8]
				opto	eye [8]
-ious	characterized by; full of; having [C]	manu	hand [11]	-or	condition; quality; state [C]
		maxi	large/long [5]		
ir	into [3]	mega	large [5]	or	mouth [8, 11]
ir	not; without [B]	megalo	large [5]	-or	person who is, has, or does [C]
-ish	characteristic of; tending to [C]	-megaly	large [5]		
		-ment	condition; quality; state [C]	orb	round; circular [6]
-ism	condition; quality; state [C]			-orium	location; place [C]
		meta	behind; beyond; later [4]	oro	mountain [12]
iso	same; equal [4]			ortho	straight [6]
-ist	person who is, has, or does [C]	micro	small/short [5]	-ory	characterized by; full of; having [C]
		milli	1,000 [2]		
-istic	characteristic of; tending to [C]	mini	small/short [5]	-ory	location; place [C]
		mis	not; wrongly [B]	-osis	condition; quality; state [C]
-itis	disease; medical condition [C]	mob	move [9]		
		mono	one [2]	-osis	disease; medical condition [C]
-itious	characterized by; full of; having [C]	mort	dead or death [10]	osm	smell [8]
		mot	move [9]	oss	bone [11]
-ity	condition; quality; state [C]	mov	move [9]	osteo	bone [11]
		multi	many [2]	ot	ear [8, 11]
-ive	characteristic of; tending to [C]	mut	change [9]	-ous	characterized by; full of; having [C]
		nas	nose [8, 11]		
-ize	act; cause; do [C]	necro	dead or death [10]		
journ	day [7]	neo	new [7]	pachy	thick [5]
juven	young [7, 10]	nephr	kidney [11]	palp	touch [8]
juxta	near; close together [4]	-ness	condition; quality; state [C]	para	beside; beyond; near [4]
		no-	not at all [B]	path	sick; disease [10]
kilo	1,000 [2]	noct	evening; night [7]	ped	foot [11]
		non	not [B]	pel	push; drive [9]
lati	wide [5]	nona	nine [2]	penta	five [2]
len	soft; gentle; weak [10]	nov	new [7]	per	through [3]
		nov	nine [2]	peri	around; near [4]

Copyright © 1996 Harcourt Brace & Company. All rights reserved.

INDEX OF WORD PARTS

petr	rock [12]	sen	old [7, 10]	tort	bent [6]
phleb	vein [11]	sens	senses [8]	tract	pull [9]
phon	sound [8]	sept	seven [2]	trans	across; through [3]
phyll	leaf [12]	sequ	follow [9]	tri	three [2]
phyt	vegetation [12]	sex	six [2]	tricho	hair [11]
pil	hair [11]	-ship	condition; quality; state [C]	-tude	condition; quality; state [C]
pisc	fish [12]	silv	tree; forest [12]	-ty	condition; quality; state [C]
platy	flat; wide [5]	simul	at the same time [7]		
plen	full [10]	sinu	bent [6]		
plet	full [10]	sol	sun [12]	-ule	small; short [5, C]
pod	foot [11]	somat	body [11]	-ulous	characterized by; full of; having [C]
poly	many [2]	-some	characteristic of; tending to [C]		
port	carry [9]	son	sound [8]	ultra	above; over; beyond [4]
post	behind; afterward [4]	spec	see; look [8]	un	not [B]
post	later; after [7]	spher	round; globe-shaped [6]	uni	one [2]
pre	earlier; in front of; before [4]	spic	see; look [8]	-ure	condition; quality; state [C]
pre	earlier; before [7]	stell	star [12]		
pro	forward; outward [3]	steno	narrow; thin [5]	vac	empty [10]
pseudo	false [10]	-ster	person who is, has, or does [C]	ven	come [9]
pul	push; drive [9]	strict	thin; narrow [5]	vent	come [9]
pulmo	lung [11]	sub	under; beneath [4]	ver	true [10]
punct	pointed [6]	super	above; over; upper [4]	-verge	turn; bend [9]
		supra	above; over [4]	vers	turn; bend [9]
quadr	four [2]	syl	with; together [4]	vert	turn; bend [9]
quart	four [2]	sylv	tree; forest [12]	vet	old; experienced [7]
quint	five [2]	sym	with; together [4]	vid	see [8]
		syn	with; together [4]	vis	see [8]
re	going back; again [3]	synchro	at the same time [7]	vit	alive or life [10]
rect	straight [6]	sys	with; together [4]	viv	alive or life [10]
retro	(going) back; behind [3]			volut	turn; roll [9]
retro	earlier; past [7]	tach	fast [10]	volv	turn; roll [9]
rhin	nose [8, 11]	tacit	quiet [10]	-ward	in the direction of; toward [3]
rot	round; circular [6]	tact	touch; feel [8]	with	away; apart; opposed [B]
rupt	break or burst [9]	-tain	hold [9]		
		tang	touch; feel [8]		
san	healthy [10]	tard	slow [10]	xyl	wood [12]
sangui	blood [11]	tele	distant; far [4]		
sap	taste [8]	tempo	time [7]	-y	characteristic of; tending to [C]
sav	taste [8]	ten	hold [9]		
sclero	hard [10]	tenu	thin; narrow [5]	-y	condition; quality; state [C]
scope	see [8]	ter	three [2]		
se	away from [3]	terr	earth; ground [12]		
seism	earthquake [12]	tetra	four [2]	zo	animal [12]
semi	half [2]	therm	heat; hot; warm [10]		

Copyright © 1996 Harcourt Brace & Company. All rights reserved.

CREDITS

Abell, George. *Realm of the Universe.* New York: Holt, Rinehart and Winston, 1976.
Ackerman, Diane. *A Natural History of the Senses.* New York: Vintage Books, 1991.
The American Heritage Dictionary of the English Language. 3rd ed. Boston: Houghton Mifflin, 1992. Entry on pages 2–3 reprinted by permission of the publisher.
"Anatomy of your Skin." *Mayo Clinic Health Letter* July 1991.
Anderson, Richard D. et al. *School Mathematics Geometry.* Atlanta: Houghton Mifflin, 1980.
Arms, Karen et al. *A Journey into Life.* 3rd ed. Fort Worth: Saunders, 1994.
"Back Care." *Supplement to Mayo Clinic Health Letter* February 1994.
Belsie, Laurent. "Computers for the Rest of Us." *Christian Science Monitor* November 15, 1994.
Bennett, W. Lance. *Inside the System.* Fort Worth: Harcourt Brace, 1994.
Berger, Kathleen. *The Developing Person Through the Life Span.* 2nd ed. New York: Worth, 1988.
Brownlee, Shannon et al. "Genes and Cancer." *U.S. News & World Report* August 22, 1994.
Burton, Maurice, ed. *World Encyclopedia of Animals.* New York: World, 1972.
Chodorow, Stanley et al. *The Mainstream of Civilization.* 6th ed. Fort Worth: Harcourt Press, 1994.
Ciardi, John. *How Does a Poem Mean?* Boston: Houghton Mifflin, 1959.
Clarke, David. "Let Them Drink Waste Water." *Garbage.* Summer 1994.
Crouse, William. *Automotive Mechanics.* New York: McGraw Hill, 1975.
Daft, Richard L. *Management.* 2nd Edition. Fort Worth: Dryden Press, 1991.
Des Jarlais, Dan C. and Friedmann, Samuel R. "AIDS and the Use of Injected Drugs." *Scientific American* February 1994.
"Diagnostic Ultrasound." *Mayo Clinic Health Letter* April 1992.
Diamond, Jared. "The Arrow of Disease." *Discover* Special Issue, 1993.
DiSilvestro, Roger. "Sweet Shadows." *International Wildlife* November-December 1994.
Donohue, Dr. "Ask Dr. Donohue." *Traverse City Record-Eagle* 12 November 1994: 3B.
"Endoscopic Surgery." *The Mayo Clinic Health Letter* September 1994.
Folger, Tim. "This Battered Earth." *Discover* January 1994.
Gould, Stephen J. "Curveball." *New Yorker* 28 November 1994.
Greulach, Victor and Chiapetta, Vincent. *Biology.* New Jersey: Scott Foresman, 1977.
Hamilton, Edith. *Mythology.* Boston: Little Brown, 1949.
Hamilton, Eva May et al. *Nutrition: Concepts and Controversies.* St. Paul: West Pub., 1985.
Harding, Caroline. "Fish Out of Water." *National Wildlife* October-November 1994.
Hartmann, Ernest. "Approaches to Insomnia." *The Harvard Medical School Mental Health Letter* March 1985.
Haviland, William A. *Cultural Anthropology.* 7th ed. Fort Worth: Harcourt Brace, 1993.
"Hearing Aids." *Mayo Clinic Health Letter* May 1994.
Heimler, Charles and Price, Jack. *Focus on Physical Science.* Columbus: Charles E. Merrill, 1974.
"Herbal Supplements." *Mayo Clinic Health Letter* December 1992.
Hole, John W. Jr. *Human Anatomy and Physiology.* 4th ed. Dubuque: Wm. C. Brown, 1987.
Illingworth, Valerie. *The Anchor Dictionary of Astronomy.* Garden City: Anchor Books, 1980.

"Indoor Air Pollution." *Mayo Clinic Health Letter* November 1993.
Kusler, John A. et al. "Wetlands." *Scientific American* January 1994.
Labich, Kenneth. "Why Companies Fail." *Fortune* 14 November 1994.
Light, Donald and Keller, Suzanne. *Sociology.* New York: Knopf, 1975.
Line, Les. "Have Wings, Can't Fly." *International Wildlife* November-December 1994.
Luoma, Jon R. "An Untidy Wonder." *Discover* Special Issue, 1993.
Lynch, Wayne. "Den Mothers and Their Cubs." *International Wildlife* November-December 1994.
McNeill, Joseph. *Homeowner's Guide.* New York: Van Nostrand Reinhold, 1979.
Mitchell, John G. "Our National Parks." *National Geographic* October 1994.
Morton, Alexandra. "Life Among the Whales." *Smithsonian* November 1994.
"Multiple Sclerosis." *Harvard Medical School Health Letter* November 1987.
"The Muscles and Bones." *The Johns Hopkins Medical Handbook.* New York, Rebus, 1992.
Naeye, Robert. "Dawn of the Dinosaurs." *Discover* January 1994.
O'Donnell, Mary Agnes. *Seething Cauldrons.* Berkeley: Pentagram Press, 1991.
"Orthodontics for Adults." *Mayo Clinic Health Letter* November 1989.
"Out of Sight, Out of Mind?" *Consumer Reports* February 1994.
Parkes, Henry. *The Divine Order.* New York: Knopf, 1969.
Plummer, Charles and McGeary, David. *Physical Geology.* Dubuque: W.C. Brown, 1985.
Polosmak, Natalya. "A Mummy Unearthed from the Pastures of Heaven." *National Geographic* October 1994.
Radetsky, Peter. "How Did Life Start?" *Discover* Special Issue, 1993.
Rathus, Spencer A. *Psychology.* 5th ed. Fort Worth: Harcourt Brace, 1993.
Rennie, John. "Insects Are Forever." *Scientific American* November 1993.
Roach, Mary. "Aliens in the Treetops." *International Wildlife* November-December 1994.
Schifferes, J.J. *Essentials of Healthier Living.* New York: Wiley, 1968.
"Second Opinion." *The Mayo Clinic Health Letter* October 1994.
Serway, Raymond, and Faughn, Jerry. *College Physics.* 3rd ed. Fort Worth: Saunders, 1992.
Spence, Alexander P. *Biology of Human Aging.* Englewood Cliffs: Prentice Hall, 1989.
Spotts, Peter N. "Micro Bugs." *The Christian Science Monitor* 15 November 1994.
Stewart, Doug. "Do Fish Sleep?" *National Wildlife* April-May 1994.
Stewart, Doug. "The Curse of the Great Eastern." *Smithsonian* November 1994.
"Stricture of the Esophagus." *The American Medical Association Family Medical Guide.* New York: Random House, 1982.
"Stroke." *The Johns Hopkins Medical Handbook.* New York: Rebus, 1992.
Swerdlow, Joel L. "America's Poet: Walt Whitman." *National Geographic* December 1994.
Tischler, Henry L. *Introduction to Sociology.* 4th ed. Fort Worth: Harcourt Press, 1993.
"Touch." *Mayo Clinic Health Letter* June 1994.
"Tuberculosis." *Mayo Clinic Health Letter* April 1993.
"Update '94." *The Mayo Clinic Health Letter* November 1994.
van denHueval, Edward P.J. and Paradijs, Jan van. "X-Ray Binaries." *Scientific American.* November 1993.
Van Lanker, Diana. "Old Familiar Voices." *Psychology Today* November 1987.
"VCRs." *Consumer Reports.* March 1994.
Vincent, Amanda. "The Improbable Seahorse." *National Geographic* October 1994.
Wallace, Robert et al. *Biology: The World of Life.* Santa Monica: Goodyear Pub. Co., 1981.
Yoon, Carol Kaesuk. "Drugs from Bugs." *Garbage* Summer 1994.
Young, Jennifer. "The Rock Fantasy." In *The Essay Connection.* Lynn Bloom, ed. Lexington: D.C. Heath, 1984.